W9-AWR-385

SS: ROLL OF INFAMY

SS: ROLL OF INFAMY

CHRISTOPHER AILSBY

Motorbooks International
Publishers & Wholesalers ®

This edition first published in 1997 by

Motorbooks International Publishers & Wholesalers,

729 Prospect Avenue, PO Box 1, Osceola, WI 54020, USA

Copyright © 1997 Brown Packaging Books Ltd

Previously published by Brown Books in the United Kingdom.

All rights reserved. With the exception of quoting brief passages for the purposes of review no part of this publication may be reproduced without prior written permission from the Publisher and the copyright holders. Motorbooks International is a certified trademark, registered with the United States Patent Office.

The information in this book is true and complete to the best of our knowledge. All recommendations are made without any guarantee on the part of the author or publisher, who also disclaim any liability incurred in connection with the use of this data or specific details.

We recognize that some words, model names and designations, for example, mentioned herein are the property of the trademark holder. We use them for identification purposes only. This is not an official publication.

Motorbooks International books are also available at discounts in bulk quantity for industrial or sales-promotional use. For details write to the Special Sales Manager at the Publisher's address.

Library in Congress Cataloging-in-Publication Data available.

ISBN 0-7603-0409-2

Conceived and produced by Vincenzo Bona

Brown Packaging Books Ltd, 255-257 Liverpool Road, London, N1 1LX

Editor: Judith Millidge

Designer: Colin Hawes

Printed and bound in Italy.

Picture acknowledgements:

All photographs Christopher Ailsby Historical Archives except:

Popperfoto: 10; *TRH Pictures:* 2-3, 24, 38, 52, 113, 127, 137, 151;

TRH Pictures via Espadon: 61, 80, 90, 104, 161, 181.

Previous pages: Troops of the Leibstandarte SS Adolf Hitler *on parade in full dress uniform at Tempelhof airport on 24 March 1934.*

Contents

Introduction

In preparing this book, I have tried to give an across the board look at the personnel of the SS and used examples that illustrate the varied and complex nature of this organisation.

Contrary to popular expectation, the members of the SS were not exclusively German but were drawn from many nationalities, from Russians to Britons and Americans. The entries are arranged so that the reader can see what awards each individual received while serving in the SS. These reflect the extent of the involvement they had during their careers. The main awards that are featured are those of the Knight's Cross of the Iron Cross, which reflects valour shown on the field of conflict, and the Knight's Cross of the War Merit Cross, which indicates the service aspect shown to the Third Reich and in particular the SS – a great number of the more disreputable characters sport this award. The party number represents the award of the Golden Party Badge, highly prized by veteran members of the NSDAP. In as many cases as possible I have tried to give the relevant dates, but this is an extremely complicated task and I would welcome any input from a reader who can give any pertinent data on any missing dates, awards, or numbers.

Special mention must be made of my assistant, John Ailsby, for without his help and input the book would have taken infinitely longer to prepare; his checking of facts and dates have been of the highest order. I hope to have the pleasure of working with him again on another project in the near future.

During the writing of the book, which I do in longhand, I had a personal disaster of the type that authors fear the most. A friend of mine dropped my fountain pen that has written everything since it was given to me as a 21st birthday present. At great expense other pens were bought but all failed to meet up to the standard. It was worse than writer's block. What was more, the pen was returned from Sheaffer's as unrepairable. Luckily, Sheaffer's managing director, after hearing about my plight, found me another pen of similar weight and dispatched it to me post haste. Without this help, the book would not have been completed.

Another debt of thanks goes to Frank Thayer, PhD. New Mexico State University Las Cruces. To Josef Charita as always a deep debt of gratitude for his input.

The dates of awards given to SS individuals are listed where known, otherwise no date is given. Similarly, death dates are only given where known. The following key gives the abbreviations used in the main text relating to how the various SS members met their end.

KEY:	
E.A.	*Executed by the Allies*
K.I.A.	*Killed in Action*
M.I.A.	*Missing in Action*
D	*Died of natural causes*
S	*Suicide*
A	*Accidental death*
E.R.	*Executed by the Reich*
M	*Murdered*
E	*Escaped*

D'ALQUEN, Gunter
RANK: SS-Standartenführer
BORN: 24 October 1910—
PARTY NUMBER: 66689
SS NUMBER: 8452
AWARDS: Golden Party Badge;1939 Iron Cross Second Class;War Merit Cross Second Class with Swords; SS Honour Ring; SS Honour Sword.

D'Alquen was editor of the SS newspaper, *Das Schwarze Korps*, founded by Heydrich (q.v.) in 1934. Under his protection, it was one of the only papers free from the heavy handed censorship of Göbbels' propaganda ministry. D'Alquen also wrote an official pamphlet for Himmler, *Die SS*, based on Himmler's magisterial address to the higher leadership of the SS on 2 July 1936, at a ceremony for the thousandth anniversary of Henry the Fowler's death.

Himmler commissioned him to orchestrate a recruiting campaign

In his capacity as war correspondent of the Wehrmacht propaganda section, d'Alquen visited Le Paradis in Normandy the day after the infamous massacre of prisoners in 1944. He saw the bodies and was told the implausible story that dumm-dumm bullets had been used by the Second Royal Norfolks. Soon after the 20 July Bomb Plot, Himmler commissioned him to orchestrate a recruiting campaign for Russian deserters. Towards the end of the war he became head of the Wehrmacht propaganda section, in succession to General Wedel, a particular enemy of Göbbels, who declared that Wedel had increased the propaganda section to the size of a division. D'Alquen also assisted Prützmann (q.v.) in the creation of the Werewolf organisation. He was fined by a Berlin de-Nazification court in July 1955 DM60 000.

AMANN, Max
RANK: Reichsleiter, SS-Obergruppenführer
BORN: 24 November 1891
DIED: 31 March 1957 (D)
PARTY NUMBER: 3
SS NUMBER: 53143
AWARDS:1914 Iron Cross Second Class; Golden Party Badge; Coburg Badge, 14 October 1932; Blood Order; Pioneer of Labour Decoration, 1 May 1941; SS Honour Ring; SS Honour Sword.

Amann, an uncouth but shrewd man, was born in Munich. During World War I he served in a Bavarian infantry regiment, where he was Hitler's sergeant. He joined the SA (Sturmabteilung, the Brownshirts), and was one of the original party members. From 1925, he was in the SA Central Office, and his business training led him to become party treasurer and to undertake the running of its paper, the *Völkische Beobachter*. When Hitler wrote a book called *Four and a Half Years of Struggle Against Lies, Stupidity and Cowardice*, it was Amann who conceived a shorter, more memorable title: *Mein Kampf*. Amann took over responsibility for the book, arranging publication, organising the royalties, which were Hitler's main source of income, and supervising the dozens of editions which were published during Hitler's lifetime.

With *gleichschaltung* of the press (with the coming to power of the Nazis in January 1933, all newspapers were required to conform to the party line or else risk punishment), Amann became president of the Reich association of newspaper publishers and president of the Reich press chamber. He also bought the Hugenbergs' press empire for the party in 1943. His toughness and greed made him a millionaire, but at the war's end he was tried by a de-Nazification court and stripped of his property; he died in Munich in poverty.

ANCANS, Roberts

RANK: Waffen-Hauptsturmführer der SS
  (Latvian Volunteer)
BORN: 11 November 1919
DIED: 1 January 1989 (D)
AWARDS: Medal for the Winter Campaign
  in Russia 1941-1942; Infantry Assault
  Badge; Close Combat Clasp Silver Class;
  1939 Iron Cross Second Class, 1 April
  1943; 1939 Iron Cross First Class,
  27 December 1944; Knight's Cross of
  the Iron Cross, 25 January 1945.

Born in Tilsa, Latvia, Ancans volunteered for service in the Latvian Defence Forces to fight with the Germans against the Soviet Union for the freedom of Latvia. He was in charge of a close-combat training school, the 19th Field Replacement Battalion 19th SS-Volunteer Division (Latvian No 2), 6th SS-Volunteer Army Corps, Army Group North. He was awarded the Knight's Cross of the Iron Cross for his bravery. He survived the war and lived in the USA, where he died in 1989.

ARENT, Prof Benno von

RANK: SS-Oberführer
BORN: 19 June 1898—
PARTY NUMBER: 1105236
SS NUMBER: 36320
AWARDS: SS Honour Ring; SS Honour
  Sword

Having served in World War I, von Arent joined the NSDAP and was also a member of the SS. He was a designer of insignia for the political bodies and was responsible for the creation of such important awards as the Danzig Cross First and Second Class, and the design drawings for the Balkan Shield in 1945.

BACH-ZELEWSKI, Erich von dem

RANK: SS-Obergruppenführer und General
  der Waffen-SS und Polizei
BORN: 1 March 1899
DIED: 8 March 1972 (D)
PARTY NUMBER: 489101
SS NUMBER: 9831
AWARDS: 1914 Iron Cross Second Class;
  1914 Iron Cross First Class; Cross of
  Honour 1914-1918 Combatants; 1914
  Wound Badge Black Class; War Merit
  Cross Second Class with Swords; War
  Merit Cross First Class with Swords;
  Knight's Cross of the Iron Cross,
  30 September 1944; German Cross in
  Gold, 23 February 1943; 1939 Iron
  Cross Second Class Bar, 31 August
  1941; 1939 Iron Cross First Class Bar,
  20 May 1942; Golden Party Badge;
  Danzig Cross First Class; SS Honour
  Ring; SS Honour Sword.

Born in Lauenburg, Pomerania, into a Junker family, Bach-Zelewski became a professional soldier serving at the front in World War I. After the war, he joined in succession the police service, the NSDAP in 1930 and the SS in 1931. When Hitler came to power, he was promoted quickly and for a time commanded the SS-District Southeast in Breslau-Silesia. Between 1932 and 1934 he was a Reichstag deputy. From 1941-42 he was senior SS and Police Leader in the Central Army Group area in Russia, where he was head of all anti-partisan units, and directly responsible to Himmler (q.v.). Despite his zeal, he became ill in 1942 due to the horrors being committed in the East, being admitted to the SS hospital in Hohenlychen suffering from a nervous breakdown. He suffered hallucinations connected with the shooting of Jews.

The change in control did not change the involvement of the Army or the Luftwaffe in these operations. Bach-Zelewski controlled the task of combatting guerrillas or partisans behind the lines on the Eastern Front and in the mountain reaches of the Balkans, and gave the SS control of the Wehrmacht and non-German soldiers fighting as volunteers in the Wehrmacht.

Bach-Zelewski was in command of all German units employed in curbing the Warsaw Uprising during August to October 1944. During the brutal suppression, the Soviet forces in the region made no attempt to aid the Poles, but stood firm on the eastern banks of the Vistula to await the predictable outcome. As with the earlier revolts, Himmler wished to see this as a battle honour for the SS, so the Warsaw Shield was instituted on 10 December 1944 to be awarded 'as a battle badge to members of the Armed Forces and non-military personnel who between 1 August and 2 October 1944 were honourably engaged in the fighting in Warsaw.' However, Bach-Zelewski was unable to award a single medal as the factory producing them was bombed out. The panzer leader

General Guderian said of the putting down of the revolt: 'What I learnt was so appalling that I felt myself bound to inform Hitler about it that same evening and to demand the removal of the two brigades from the Eastern Front.'

In order to prevent his extradition to Poland after the war, Bach-Zelewski became a prosecution witness during the Nuremberg Trials. He was sentenced by the Allies in 1951 to 10 years' special labour, which in effect meant house arrest. In 1958, he was re-arrested and charged with murders committed in 1941-42. As more evidence about his wartime activities emerged, he was again retried and sentenced in 1961 to life for murders which had occurred in Breslau-Silesia during the period 1942-44 when it was under his command. He died in Munich-Harlaching in 1972.

BACKE, Herbert

RANK: SS-Obergruppenführer
BORN: 1 May 1896
DIED: 6 April 1947 (S)
PARTY NUMBER: 22766
SS NUMBER: 87882
AWARDS: Golden Party Badge; War Merit Cross Second Class without Swords; War Merit Cross First Class without Swords; SS Honour Ring; SS Honour Sword.

Born in Batum in the Caucasus, Backe was educated at the Russian Tifliser Gymnasium and Göttingen University. He was imprisoned

by the Russians for most of World War I. An agricultural specialist, he served as State Secretary in the Ministry of Food from 1933 until 1942, when he assumed the position of Food Minister, a post he held until the end of the war. One of the ministers named in Hitler's last testament, he was imprisoned in Nuremberg after the war and hanged himself on 6 April 1947.

BARBIE, Klaus

RANK: SS-Obersturmführer
BORN: 25 October 1913
DIED: 23 September 1991 (D)
PARTY NUMBER: —
SS NUMBER: —
AWARDS: 1939 Iron Cross Second Class.

The infamous 'Butcher of Lyons', Barbie was born in Triers, the son of a village school master. He joined the SS and was assigned to the SD, beginning a long career in espionage that survived the Third Reich.

On 2 May 1941, Barbie was posted to the Bureau of Jewish Affairs in the Hague as an intelligence officer. His next appointment was the Amsterdam Gestapo headquarters in Euterpestraat. Barbie's orders were to concentrate on the Zionists, Jewish financiers, Marxists and, especially, Freemasons, whom the Nazis

regarded as a special threat. Eichmann (q.v.) was impatient, intelligence gathering was a slow, laborious business and he wanted the RSHA section IVB4 to be providing the cargoes for the deportation trains. By May 1942 the first had arrived in Holland, but Barbie had moved to France by then and took up his appointment in Lyons in November 1942.

Barbie's first commander was SS-Sturmbannführer Rolf Müller, who took an immediate dislike to him and distanced himself from Barbie, leaving him uncontrolled in Lyons, well away from his supremo, SS-Standartenführer Helmut Knochen (q.v.) of Amtix at Sipo-SD headquarters in Paris. Barbie's brief from Knochen was crudely simplistic: penetrate and smash the Resistance in Lyons. Barbie chose as his headquarters the Hotel Terminus, a luxurious four-star establishment. Those who had dealings with him encountered a person with a split personality. He affected a pose of informality, sometimes refusing to use an official protected car so he could meander through the streets, meeting fellow pedestrians as acquaintances. Barbie had a love of good food, and the waitress who served him found him generous, but this side to him could be replaced by uncontrollable rages and sadism.

Two incidents stand out in Barbie's unspeakable career. On 2 June 1943, information gleaned from an unknown source led him to the local doctor, Dugougon, who was using his house for a meeting of prominent Resistance members. The most influential was a Monsieur Martel, whose cover was that he was a patient needing treatment for rheumatism. When the Gestapo broke in they savagely arrested all inside, but had particular interest in 'Jean Martel', or Jean Moulin, the organiser and coordinator of the various Resistance cells in the area. Moulin, one of the great heroes of the French Resistance, endured a long, slow death at the hands of Barbie, who knew all the refinements of torture. An eyewitness recounted: 'he was unconscious, his eyes dug in as though they had been punched through his head. A mute rattle came out of his swollen lips.' Desperately ill with a fractured skull and suspected brain damage, he was transported to Paris where he spent several days in a coma at the residence of SS-Standartenführer Boemelberg. Early in July, the barely conscious Moulin was transported to Germany, and died en route. His death certificate verified he died at Metz of heart failure on 8 July 1943.

Barbie's reign of terror knew no bounds, and he was responsible for the deportation of 842 people to concentration camps, of whom at least 373 were known to have perished. Of that total, 52 were children, with 44 of them being sent to the gas chambers from the children's home at Iziev. A special haven for Jewish children from all over France, Iziev was betrayed by informers, and the home was raided by Barbie and his forces in April 1944.

Barbie was so shaken by the beating he vowed never to work for the British again

After the war some of the strangest, and as yet unexplained, events occurred. John Loftus, former prosecutor with the US Office of Special Investigations, stated that both America and Britain recruited ex-SS men to infiltrate communist cells in Eastern Europe. In 1945, MI6, the British intelligence-gathering organisation, secretly flew SS-Brigadeführer Walter Schellenberg (q.v.) to London, where he provided a list of all his most important agents. Barbie's contact with MI6 was through SS-Untersturmführer Hans Markus, one of Schellenberg's key men. At first Barbie was used as a 'runner', distributing supplies and money to new agents. Later, with numerous contacts he set up his own intelligence operation and the network grew. The supreme irony was that while MI6 had no qualms about using Barbie, MI5 and British military intelligence were trying to track him down for war crimes. Barbie knew he was living dangerously and went to a doctor in Hamburg to have his SS blood group tattoo removed. Shortly afterwards he was arrested in the city by British soldiers and beaten up. He and two other SS men were locked in the coal cellar of a house for three days, but were allowed to escape. Conveniently, they found an iron bar to force open the door. There was only one guard on duty and he was playing a flute when they fled. Barbie was so shaken by the beating he vowed he would never work for the British again, so he switched his allegiance to the Americans from 1947 to 1950.

Asked to penetrate the German Communist Party and detect Soviet agents, Barbie was given his own office in Augsburg and 100 informers. The Americans described him afterwards as 'invaluable'. He used his new position with the Americans to help ex-SS men escape from Germany. Years later he boasted how easy it had been to fool the Allies. Towards the end of 1950, the Americans found Barbie too 'hot' to keep. The French knew he was in the American zone and demanded that he should be made to pay for his atrocities, so Barbie slipped out of Augsburg in June 1951 in a US Army truck. American agents gave him false papers and a new identity, Klaus Altman. He eventually turned up in Bolivia and remained safe for over 30 years, until 5 February 1983, when he was handed over to the French.

Klaus Barbie was tried for his war crimes in 1987. He put up no defence and for much of the proceedings insisted on withdrawing from the dock altogether. The survivors who testified said, 'he loved to play God,' and recalled the Gestapo chief's devotion to cruelty and inflicting pain. Barbie's family spoke of an apparently devoted husband and a father who had been inconsolable after the death of a son. He was found guilty and sentenced to life imprisonment, dying in prison in 1991.

BARKMANN, Ernst (now goes under the name of E. Schmuck-Barkmann)

RANK: SS-Oberscharführer
BORN: 25 August 1919—
PARTY NUMBER: —
SS NUMBER: —
AWARDS: 1939 Iron Cross Second Class, 14 July 1941; 1939 Iron Cross First Class, 1 August 1944; Knight's Cross of the Iron Cross, 27 August 1944; '50' Tank Combat Badge; Infantry Assault Badge Silver Class; 1939 Wound Badge Gold Class.

A courageous soldier, Barkmann was born in Kisdorf near Bad Segeberg, Holstein, the son of a farmer. After leaving school in 1935, he worked on his father's farm until his call-up on 1 April 1939, when he joined the SS-Standarte *Germania*. He went to Hamburg for three months of basic training and was then posted to 111 Battalion of the Standarte at Radolfzell on Bodensee. He served in the Polish campaign as a machine gunner with 9 Kompanie, and was wounded while later fighting in Russia. After recovering, he spent a period with European SS volunteers in Holland as an instructor. In 1942, he volunteered for service with the SS Panzer Division Regiment and was posted to 2 Kompanie, SS Panzer Regiment 2, *Das Reich*, on the Russian Front.

At the beginning of 1944 the division was transferred to Bordeaux for rest and refitting, but moved north to Normandy to engage the enemy after D-Day. Barkmann and his crew wrought havoc on the American tanks, and he is credited with destroying 50 tanks. For his gallantry he was awarded the Knight's Cross of the Iron Cross. He was in action during the Ardennes Offensive, before being returned to the Eastern Front, and continued fighting south of Vienna in the last days of the war, when he was captured by the British.

BAUM, Otto
RANK: SS-Oberführer
BORN: 15 November 1911—
PARTY NUMBER: 4197040
SS NUMBER: 237056
AWARDS: 1939 Iron Cross Second Class, 25 September 1939; 1939 Iron Cross First Class, 15 June 1940; German Cross in Gold, 26 December 1941; Knight's Cross of the Iron Cross, 8 May 1942; Oakleaves, 12 August 1943; Swords, 2 September 1944; Demjansk Shield; SS Honour Ring; SS Honour Sword.

Otto Baum was born in Stetten-Hechingen, Swabia. In 1936, he volunteered as an officer candidate to join the SS-Verfügungstruppe and was commissioned as an Untersturmführer. He served in the

Polish campaign and in France in 1940. Posted to Russia, he demonstrated exceptional bravery during the heavy fighting at Demjansk and was awarded the Knight's Cross while serving as commanding officer of the 3rd Battalion 3rd SS-Totenkopf Infantry Regiment in 1942. In the most serious combat conditions he rallied his troops to

attack, throwing the Soviets off guard and causing them to waver. He repeatedly counterattacked against superior odds.

In 1943 he was severely wounded, but returned as the commanding officer of the 5th SS-Panzergrenadier Regiment *Totenkopf* and was the 377th recipient of the Oakleaves. His command was transferred to the Western Front after the Allied invasion of Normandy in 1944. Baum fought a continuous delaying action, and while serving as commander of the 2nd SS Panzer Division *Das Reich* was awarded the Swords, becoming the 95th recipient. His last command was of the 16th SS Panzergrenadier Division *Reichsführer-SS* on the southern front.

BAUR, Hans
RANK: SS-Brigadeführer
BORN: 19 June 1897
DIED: 17 February 1993 (D)
PARTY NUMBER: 48113
SS NUMBER: 171865
AWARDS: Combined Pilot and Observer Badge in Gold with Diamonds; SS Honour Ring; SS Honour Sword.

Baur was a pilot in World War I and afterwards joined Lufthansa. He made many international flights and showed great expertise in the commercial flying world, earning a reputation that brought him to Hitler's notice. Baur joined his personal staff and Hitler seldom flew with any other pilot, admiring not only his aeronautical skills but also enjoying his company.

Baur was in the bunker at the end of the war and implored

Hitler to let him fly him to Japan or Argentina, assuring him that they could still escape. Hitler's response was unequivocal: 'one must have the courage to face the consequences. I am ending it all here. I know that by tomorrow millions of people will curse me.' In recognition of his long and faithful service Hitler shook his hand and gave him his treasured portrait of Frederick the Great. Baur attempted to break out of Berlin and was captured by the Soviets, losing a leg. Imprisoned by the Allies after the war, he was released in 1955, when he confirmed Hitler's suicide.

BECHER, Kurt
RANK: SS-Obersturmbannführer
BORN: 12 September 1909—
PARTY NUMBER: 4486195
SS NUMBER: 234478
AWARDS: German Cross in Gold; 1939 Iron Cross Second Class; 1939 Iron Cross First Class; War Merit Cross Second Class with Swords.

A former grain salesman from Hamburg, Becher was a skilled negotiator and head of an SS Remount Purchasing Commission from 1942. Fegelein (q.v.) noticed his skill in acquiring the Baron Oppenheim racing stud for the SS. Becher served in Budapest in the SS personnel office, and was introduced to Himmler's (q.v.) intimate circle of advisers, probably by Schellenberg (q.v.) after the 'occupation' of Budapest, when Becher once more handled a negotiation for the SS, acquiring the Jewish Mannfred Weiss steel combine.

In 1944-45 Himmler dreamt up an alternative method of disposing of the Jews: he proposed selling them to the Western Allies. Becher was required to go to Istanbul to offer the lives of 700,000 Jews in exchange for 10,000 lorries to be delivered by the Allies to the port of Salonika. Accompanied by Brand, Becher departed for Istanbul and tried to make contact with the British Embassy in Ankara and the Jewish Agency in Palestine. British military intelligence arrested him on the Turkish-Syrian border and interned him in Cairo. He was permitted to see the Jewish Agency representative, Moshe Sharell, who forwarded proposals to London, but they fell on stoney ground. Once made public, however, the proposals caused Himmler acute embarrassment in Germany.

Becher also visited Switzerland in his efforts to obtain foreign currency for Jewish lives. This was partly successful, and two trains left Belsen in 1944 and another in February 1945.

BECKER, Helmuth
RANK: SS-Brigadeführer und Generalmajor der Waffen-SS
BORN: 12 August 1902
DIED: 28 February 1952 (E.A.)
PARTY NUMBER: 1592593
SS NUMBER: 113174
AWARDS: 1939 Iron Cross Second Class, 24 May 1940; 1939 Iron Cross First Class, 22 June 1940; Knight's Cross 7 September 1943; Oakleaves, 21 September 1944; German Cross in Gold, 26 September 1942; 1939 Wound Badge Black Class; 1939 Wound Badge Silver Class; SS Honour Ring; SS Honour Sword.

Becker was born in Alt-Ruppin, Brandenburg, and saw service in the Reichswehr before joining the SS-Totenkopf Standarte *Oberbayern*. He soon assumed command of its first battalion and saw service in Poland and France before being transferred to Russia. During the battle of Demjansk he commanded a battle group with considerable success. He replaced Hermann Priess (q.v.) and, taking over I SS Panzer Corps, he commanded the remnants of the 3rd SS Panzer Division *Totenkopf*, where he and his men were involved in bloody battles. He was awarded the Knight's Cross of the Iron Cross in recognition of these activities and four years later was the 595th recipient of the Oakleaves.

Becker's excesses in Russia, before and during his stint as commander of the *Totenkopf* Division, were bad enough to embarrass even the SS. In July 1944, Himmler (q.v.) launched an investigation into allegations of his sexual and military misconduct. Evidence showed that Becker organised and led an orgy in his regimental office canteen in France at Christmas 1942. While drunk, Becker allegedly broke furniture, smashed windows and rode a horse to death in the canteen before fornicating with revellers. He kept prostitutes in his forward command post in the Ukraine in the spring of 1943 and then, to celebrate Hitler's birthday in April 1943, a drunken Becker ordered a 10-minute salvo salute from all the heavy guns in his regiment, wasting precious ammunition and forcing the men in adjacent units to take cover. He publicly raped Russian women and was insensibly drunk while in frontline command. Himmler was unable or unwilling to punish Becker, or even prevent him from obtaining command of the *Totenkopf* Division. Becker's combat successes, the attrition of capable SS field commanders, plus Hitler's personal admiration, all combined to keep him in authority until the end of the war. After the war Becker was sentenced by the Russians to 25 years' hard labour. While commanding a reconstruction brigade, he was reported for allowing an unexploded grenade to be cemented into a wall. He was tried by a military court, found guilty and shot on 28 February 1952.

BEHRENDS, Dr Hermann

RANK: SS-Gruppenführer
BORN: 11 May 1907
DIED: 1946 (E.A.)
PARTY NUMBER: 981960
SS NUMBER: 35815
AWARDS: 1939 Iron Cross Second Class; War Merit Cross Second Class with Swords; War Merit Cross First Class with Swords; 1939 Wound Badge Black Class; SS Honour Ring; SS Honour Sword

Behrends was the first leader of the Berlin SD, when it was officially only a party office with no foreign intelligence or military section. He was probably responsible for preparing the death lists for the purge of the SA in 1934. On 17 January 1937 Himmler (q.v.) addressed an army officers' group, stating that 'detailed problems of execution do not concern the SD, but only ideological problems'. In contradiction to this, Behrends controlled the Tuchachewski forgeries (a Russian opponent of Stalin; the letters purported to show his group in contact with the Wehrmacht). At the end of 1936, Heydrich (q.v.) had invented an ingenious scheme that resulted in the notorious Moscow Generals' Trials,

and the execution of the generals Tuchachewski, Uberewitch, Eideman and Putna on 12 June 1937. Heydrich thought he had destroyed the Russian high command.

Behrends went on to direct the racial German office in Yugoslavia. The worst excesses were committed by him in Slovenia. He was tried in 1945 and hanged in Belgrade in 1946.

BENDER, Horst

RANK: SS-Standartenführer
BORN: 24 February 1905—
PARTY NUMBER: 1261871
SS NUMBER: 122746
AWARDS: War Merit Cross Second Class with Swords; War Merit Cross First Class with Swords; SS Honour Ring; SS Honour Sword

Bender was the head of the Waffen-SS Judge Advocate's department. When Otto Thierack became Minister of Justice on 20 August 1942, Hitler empowered him to deviate from any existing law to establish a National Socialist Administration of Justice. Göbbels suggested that in addition to the Jews and gypsies, many more 'undesirables' could be 'exterminated by work'. Bormann (q.v.) gave his approval for Thierack to see Himmler (q.v.) at Zhitomir, and with Streckenbach (q.v.) and Bender (q.v.) they reached an agreement on a principal entitled 'the delivery of a-social elements to the Reichsführer-SS to be worked to death'. The initial proposal was to be applied to all Jews and gypsies, to Poles imprisoned for three or more years and to Czechs and Germans serving life sentences. Himmler's meeting refined this to all Germans serving sentences of eight years and over, as well as all persons already in 'protective custody'. Bender made further recommendations on penal detention. Himmler regarded the Dirlewanger (q.v.) Penal Unit as an essential component of Waffen-SS discipline, linking it with the 501st SS-Parachute Battalion as a way to redeem lost honour. The practice was opposed by Bender. When, in March 1944, Berger (q.v.) wanted to transfer all the SS men in detention at Marienwerder to the Dirlewanger Unit, he advised Himmler to send only those convicted of criminal offences who would not be accepted by the parachute unit.

BERGER, Gottlob

RANK: SS-Obergruppenführer
BORN: 16 July 1896
DIED: 5 January 1975 (D)
PARTY NUMBER: 426875
SS NUMBER: 275991
AWARDS: 1914 Iron Cross Second Class;
1914 Iron Cross First Class; Cross of
Honour 1914-1918 Combatants; 1914
Wound Badge Silver Class; War Merit
Cross Second Class with Swords;
War Merit Cross First Class with
Swords; Knight's Cross of the War
Merit Cross with Swords, 15 November
1944; German Cross in Silver, 1 July
1943; 1939 Iron Cross First Class Bar;
Golden Party Badge; SS Honour Ring;
SS Honour Sword.

Born in Gerstetten, Württemberg, the son of a sawmill owner, Berger served as an officer in World War I and was seriously wounded. After the war he joined the Freikorps; he was a teacher in Gerstetten and also held the post of director of the Regional Gymnastic Institute in Stuttgart. Berger wormed his way into Himmler's (q.v.) confidence and became his chief adviser, as well as an adviser to Alfred Rosenberg, the anti-Semitic writer. He was an early member of the SA, but after the murder of Röhm gave his loyalty to the SS. He became head of the SS Sports Office on 1 August 1938; once in charge the SS main office began a reorganisation. From 1 April 1940 he was head of the main recruiting office for the Waffen-SS, and it was he who exploited the availability of non-ethnic Germans for recruitment into the Waffen-SS, particularly as the other branches of the military had no call on their service. He was also responsible for the welfare of German and non-German members of the Waffen-SS, and was Himmler's liaison representative to Rosenberg's ministry.

For a short time Berger held the post of commanding general in Slovakia, where he 'imposed the peace of the graveyard' during the Slovak uprising. He was relieved part-way through the uprising by General Höfle, and from 20 July 1944 was responsible for all POW affairs. He was tried at Nuremberg for the wartime murder of Jews and was sentenced to 25 years' imprisonment in 1949. He was released in 1951 and died in Gerstetten in 1975.

BEST, Dr Werner

RANK: SS-Obergruppenführer
BORN: 10 July 1903—
PARTY NUMBER: 341338
SS NUMBER: 23377
AWARDS: Golden Party Badge; War Merit
Cross Second Class with Swords; War
Merit Cross First Class with Swords;
SS Honour Ring; SS Honour Sword.

A law student from the Rhineland, Best was imprisoned during the French occupation of the Ruhr after World War I for his outspoken nationalist views. He became a legal adviser to the NSDAP and was the drafter of the Boxheim Papers, a plan for a Nazi putsch, which was disclosed in 1931 and caused no little embarrassment to them. In 1933 he became police commissioner for Hesse and in July of that year state governor. He strengthened his career by becoming deputy to Heydrich (q.v.), and as first legal adviser to the SD and Gestapo he laid the foundations of their strength. He was a disciple of Ernst Jüttner (q.v.) and an ardent admirer of Hitler. RSHA was divided into seven departments and Best controlled the personnel department, Amt I, from 1939 to

1940. At the start of the war, however, Best found himself opposed to the new tendencies in National Socialism, and from 1940 to 1942 he led the SD in France. He was then made Plenipotentiary to Denmark, arriving in Copenhagen on 5 November 1940 to take up his duties. His rule was lenient by

Nazi standards, and he seems to have tried to soften the effect of the 'Final Solution' in Denmark. There is evidence that he leaked a warning to the Danish resistance, which enabled them to effect the escape of almost all of Denmark's Jews to Sweden. On 30 December 1943, Best was summoned to Hitler's headquarters, where the Führer reiterated that the most effective deterrent to 'terror' was the use of greater 'terror'. Best tried to counter this argument, but Hitler was adamant that for every victim of resistance, five Danish hostages must die. Best returned to Copenhagen, determined to thwart this directive as far as possible. His enlightened attitude was not, however, shared by the military governor von Hanneken or the SD, and 1944 was to prove one of the bloodiest in Danish history.

In 1946, Best was found guilty of murder by a Danish court and condemned to death, commuted to life imprisonment. Released from Copenhagen prison on 29 August 1951 he returned to Germany, where in 1958 he was found guilty of mass murder and imprisoned. He was released in 1972 due to ill health.

BITTRICH, Willi

RANK: SS-Obergruppenführer und General der Waffen-SS
BORN: 26 February 1894
DIED: 19 April 1979 (D)
PARTY NUMBER: 829700
SS NUMBER: 39177
AWARDS: 1914 Iron Cross Second Class; 1914 Iron Cross First Class; Cross of Honour 1914-1918 Combatants; 1914 Wound Badge Black Class; 1939 Iron Cross Second Class Bar, 25 September 1939; 1939 Iron Cross First Class Bar, 7 June 1940; Knight's Cross, 14 December 1941; Oakleaves, 23 August 1944; Oakleaves with Swords, 6 May 1945; SS Honour Ring; SS Honour Sword.

A dedicated professional soldier, Bittrich was born in Wenigerode in the Harz mountains. During World War I he served as an army officer and then qualified as a pilot. He volunteered to serve with the Grenzschütz Ost and subsequently joined the Reichswehr; he continued his flying in Russia under an agreement with the Soviets, which circumnavigated the aviation ban in the Treaty of Versailles. He joined the SS-Verfügungstruppe in 1934 and the *Leibstandarte* in 1939. During the Polish and French campaigns he commanded the regiment *Deutschland*, and was awarded the Knight's Cross for actions on the Russian Front. His divisional commands included the *Das Reich* and *Hohenstaufen* Divisions. In his role as commander of II SS Panzer Corps he was awarded the Oakleaves, becoming the 563rd recipient.

Bittrich's greatest victory came while commanding this corps at Arnhem in 1944, the last German battlefield victory. His name is etched on the memory of every British paratrooper who landed there, for it was his troops who destroyed the airborne division. While still in command of the corps, he was awarded the Swords, becoming the 153rd recipient. After the war he was tried by the French for war crimes and acquitted in 1954. He died in Wolfratshausen, Bavaria, in 1979.

BLANKENBERG, Werner

RANK: SS-Gruppenführer
PARTY NUMBER: —
SS NUMBER: —

Blankenberg worked as a liaison officer within the Department of Health and became head of the secret Euthanasia Office in the Führer's Chancellery. The programme involved the 'mercy killings' of the mentally and physically handicapped. He was recruited by Bouhler, (q.v.) a man who, along with Brach (Blackenberg's predecessor), has been described as a dehumanised bureaucrat. The euthanasia programme had been stopped by Hitler in 1941 after intense public protest (though by then 75,000 had been murdered), and gradually the Führer Chancellery was absorbed by the Party Chancellery under Martin Bormann. However, in the autumn of 1943, on Himmler's (q.v.) direct orders, SS Judge Advocate Konrad Morgen (q.v.) carried out an investigation into the running of the concentration camps, brought about by Globocnik's (q.v.) self-enrichment and an unsatisfactory audit. Morgen discovered that Blankenberg sent daily orders to Wirth (q.v.) in Poland: Bouhler had not relinquished his men two years after the end of the euthanasia programme as planned. He expected to recover them with the express purpose of resuming 'mercy killings' after the war and Blankenberg was active in its contin-uation. After the war his whereabouts were not discovered.

BOCHMANN, Georg

RANK: SS-Oberführer
BORN: 18 September 1913
DIED: 8 June 1973 (D)
PARTY NUMBER: 1907565
SS NUMBER: 122362
AWARDS: 1939 Iron Cross Second Class,
    20 June 1940; 1939 Iron Cross First
    Class, 8 July 1941; Knight's Cross of the
    Iron Cross, 3 May 1942; Oakleaves,
    17 May 1943; Oakleaves and Swords
    30 March 1945; General Assault Badge;
    Demjansk Shield; SS Honour Ring;
    SS Honour Sword.

Born in Albernau, the Aue district of Saxony, Bochmann was the son of a factory worker. In 1934 he joined the SS-Totenkopf and was promoted in 1936 to join the SS-Totenkopf Standarte *Oberbayern*. He was a prime mover in the creation and outfitting of the SS *Totenkopf* Division, 1939-40. While serving as commanding officer of Battle Group *Bochmann*, he was awarded the Knight's Cross of the Iron Cross for actions of the Russian Front. He was present at the battle of Demjansk and the recapture of Kharkov. While in command of motorcycle regiment *Thule*, he was awarded the Oakleaves, becoming the 246th recipient, and receiving the award from Hitler personally. Bochmann temporarily commanded the SS-Officers' School for Administration in Arolsen, Hesse. While in command of the 18th SS Panzergrenadier Division *Horst Wessel*, he was awarded the Swords, becoming the 140th recipient.

BOCK, Friedrich-Wilhelm

RANK: SS-Oberführer und Oberst der
    Schutzpolizei
BORN: 6 May 1897
DIED: 11 March 1978 (D)
PARTY NUMBER: 2223186
SS NUMBER: 405821
AWARDS: 1914 Iron Cross Second Class;
    Cross of Honour 1914-1918 Combatants;
    1914 Wound Badge Black Class; 1939
    Iron Cross Second Class, Bar, 21 August
    1941; 1939 Iron Cross First Class,
    16 September 1941; Knight's Cross of
    the Iron Cross, 23 August 1943;
    Oakleaves, 2 September 1944.

A Prussian from Wreschen on the Warthe river near Posen, Bock volunteered for service on 2 August 1914 and fought throughout World War I. Afterwards, he joined the Freikorps and, in 1922,

BORMANN, Martin

RANK: Reichsleiter and
        SS-Obergruppenführer
BORN: 17 June 1900
DIED: unknown
PARTY NUMBER: 60508
SS NUMBER: 555
AWARDS: Blood Order, 17 February 1939;
        Frontbann Badge; SS Honour Ring;
        SS Honour Sword.

Born in Halberstadt in Lower Saxony, Bormann was one of Hitler's closest confidantes. Called up as a gunner towards the end of World War I, he did not see action. After the war he was unemployed and then worked as a steward on an estate. He joined the Rossbach Freikorps and later the Frontbann, the paramilitary force organised by Röhm after the banning of the SA in 1923. He and Höss (q.v.) were jailed for the murder of Walter Kado, a teacher they claimed was an informant in the French-occupied Ruhr. He was released in 1925 and he joined the NSDAP working first as head of the press service in Gau Thüringen, then rising to become Gauleiter in 1928, before transferring to the staff of the supreme SA leadership towards the end of that year.

Bormann's fund-raising abilities became legendary; he was made party treasurer and was Hitler's intermediary as overseer of the 'Adolf Hitler Fund'. Donations and extortions were deposited and used for multifarious enterprises. He ensured that the scandal surrounding the mysterious death of Hitler's niece, Geli Raubel, was hushed up by using the fund to pay off the police inspector, Heinrich Müller (q.v).

In September 1929 Bormann married Gerda Buch who was, if possible, even more fanatical in her beliefs than her husband. Bormann hated everything about Walter Buch, her father, coveting only his Blood Order, the award worn by veterans of the 1923 Putsch. On 30 May 1938 Bormann considerably expanded the conditions for the award of the Blood Order, much to the dismay of the Alter Kämpfers (veterans). New conditions for recipients included: the imposition of a death sentence which was later commuted to life imprisonment; to have served at least a one-year jail sentence for political crimes; or to have been severely wounded. Thus, not eligible for his involvement in the putsch,

the police service, becoming a captain in 1933 and a major in 1934. He joined the newly raised police division, and in the 1940 Western campaign took command of the second detachment of the artillery regiment.

During the Russian campaign he was considered to be one of the most accomplished artillery officers of the division and was awarded the Knight's Cross of the Iron Cross. He stayed with his unit until 1944, when he became artillery commander of II SS Panzer Corps in the West. When SS-Brigadeführer Stadler (q.v.) was wounded in late July, his command of the 9th SS Panzer Division *Hohenstaufen* was given to Bock, who held it temporarily from 1 August to 10 October 1944, when Stadler returned to the unit. During his tenure, Bock participated in the fighting around Hill 112, as well as at Cheau and Estry. In recognition of his leadership he was awarded the Oakleaves, becoming the 570th recipient. He died in Hanover in 1978.

Bormann was able to confer the award on himself under either clause one or two and his ambition was fulfilled.

Hitler trusted him to conduct his financial affairs, and Bormann was responsible for rebuilding the Berghof. He may also have encouraged or facilitated Hess's (q.v.) flight to Scotland in 1941. On Hitler's command, Hess's office was renamed Parteikanzlei and Bormann was promoted to head it and to act as chief of staff to the Führer's deputy. He also became a member of the Council of Ministers for the Defence of the Reich.

Bormann (far right in picture) possessed a ruthless and crafty mind, and during the war he became an almost invisible courtier who wielded enormous power. After his appointment as Hitler's Secretary on 12 April 1943 he controlled access to Hitler, preventing even the most senior leaders from seeing the Führer. He witnessed Hitler's will and marriage, and attempted to have Göring executed. He transmitted Dönitz's succession as Führer and ordered the mass breakout from the bunker. His fate is unknown, there was one theory that he died at the Lehrta bridge. An American investigator, McCabe, concluded that he could have committed suicide, been killed in Berlin, been a Russian or British agent, or escaped to Argentina. He was tried in absentia at Nuremberg, found guilty and sentenced to death.

BOUHLER, Philipp

RANK: SS-Obergruppenführer
BORN: 2 September 1899
DIED: 10 May 1945 (S)
PARTY NUMBER: 12
SS NUMBER: 54932
AWARDS: Golden Party Badge; Blood Order No 29; Culture Badge; SS Honour Ring; SS Honour Sword.

After being severely wounded in World War I, Munich-born Bouhler (left in picture) became involved in publishing. In 1921 he became an early member of the NSDAP, which subsequently entitled him to be known as an Alter Kämpfer and worked on the *Völkischer Beobachter*, being its business manager from 1925 to 1934. In 1933 he was promoted to Reichsleiter and followed Himmler (q.v.) as Police President of Munich in 1934. Later in the year, he was appointed head of Hitler's private Chancellery, a most important move, effectively making him part of Hitler's secretariat. Holding a number of posts associated with the publishing industry, Bouhler also became chairman of the Censorship Committee, which nominated books to be approved or damned according to Nazi policy.

Hitler entrusted Bouhler and Dr Karl Brandt (q.v.) with responsibility for the programme of euthanasia in 1939. However, public concern about the programme forced Hitler to abort it. Bormann's (q.v.) ambitions contributed to the absorption of the private Chancellery by the party Chancellery, and by 1944 Bouhler was sidelined. He and his wife committed suicide at Zell am See when the Americans tried to arrest him in 1945.

BRANDT, Prof Dr Karl

RANK: SS-Gruppenführer
BORN: 8 January 1904
DIED: 2 June 1948 (E.A.)
PARTY NUMBER: 1009617
SS NUMBER: 260353
AWARDS: SS Honour Ring; SS Honour
   Sword.

Having been asked to treat SA-Obergruppenführer Wilhelm Brüchner, who had been injured in a car crash in 1933, Brandt made such as impression on his patient, who was Hitler's chief personal adjutant, that he quickly became part of Hitler's inner circle. In September 1939 Brandt and Bouhler (q.v.) were given command of the programme of euthanasia. On its cessation, Brandt was appointed Reich Commissioner for Sanitation and Health in 1942 and became one of Hitler's doctors.

Hitler's personal physician was Theodor Morell, who had taken a post as ship's doctor after graduation from medical school, then began a practice as a specialist in skin and venereal diseases in Berlin. Heinrich Hoffman, Hitler's court photographer, developed a dangerous infection in 1936 and Morell cured it with sulphanilamide, a new wonder drug he had imported from Hungary. Morell was engaged by Hitler on this recommendation.

His farewell address from the scaffold was curtailed by the hood placed over his head

Brandt competed with Morell for Hitler's favours, advising him against the use of countless drugs which Morell was administering by injection. Hitler refused all criticism of Morell, and Brandt was dismissed in October 1944, being replaced by Ludwig Stumpfegger (q.v.).

During his tenure in office Brandt was continually criticised by the Bishop of Münster, Clemens von Galen, one of the bravest opponents of the Third Reich in Germany. It was the bishop who had first raised doubts about the euthanasia programme, and his sermons on the matter had led to its suspension. Later, Brandt reported to Himmler that the bishop was raising doubts about the evacuation of mental patients from institutions in areas subject to air raids. Himmler himself had wanted to arrest the bishop in 1941, but had not for fear of the trouble this might cause in Westphalia. In this he would have been supported by both Hitler and Heydrich (q.v.), who despised what they called the 'black crows' of the Christian churches. Hitler himself saw Nazism itself as a religious faith, but the whole religious debate bored him. However, he was impressed by the machinery of the faiths, Roman Catholicism in particular. Needless to say, those religious groups which fell foul of Nazism, such as the Jehovah Witnesses, who refused to do military service, were ruthlessly suppressed.

Two weeks before his suicide Hitler became aware that Brandt had secreted his family in a position of safety where they could surrender to the Americans rather than fall into Soviet hands. Hitlerian rage resulted in Brandt being summarily tried for treason, found guilty and condemned to death, although Himmler (q.v.) and Speer succeeded in staying the execution by calling for new witnesses. Although he dodged the sentence imposed by Hitler's court, Brandt was tried by a US court for having approved medical experiments by SS doctors at concentration camps. His defence was that 'any personal code of ethics must give way to the total character of the war'. He was found guilty and condemned to death. He offered his body for experimental purposes similar to those he had sanctioned, but this was declined. He remonstrated that his execution was political revenge, and his farewell address from the scaffold was curtailed as the black hood was placed over his head.

BRANDT, Dr Rudolf

RANK: SS-Standartenführer
BORN: 2 June 1909
DIED: 2 June 1948 (E.A.)
PARTY NUMBER: 1331536
SS NUMBER: 129771
AWARDS: War Merit Cross Second Class
with Swords; War Merit Cross First
Class with Swords; SS Honour Ring;
SS Honour Sword.

Rudolf Brandt was Himmler's personal chaplain and head of the minister's office. He was found guilty at the war's end and hanged in Landsberg Prison in 1948.

BRAUN, Prof Dr Wernher von

RANK: SS-Sturmbannführer
BORN: 23 March 1912
DIED: 16 June 1977 (D)
PARTY NUMBER: 5738692
SS NUMBER: 185068
AWARDS: War Merit Cross Second Class
with Swords; War Merit Cross First
Class with Swords; Knight's Cross of
the War Merit Cross with Swords,
28 October 1944.

Wernher von Braun (right in picture) was the Third Reich's most celebrated rocket scientist. He was born in Wirsitz, Westpreussen, which is now part of Poland. He belonged to the Verein für Raketen as an 18-year-old student and, by the end of the 1920s, to a group of technicians researching rocket propulsion, as an assistant to Nebel and Riedel. From 1 October 1932 he was an employee of the army's weapons department at the testing grounds in Kümmersdorf. As technician in charge, he was prominent in the founding of the Army Technological Research Institute from 1936, and took part in creating the 'wonder weapons'.

While Director of Rocket Research at Pennemünde, he created the Flüssigkeitsgrossrakete 'A4', better known as the V-2 rocket. In July 1943, at the instigation of Armaments Minister Albert Speer, a colour film showing the successful start flight of a V-2 missile was shown to Hitler himself, who until then had been against the project. After the presentation Hitler said to von Braun, 'I thank you. In the face of this missile one can only say that Europe and the world, from this point onwards, are too small for a war. With these weapons a war would be unbearable for mankind.' For his contributions von Braun received the title of Professor on 21 July 1943. Between January 1944 and April 1945 around 6000 V-2s were built, with some 2315 being launched against Antwerp, London, and other British targets.

Von Braun surrendered to the Americans on 2 May 1945, together with his entire staff and a goods train full of technical documents, and he was taken to the USA. There he entered the service of the US Missile Department and accepted American citizenship in 1955. The basis for this was a decree from President Truman about the employment of captured German scientists in the USA: 'They receive special treatment because of their technical or scientific expertise. A personality from the Nazi regime who holds a high position or has been awarded honours will not receive exceptional treatment on that basis alone.'

When a reporter asked von Braun his reasons for changing citizenship, he answered: 'My country has lost two world wars. Next time, I would like to be on the winning side.' As the leader of a development team, which worked with technicians of the HVP under the control of the US Army, he succeeded in launching the first American satellite, *Explorer*. At the beginning of 1970, von Braun was appointed Deputy Director of NASA and Leader of Planning. He died in 1977.

BREMER, Gerhard

RANK: SS-Sturmbannführer
BORN: 25 July 1917
DIED: 29 October 1989 (D)
PARTY NUMBER: 5274225
SS NUMBER: 310405
AWARDS: 1939 Iron Cross Second Class,
      1 October 1939; 1939 Iron Cross First
      Class, 7 June 1940; German Cross in
      Gold, 30 August 1944; Knight's Cross of
      the Iron Cross, 30 October 1941;
      Oakleaves 25 November 1944; Close
      Combat Clasp Silver Class, June 1944;
      SS Honour Ring; SS Honour Sword.

An exceptional soldier, Gerhard Bremer was born in Dusterntal, joined the SS-Verfügungstruppe in October 1936 and was assigned to the SS-Standarte *Germania*. He went to the SS-Junkerschule at Bad Tölz, and was then posted to the *Leibstandarte SS Adolf Hitler*. He took part in the Polish and Western campaigns, was transferred to the east in Operation 'Barbarossa'. Here, he commanded the Kradschützen company of the *Leibstandarte*. The fluidity of the front in the early days of the campaign gave the motorcycle units an edge in chasing the fleeing Soviet forces. In one single engagement, for example, Bremer captured over 500 prisoners and a cache of military equipment. His unit rushed on through two Soviet defence lines and outflanked another, breaking into the town of Mariupel. In recognition of his bravery and leadership he was awarded the Knight's Cross of the Iron Cross.

In 1943 Bremer was transferred to the newly formed 12th SS Panzer Division *Hitlerjugend*. During the hectic fighting after the D-Day landings, the *Hitlerjugend* suffered heavy casualties. Caught in the Falaise cauldron, only a few of the unit fought their way out; in recognition of his leadership Bremer was awarded the Oakleaves, becoming the 668th recipient. Having reformed and fought in the abortive Ardennes Offensive, *Hitlerjugend* was subsequently transferred to Hungary. It was pushed back to Austria, where Bremer surrendered with the remnants of his division to the American forces. He went into French captivity and was released in 1947. He lived in Spain, where he died in Denia las Rotas in 1989.

BRUINS, Derk-Elsko

RANK: SS-Oberscharführer
BORN: 20 March 1923
DIED: 5 February 1986 (D)
PARTY NUMBER: —
SS NUMBER: —
AWARDS: 1939 Iron Cross Second Class;
      1939 Iron Cross First Class; Knight's
      Cross of the Iron Cross, August 1944;
      Medal for the Winter Campaign in
      Russia 1941/1942; 1939 Wound Badge
      Black Class; General Assault Badge.

A Dutchman, Bruins volunteered for the Waffen-SS and served as a gunner in the 1st Company, SS-Panzer Jäger-Abteilung 54, 23rd SS Freiwilligen Panzergrenadier Division *Nederland*. Over a number of days during the fierce fighting around Narwa-Hilgerrburg against the Red Army, acting calmly and with a pronounced sense of duty, Bruins destroyed 12 or more Soviet tanks, with total disregard for his own life or safety, rejoining his comrades as if nothing had happened. For his bravery he was awarded the Knight's Cross of the Iron Cross. After the war he was imprisoned and then made his home in Germany, dying in Gerolstein Elfel in 1986.

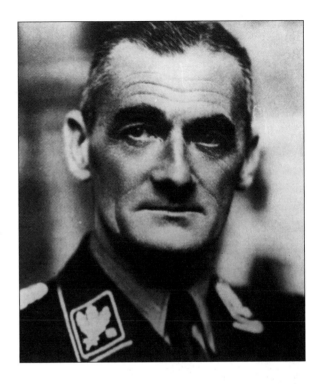

BUCH, Walter

RANK: SS-Obergruppenführer
BORN: 24 October 1883
DIED: 15 September 1949 (S)
PARTY NUMBER: 7733
SS NUMBER: 81353
AWARDS: Golden Party Badge; Coburg
    Badge, 14 October 1932; Blood Order;
    NSDAP Long Service Medal 25 Years;
    NSDAP Long Service Medal 15 Years;
    NSDAP Long Service Medal 10 Years;
    SS Honour Ring; SS Honour Sword.

The son of a prominent judge, Buch was born in Bruchsal, Baden. He saw service in the army in World War I, rising to the rank of major, a title he used throughout his career. After the war he was a member of several ex-servicemen's organisations. In 1922 he joined the SA, becoming the commander of the Nuremberg force in 1923 and fighting in the 1923 Putsch. He was made president of the USCHLA, the NSDAP disciplinary tribunal. He was to become 'lord high executioner' of the party, a vengeful man from whom nobody was immune. In this capacity he accompanied Hitler on the arrest of Röhm at Weissensee, and he took charge of the liquidations at Stadelheim prison. Eyewitnesses recounted his enjoyment as he watched his victims die, some of them old comrades whom he butchered with his own hands.

As president of the tribunal he judged all cases in accordance with Hitler's views. Buch's article in *German Justice* on 21 October 1938, stating: 'the Jew is not a human being. He is an appearance of putrescence. Just as the fission-fungus cannot permeate wood until it is rotten, so the Jew was able to creep into the German people, to bring a disaster only after the German nation had begun to rot from within', provoked anti-Semitic riots on 9 November 1938. Buch decreed that Nazis who raped Jewish women were to be expelled from the NSDAP and surrendered to the courts, whereas murderers were given minor punishments. Party members who killed Jews were merely carrying out orders.

After the war he was arrested, tried and given five years' hard labour

Hated, despised and ignored by his son-in-law Martin Bormann, he was nevertheless made Reichsleiter, but his power was short-lived, as most of his functions were taken over by the SD and he became an irrelevance. After the war he was arrested, tried and given five year's hard labour. Whilst in captivity he committed suicide, slashing his wrists and drowning in Ammer Lake in Bavaria.

CHRISTEN, Fritz

RANK: SS-Unterscharführer
BORN: 29 June 1921—
PARTY NUMBER: —
SS NUMBER: —
AWARDS: 1939 Iron Cross Second Class, 20 July 1941; 1939 Iron Cross First Class, 24 September 1941; Knight's Cross of the Iron Cross, 20 October 1941.

Christen was a gunner with the 2nd Company, SS-Antitank Detachment of the *Totenkopf* Division; he was born in Wredenhagen, Mecklenburg.

His battery was located just north of Lushno, taking the full brunt of the first Soviet armoured assault on the morning of 24 September 1941. Christen was the only member of the battery to survive. He stayed at his post firing feverishly until he had driven off the attacking tanks, and destroyed six. Christen remained alone in the emplacement for the next two days. He repeatedly repulsed Russian infantry and tank attacks with his 50mm cannon while exposed to a continual hail of artillery, mortar and machine-gun fire. He hung on grimly, cut off completely from the rest of his unit and the division. He refused to abandon his post, carrying shells to his gun from the disabled batteries around him during the hours of darkness.

On 27 September the Russians were finally driven out of Lushno, and his astonished SS comrades found Christen still crouched behind his anti-tank cannon. In 72 hours he had killed 100 enemy soldiers and knocked out 13 Soviet tanks. For this feat he was awarded the Knight's Cross – the first and youngest enlisted man from the ranks of the Waffen-SS to be so honoured.

Left:A snow-covered member of the SS-Polizei *Division on the Leningrad Front during the winter of 1941-42. His weapon is the Kar 98 bolt-action rifle.*

CHRISTOPHERSEN, Egon

RANK: SS-Unterscharführer
BORN: 8 February 1919
DIED: 15 January 1988 (D)
PARTY NUMBER: —
SS NUMBER: —
AWARDS: 1939 Iron Cross Second Class, 26 March 1943; 1939 Iron Cross First Class, 28 May 1944; Knight's Cross of the Iron Cross, 11 July 1944; Medal for the Winter Campaign in Russia 1941-1942.

From Stroeby in Denmark, Christophersen volunteered for the Waffen-SS and became a platoon NCO in the 7th Company, 24th SS-Panzergrenadier Regiment, 11th SS Freiwilligen-Panzergrenadier Division *Nordland*, III (Germ.) SS Panzer Corps.

During January 1944, *Nordland* fought rearguard actions, past Kingisepp and westwards to Narva, the scene of very bitter defensive fighting until April, when the Narva Bridgehead was

established. Static warfare continued until July, when the non-German Waffen-SS held up the Red Army. For his bravery and his decisive action while engaged in repulsing a Russian attack and the resultant counterattack in the Narva Bridgehead, Christophersen was awarded the Knight's Cross of the Iron Cross. He survived the war and died in Denmark in 1988.

CLAUBERG, Karl
RANK: SS-Oberführer
BORN: 1898
DIED: 9 August 1957 (M or S)
PARTY NUMBER: —
SS NUMBER: —
AWARDS: Golden Party Badge (Honour Award)

Clauberg was the oldest son of a rural craftsman who later established a weapons business. He joined the army in 1916, seeing action in France and being taken prisoner by the British. After the war he became a gynaecologist and later a professor whose early researches on female hormones during the 1920s and early 1930s led to the discovery of the chemicals progynon and prolutons for the treatment of infertility. He joined the NSDAP in 1933 and, after being introduced to Himmler (q.v.) in 1940, began to concentrate his researches on methods of mass sterilisation. He was a member of the SD and Himmler employed him in experiments of mass sterilisation on Jewish women from July 1942, first at Ravensbrück and then Auschwitz. This led to the infamous 'Auschwitz sterilisation experiments'. In the latter part of 1944, Clauberg was engaged in a new project on sterility and reproduction as chief of a new institution known as the 'City of Mothers'.

Captured by the Russians on 8 June 1945, Clauberg was imprisoned for three years in the Soviet Union before being tried for war crimes. He was sentenced to 25 year's imprisonment, but was repatriated with others in October 1955, totally unrepentant. Charges were brought against him in November 1955 by the Kiel Court, but suddenly and mysteriously he died in his cell on 9 August 1957. It was generally believed that he was about to name names at the top of the Nazi medical hierarchy, and as a result medical colleagues helped bring about his demise.

COLLANI, Hans
RANK: SS-Standartenführer
BORN: 13 December 1908
DIED: 29 July 1944 (K.I.A.)
PARTY NUMBER: —
SS NUMBER: —
AWARDS: 1939 Iron Cross Second Class, 25 September 1939; 1939 Iron Cross First Class, 18 October 1942; German Cross in Gold, 24 April 1944; Knight's Cross of the Iron Cross, 19 August 1944.

A Pomeranian, Collani joined the SS and saw service in the *Leibstandarte* where he was 'Sepp' Dietrich's (q.v.) adjutant. He was engaged in the Polish campaign and went on to command Finnish volunteers. In 1944 he was the commanding officer of the 49th SS-Freiwilligen Panzergrenadier Regiment *de Ruyter*, SS-Freiwilligen Panzergrenadier Brigade *Nederland*, III (Germ.) SS Panzer Corps, Army Group North. From January to June of that year German forces were able to hold the Narva Bridgehead (Narva had great significance for the Nazis, for it was there that the Teutonic Knights had fought against the Slavs in the Middle Ages). In the early hours of the morning of 27 June the Russians attacked north of the town, threatening the main supply line to Narva. A successful counterattack was mounted against the Soviets by the first battalion of the 49th SS-Volunteers Regiment commanded by Hans Meyer. Meyer was killed, and Collani was severely wounded and died two days later in a field hospital. For his bravery in the counterattack he was posthumously awarded the Knight's Cross of the Iron Cross.

The Waffen-SS defence at Narva resulted in the award of no fewer than 29 Knight's Crosses to personnel of the volunteer divisions. The fighting around Narva ended during the evening of 18 September 1944, when all Waffen-SS units were pulled out and ordered west towards Estonia.

CONTI, Dr Leonardo

RANK: SS-Obergruppenführer
BORN: 24 August 1900
DIED: 6 October 1945 (S)
PARTY NUMBER: 72225
SS NUMBER: 3982
AWARDS: Golden Party Badge; War Merit Cross Second Class without Swords; War Merit Cross First Class without Swords; SS Honour Ring; SS Honour Sword.

Conti was born in Lugano, Switzerland, and after taking his medical degree he moved to Berlin where he joined the Nazi Party, becoming in 1923 the first SA physician in Berlin. Hitler appointed him to be Reich Health Leader and State Secretary for Health in 1939. He instituted the euthanasia programme for killing Germans of unsound mind and mental defects with the avowed intention of cleansing the Nordic race. Conti committed suicide while awaiting trial in Nuremberg Prison. The Berlin de-Nazification Tribunal fined his estate DM3000 four years after his death.

COOPER, Thomas Hellor

RANK: SS-Unterscharführer
BORN: 29 August 1919—
PARTY NUMBER: —
SS NUMBER: —
AWARDS: 1939 Wound Badge Silver Class.

The only Englishman to receive a German combat award during World War II, Cooper was the son of a British soldier/photographer and a German mother. After World War I his parents returned to Britain, where Thomas was born. Unable to join the police because of his mother's nationality, an embittered Cooper joined the BUF (British Union of Fascists) and subsequently looked to Germany for work. In 1939 he sought the help of the German academic exchange organisation in London and was eventually sent to Stuttgart.

He was offered a teaching job at a school in the Taunus Mountains and he started on 20 August. With the outbreak of war he was dismissed as an enemy alien, but secured a post as a private tutor. It was suggested that he might join the German Army, and eventually he was presented to Gottlob Berger (q.v.), who enrolled him in the SS. On 1 February 1940 he reported to the *Leibstandarte* for basic training. He found life difficult and had run-ins with members of the unit. He was moved to a new unit, SS-Totenkopf, based at Radolfzell and repeated his basic training. In July 1940 Cooper was transferred to the 8th company of the 5th Totenkopf Infantry Regiment where he received temporary NCO rank and acted as an instructor, remaining with the regiment until 1941, with the rank of Rottenführer.

Cooper finally saw action in February 1943. In the face of a heavy barrage and onslaught by infantry and tanks, Cooper collected his unit together and withdrew. Having travelled only 500m (1640ft), he fell, his legs severely wounded by shrapnel. However, he qualified for a wound badge, becoming the only Englishman to win a German combat decoration. He was subsequently placed in charge of the British Freikorps. In 1945 he was tried at the Old Bailey for high treason, found guilty and condemned to death. This was commuted to life imprisonment.

DALUEGE, Kurt

RANK: SS-Oberstgruppenführer und
Generaloberst der Polizei
Chef der Ordnungspolizei
BORN: 15 September 1897
DIED: 20 October 1946 (E.A.)
PARTY NUMBER: 31981
SS NUMBER: 1119
AWARDS: 1914 Iron Cross Second Class;
Cross of Honour 1914-1918
Combatants; 1914 Wound Badge Silver
Class; Gau Berlin Badge, Gold Class;
Frontbann Badge; German Cross in
Silver, 10 September 1942; Knight's
Cross of the War Merit Cross with
Swords, 1 September 1943
(6 September 1943); SS Honour Ring;
SS Honour Sword.

Born in Kreuzberg-Oberschlesien, Daluege was wounded several times during World War I.

Professionally Daluege was an engineer, having studied at the Berliner Technischer Hochschule and passing the state exams for the Engineering Diploma in 1923. He worked as a site manager with different canal and tram constructions, later changing to be a technical assistant in the Prussian Ministry of Agriculture. From 1927 until 1933 Daluege worked at the Berlin Refuse Collection Department as an engineer. Politically, he was involved in the growing success in different right-wing radical groups from the end of World War I, in particular the National Socialists, where he rose to the level of leader. He entered the Freikorps Rossbach in 1922, as well as the NSDAP after the banning of the Grossdeutschen Arbeiterpartei in 1923. After the legalisation of the NSDAP and Sturmabteilung (SA) in 1925, he was promoted to deputy gauleiter and leader of the first SA unit in Berlin. During

the re-banning of the SA, he was the founder and leader of the Frontbanns-Nord. At the end of 1928 Daluege left the Berlin SA and joined the SS. On 25 July 1930, he was promoted to SS-Oberführer, then to SS-Gruppenführer on 1 July 1932, remaining leader of the SS-Gruppe Ost until August. From 24 April 1933 until its dissolution, he belonged to the Prussian Landtag as a specialist of the NSDAP coalition party for police matters, and was a representative from 12 November 1933. In June 1933, he was elected to the Prussian Staatsrat.

On 30 January 1933, the day the National Socialists assumed power, Daluege began his appointment as Kommissar by special appointment in the Prussian Home Office through Hermann Göring, and was promoted to the chief of all police informers. On 11 May, he took over the leadership of the police in Prussia, simultaneously being appointed as Ministerialdirektor. On 15 September 1933, he was promoted to Generalleutnant of the Prussian Landespolizei. Two months later he took on the leadership of the police department in the Reich Home Office. Daluege was promoted to SS-Obergruppenführer in the same month. In June 1936, he was appointed to the position of Chef der Ordnungspolizei in the newly created Hauptamt Ordungspolizei (the civil police, known as Orpo), and on 17 June he was promoted to the rank of General der Ordnungspolizei. On 20 April 1942, he was promoted to Generaloberst der Ordnungspolizei and SS-Oberstgruppenführer, the only police officer with this rank.

Heydrich (q.v.) loathed Daluege and scathingly nicknamed him 'Dummi-Dummi', so it is ironic that his successor as Deputy Reichsprotektor of Bohemia and Moravia was none other than Daluege, who took over on 30 May 1942. He remained until 14 October 1943, and ordered the massive reprisals, murders and imprisonments that followed the assassination. From the summer of 1943 he was continually ill.

After the war Daluege was charged by the Czechs as a war criminal, found guilty and condemned to death. Due to his ill health he was only semi-conscious when he was hanged in Prague on 24 October 1946.

DARGES, Fritz

RANK: SS-Obersturmbannführer
BORN: 8 February 1913—
PARTY NUMBER: —
SS NUMBER: —
AWARDS: 1939 Iron Cross Second Class,
    15 July 1940; 1939 Iron Cross First
    Class, 19 August 1942; Knight's Cross
    of the Iron Cross, 5 April 1942.

Born in Dülseberg near Salzwedel, Altmark, Darges was Martin Bormann's (q.v.) SS adjutant from 1936 to 1939, and from October 1940 was an SS aide with periods of frontline duty until he was wounded. He was Hitler's personal adjutant from 1 March 1943 until 18 July 1944. During one conference, a house fly kept returning to a point on the map Hitler was concentrating upon, producing an angry Hitlerian outburst with attempts to shoo it away. Darges was grinning as Hitler looked his way. Immediately taking him aside, he had him transferred to the Eastern Front. Here, as the commander of the 5th Panzer Regiment, 5th SS Panzer Division *Wiking*, he was awarded the Knight's Cross of the Iron Cross.

DARRÉ, Richard Walther

RANK: SS-Obergruppenführer
BORN: 14 July 1895
DIED: 5 September 1953 (D)
PARTY NUMBER: 248256
SS NUMBER: 6882
AWARDS: 1914 Iron Cross Second Class;
    Cross of Honour 1914-1918
    Combatants; Golden Party Badge;
    War Merit Cross Second Class with
    Swords; War Merit Cross First Class
    with Swords; SS Honour Ring;
    SS Honour Sword.

Darré was born in the German colony near Belgrano, Argentina. He attended the colonial schools in Witzenhausen and Wimbledon, and several universities, including Heidelberg. He served in World War I, and afterwards led the young farmers in Insterburg. He decided to become an agriculturist and became interested in stock rearing problems. In 1929 he wrote his first book, *Blood and Soil*, setting out his views of agriculture and selective breeding. In 1930 he joined the NSDAP and met Himmler (q.v.), who absorbed his racist ideas and persuaded Darré to join the SS. He became the first head of RuSHA in 1932.

Darré became Minister of Agriculture in June 1933 with the resignation of Dr Hugenberg. His philosophy was that the Germans were both farmers and warriors. He recognised no clear division between nobility and peasantry, and his views brought him into conflict with Himmler in 1936, forcing Darré to resign the leadership of RuSHA in 1938.

Darré established the Reich Food Estate in 1933. This afforded him an opportunity for corruption on a grand scale. In 1942 an investigation discovered that he was covertly implementing black marketeering. He was dismissed from his ministry. He was tried, found guilty and sentenced to five years' imprisonment. He died of a liver disorder in Munich in 1953.

DEGRELLE, Léon

RANK: SS-Standartenführer der Reserve
BORN: 15 June 1906
DIED: 31 March 1994
PARTY NUMBER: —
SS NUMBER: —
AWARDS: 1939 Iron Cross Second Class,
2-13 March 1942; 1939 Iron Cross First
Class, 18-21 May 1942; Knight's Cross
of the Iron Cross, 20 February 1944;
Oakleaves, 27 August 1944; Close Combat
Clasp Gold Class, 14 September 1944;
Infantry Assault Badge Silver Class, 30
August 1942; Belgium Badge of Honour
of 'Rex' Gold Class.

Léon Degrelle was born in Bouillon, Belgium, and became the most famous foreign volunteer in the Waffen-SS. He entered Belgian politics in May 1935 calling his movement 'Rexisme', for he disliked the term 'political party'. In the general election of May 1936 the Rexists won a sensational victory, gaining 21 seats in the lower house and 8 in the senate. Degrelle was offered a cabinet post by the King of the Belgians, which he later declined. He wanted much more than just a ministerial portfolio for himself and some minor positions for his party.

The ascendance of Degrelle's movement was meteoric; so, equally, was its decline: the Rexists lost most of their gains in the April 1939 general election, holding on to only four seats with Degrelle suffering defeat at the hands of the then prime minister, Paul van Zeeland, in a straight fight for a Brussels seat. Degrelle looked set for political oblivion until the occupation of his country in May 1940 catapulted him once more onto the political stage. The Rexist party was the main collaborationist faction in Wallonie under the occupation, but was never entrusted with political power, although some members held minor posts in the civic administration.

Degrelle spent most of the war on the Russian Front with a legion of Walloon Volunteers, and in May 1943 Himmler (q.v.)

decided that they had proved themselves worthy of admission into the Waffen-SS. This did not imply any question of merging them with the existing Flemish Waffen-SS. On 1 June 1943 the Walloon legion became the SS-Sturmbrigade *Wallonie* and joined the *Wiking* Division in the southern Ukraine in November.

Hitler said of him: 'If I had a son, I would wish him to be like you'

In January 1944, 56,000 German troops were trapped in the action at Cherkassy, where their effort to fight their way out lasted for several weeks and was enormously costly. On 14 February, over 200 members of the Walloon assault brigade were killed, including the commander, Lucien Lipert, and Degrelle was promoted to replace him. When the Germans finally broke out, the *Wiking* Division was down to 4000 men, and only 632 of the original 2000 Walloons came through unscathed. The survivors were sent to Wildflecken in Franconia to regroup but, in fact, received little respite. A desperate situation had developed in Estonia and the Walloon assault brigade was rushed in to take part alongside their Flemish compatriots in the Battle of the European SS at Narva in July 1944. Degrelle won the Knight's Cross of the Iron Cross, and had the Oakleaves conferred upon him by Hitler personally, becoming the 355th recipient. Hitler held Degrelle in high esteem, saying: 'If I had a son, I would wish him to be like you'.

In January 1945, the newly created panzergrenadier division was ordered to the front with two other badly under-strength volunteer divisions, the Flemings and the French, which made up the grandly titled, SS Army Corps West. They joined battle with the Russians in the region of Stettin and within a matter of weeks were reduced to a strength of little more than 700 men. By mid-April, what was left had been almost completely destroyed on the west bank of the River Oder. Some remnants of this shattered division were evacuated by sea to Denmark. Degrelle escaped to Norway, and flew on to Spain in Speer's plane. After the war he was tried in absentia by the Belgians and sentenced to death. He lived in Spain until his death. When Degrelle died, the Belgian Government took active measures to prevent Belgians who had fought beside him attending the funeral.

DIEBITSCH, Prof Karl
RANK: SS-Oberführer
BORN: 3 January 1899—
PARTY NUMBER: 4690956
SS NUMBER: 141990
AWARDS: SS Honour Ring; SS Honour Sword.

Professor Diebitsch was the head of the Hauptamt Persönlicher Stab Reichsführer-SS, Chefamt Munich. It was his job to deal with 'all artistic and architectural questions' which interested the Reichsführer-SS.

Diebitsch's creations included the police and SS sword, as well as the much sought-after 1936 chained dagger. He was also responsible for the 'touch mark', commonly referred to as the 'SS proof mark' which was the logo denoting his work. It has also been observed on some of the ceramic works decorating the walls of the SS-Junkerschule in Bad Tölz. He was also responsible for the design of SS uniforms, coats of arms for senior SS leaders and insignia, such as the long-service medals.

The famous Allach SS porcelain factory came under his control in 1939

The famous Allach SS porcelain factory came under his control in 1939, when he was named director and he used a similar touch mark as its logo on the base of all its creations. The SS acquired the small porcelain factory in Allach in 1937, and it was one of its first economic enterprises. The factory had been established as a small private concern in 1935 – Himmler viewed its acquisition as a major triumph. It was moved to the SS complex at Dachau where it produced high quality porcelain and official SS gifts, such as the pseudo-Germanic Yuletide candle holder.

Diebitsch's summed up his sense of artistic and architectural excellence when he stated: 'we know that all we may produce will be critically examined by those who come after us and we do not want these later generations to give a poor verdict on our work.' His perception of stylistic lines and runic forms intricately laced together has left a legacy of some of the finest collectables of the Third Reich period.

DIECKMANN, August

RANK: SS-Standartenführer
  (posthumously awarded)
BORN: 29 May 1912
DIED: 10 October 1943 (K.I.A.)
PARTY NUMBER: —
SS NUMBER: 183917
AWARDS: 1939 Iron Cross Second Class,
  28 September 1939; 1939 Iron Cross
  First Class, 3 June 1940; German Cross
  in Gold, 28 February 1942; Knight's
  Cross of the Iron Cross 23 April 1942;
  Oakleaves, 20 April 1943; Swords,
  10 October 1943 (posthumously).

Born in Cadenberge on the Elbe River, Dieckmann entered the SS-Verfügungstruppe in 1934 and was selected to become a cadet at the SS officer cadets' school at Brünswick; he was commissioned as an Untersturmführer on 20 April 1936. He fought in the Polish campaign and the following year in France. His unit was transferred to the Russian Front and he was awarded the Knight's Cross while commanding the first battalion SS-Panzergrenadier Regiment *Germania*. Dieckmann became the 233rd recipient of the Oakleaves while commanding the 10th SS-Panzergrenadier Regiment *Westland*. While commanding the same unit, he was killed on the fourth day of heavy fighting in the vicinity of the Dnieper river by a grenade fragment. The Russians had been constructing a large base on the so-called 'Foxtail Island' in the river, from where they had established a small bridgehead on the German bank. Dieckmann's attack was designed to destroy the bridgehead and take the island, which it did brilliantly in the face of savage fighting. His troops held him in very high esteem and considered him a brave and loyal commander. He was rightfully awarded the Swords posthumously on the day of his death.

DIELS, Rudolf

RANK: SS-Oberführer
BORN: 16 December 1900
DIED: 18 November 1957 (D)
PARTY NUMBER: 3955308
SS NUMBER: 187116
AWARDS: Cross of Honour 1914-1918
  Combatants; SS Honour Ring;
  SS Honour Sword.

The first chief of the organisation that became the Gestapo, Diels was a survivor who somehow outwitted his former agents after the 20 July Bomb Plot. He was born in Berghaus in Taunus, the son of a prominent landowner. He studied medicine and law at the Universities of Giessen and Marburg, but his preoccupations, however, were seen to be anything but academic. His interests encompassed fighting duels, being a prodigious drinker, and, rumour had it, a glass chewer.

Diels joined the Prussian Ministry of the Interior in 1930, becoming a high-ranking police official. In 1932 he became a party member and subsequently married Göring's cousin. Diels persuaded Göring, a good friend, that a secret police force was necessary to monitor the activities of the communists, and on 26 April 1933 the Geheime Staats Polizeiamt (GESTAPA) was established, (later renamed Geheime Staats Polizei, or Gestapo), as a new department of the Prussian State Police, affiliated to the Ministry of the Interior, and headed by Diels.

The Nazi Party was engaged in widespread illegal practices, of which Diels became aware. The Gestapo became the target for Himmler (q.v.), who was rising to power and was desperate to control it, bringing Diels in conflict with him. On the eve of the arsonist's attack on the Reichstag, 27 February 1933, Diels reported to Hitler that it was the work of a single demented pyromaniac and that the culprit, Marinus van der Lubbe, was in custody. Hitler, however, blamed the communists and bleated out in fury: 'This is a cunning plot! Every communist official must be shot. All communist deputies must be hanged this very night.' As a result, Diels was ousted from his position in the Gestapo, but with Göring's help still managed to hold a number of government posts, including Assistant Police Commissioner of Berlin and Administrative President of Köln. During the 1940s, he refused to participate in anti-Jewish measures. He eventually became reconciled with Himmler, however, and was allowed to wear an honourary Standartenführer's uniform.

After the 20 July Bomb Plot, Diels was seized by the Gestapo and thrown into prison. After the war he went back to the role which he played best: that of the loyal civil servant, in Lower Saxony. He accidentally shot and killed himself while on a hunting expedition on 18 November 1957.

DIETRICH, Josef 'Sepp'

RANK: SS-Oberstgruppenführer, Panzer-Generaloberst der Waffen SS, zuletzt Oberbefehlshaber der Panzer Armee

BORN: 28 May 1892

DIED: 21 April 1966 (D)

PARTY NUMBER: 89015

SS NUMBER: 1177

AWARDS: Golden Party Badge; 1914 Iron Cross Second Class; 1914 Iron Cross First Class; Cross of Honour 1914-1918 Combatants; First World War Commemorative Tank Battle Badge; 1939 Iron Cross Second Class Bar, 25 September 1939; 1939 Iron Cross First Class Bar, 27 October 1939; Knight's Cross of the Iron Cross, 4 July 1940; Oakleaves, 31 December 1941; Oakleaves with Swords, 16 March 1943; Diamonds, 6 August 1944; Combined Pilot and Observer Badge in Gold with Diamonds 1943; Blood Order No 10; SS Honour Ring; SS Honour Sword.

A Bavarian, Dietrich enlisted at 19 in the 4th Field Artillery Regiment. During World War I he served first with the artillery, then the infantry and, finally, with the newly introduced tank units. At the war's end he was demobbed with the rank of sergeant. He had a number of jobs, including a runner and hat maker.

Dietrich joined the Bund Oberland and was present at the 1923 Putsch. In June 1932 he became head of Hitler's bodyguard. He was noted as being a stern but fair commander, and his overriding ambition was to train and maintain the best political and combat personnel possible. His *Leibstandarte* saw service in the Polish campaign in 1939, suffering heavy casualties due to lack of experience and military training. They were transferred to the Western Front and saw action in the Low Countries and France in 1940. Dietrich was awarded the Knight's Cross of the Iron Cross for actions in this campaign. The *Leibstandarte* was later employed in Yugoslavia, and then conducted a brief but costly campaign in Greece and pressed on into the Soviet Balkans, where he was awarded the Oakleaves, becoming the 41st recipient. The *Leibstandarte* fought on the Russian Front, often with heavy casualties, and for these activities he was awarded the Swords. His unit was transferred to France in 1944 where he was to achieve his greatest level of recognition.

While commanding I SS Panzer Corps his units were engaged in a bitterly contested two-month battle in the Caen region. In recognition of the bravery of his troops Hitler awarded him the Diamonds, making him the 16th recipient. He assumed command of the 6th SS Panzer Army and his units fought during the Ardennes Offensive. It is still remembered for incidents such as the Malmédy Massacre, when some of Dietrich's troops shot US prisoners of war. As the war closed, his units again turned eastwards, this time

with the hope of halting the tide of the 3rd US Army through Austria. Eventually Dietrich's forces surrendered to the Americans.

After the war, 'Sepp' Dietrich was imprisoned in Landsberg and tried for the Malmédy Massacre. He was given a 25-year sentence on 16 May 1946. Released in 1956, he was re-arrested for complicity in the murder of Ernst Röhm. He served a further 18 months, was released and died in Ludwigsburg in April 1966.

DIETRICH, Dr Otto
RANK: SS-Obergruppenführer
BORN: 31 August 1897
DIED: 22 November 1952 (D)
PARTY NUMBER: 126727
SS NUMBER: 101349
AWARDS: 1914 Iron Cross Second Class; 1914 Iron Cross First Class; Cross of Honour 1914-1918 Combatants; Golden Party Badge; SS Honour Ring; SS Honour Sword.

Otto Dietrich graduated as a doctor after serving in World War I, turning to news work as Munich representative for several large newspapers, which brought him into contact with the NSDAP. He was appointed press chief of the NSDAP in 1931, and from 1937 was Göbbel's state secretary in the Ministry of Propaganda.

Time and again, he showed extraordinary talent for fabrication and dissimulation. He devised the 'editor's law', which made each editor responsible for any anti-Nazi articles in their papers. After the Röhm purge he eloquently described Hitler's shock at the moral degeneracy of the old comrades he had liquidated. When Hess (q.v.) flew to Scotland, Dietrich reported his death in an accident over enemy territory. In October 1941, Dietrich boasted that 'Soviet Russia is done with and the British dream of war on two fronts is dead.' This pronouncement ultimately proved fallacious, and cast a shadow over Nazi propaganda. Hitler dismissed him from his position of President of the Reich Press Chamber in March 1945. He was tried at Nuremberg by a military tribunal in 1949, being sentenced to seven year's imprisonment. He was released from Landsberg Prison in December 1949 and died in Düsseldorf in 1952.

DING, Dr Erwin
RANK: SS-Sturmbannführer
BORN: 19 September 1912
DIED: 1945 (S)
PARTY NUMBER: 1318211
SS NUMBER: 280163
AWARDS: 1939 Iron Cross Second Class; SS Honour Ring; SS Honour Sword.

Before the war Ding had served as a surgeon in the SS-Totenkopf Verband and as camp physician in Buchenwald concentration camp. In October 1939 he was transferred to the *Totenkopf* Division as adjutant to the chief surgeon of the division and remained with the unit until August 1940. He joined the staff of the Hygiene Institute of the Waffen-SS and was assigned the job of organising and conducting the infamous typhus experiments carried out on prisoners at Buchenwald in 1942 and 1943. As a result of his experiments with injections of typhus bacilli, Ding was responsible for the deaths of nearly 600 inmates at the Buchenwald camp. After being arrested and charged by the American military authorities in 1945, he committed suicide before being brought to trial.

DIRLEWANGER, Dr Oskar
RANK: SS-Oberführer
BORN: 26 September 1895
DIED: 7 June 1945 (M)
PARTY NUMBER: 1098716
SS NUMBER: 357267
AWARDS: 1914 Iron Cross Second Class; 1914 Iron Cross First Class; Knight's Cross 30 September 1944; 1939 Iron Cross Second Class Bar, 24 May 1942; 1939 Iron Cross First Class Bar, 16 September 1942; German Cross in Gold, 5 December 1943; Knight's Cross of the Iron Cross, 30 September 1944; Close Combat Clasp Bronze Class; Slovakia – War Victory Cross Order First Class with Swords.

Dirlewanger, a totally unsavoury character, was born in Würzburg, Franconia. He was a former member of a Freikorps unit and later joined the French Foreign Legion. Gaoled for sex crimes in 1935, on his release he volunteered for the Condor Legion in the Spanish Civil War. He approached the head of the SS recruitment office, Gottlob Berger (q.v.), and suggested that a special unit be set up to recruit convicted criminals incarcerated in concentration and penal camps, thus enabling felons to atone for their crimes. This unit, which was to be a Sonderkommando, was responsible for operations against the partisans in Eastern Europe from 1942. Its reputation became notorious, peopled as the division was by murderers, rapists and other criminals. The brigade was most notorious for its actions in Warsaw during the Polish Uprising. Dirlewanger apparently entertained the officers of his mess with the death struggles of Jewish girls to whom he had given strychnine injections. At the end of the war all the members of his brigade were executed by the Russians. Dirlewanger's fate is unclear. He was either killed by former brigade members or concentration camp inmates in 1945 at Altshausen. He is buried in the local cemetery.

DOEHLE, Dr Heinrich
RANK: SS-Oberführer
BORN: 23 September 1883—
PARTY NUMBER: 3934062
SS NUMBER: 309078
AWARDS: SS Honour Ring; SS Honour Sword.

Doehle worked in the Chancellery. It was his task to produce a detailed reference book enumerating the awards permitted by the Nazi Government. The book's exhaustive title was *Die Auszeichnungen des Grossdeutschen Reichs, Orden & Ehrenzeichen & Abzeichen.*

After the end of World War I, the Weimar Republic banned all the awards of the old Second Reich empire and only the civilian grade of the *Pour le Mérite* was allowed. In the chaotic period leading up to the National Socialist takeover in January 1933, only this, certain approved Freikorps awards and orders from some of the old ducal states were permitted to be worn. The Nazis realised the importance of orders and decorations, and reconstituted the various official orders, decorations and medals that applied to all aspects of German military, diplomatic, political and civil life. By 1936 Hitler had issued a number of directives, formalising what was permitted. He had also made the central government responsible for the design and award, virtually eliminating the authority of the individual states to produce and award medals. Doehle produced his first work in May 1939, which contained 88 pages and had only black and white photos of the awards. By 1943 a number of new awards and decorations were established, and despite wartime shortages, the new edition contained plates printed in colour. Awards and decorations were considered of immense morale value, so scarce resources and manpower were employed in this undertaking. A fifth edition was in preparation in 1944, but bombing prevented publication.

DOLLMANN, Dr Eugen
RANK: SS-Standartenführer
BORN: 21 August 1900—
PARTY NUMBER: 3402541
SS NUMBER: 289259
AWARDS: War Merit Cross Second Class with Swords; SS Honour Ring; SS Honour Sword.

Himmler appointed Dollmann as police attaché to the Rome embassy in 1941. Why Dollmann was attracted to the SS is unclear. He had been brought up in Rome and spoke fluent Italian; he was an art historian, tolerated by Mussolini and a confidante of Count Ciano. He was described by Höttl as a 'drawing room hero'. In fact he was one of Himmler's intellectuals. In 1943 he became the adjutant to Karl Wolff (q.v.) when he was military governor of northern Italy. In 1945, when Wolff independently negotiated the surrender, Dollmann was a mediator in Switzerland and Italy.

DÖRNER, Helmut

RANK: SS-Oberführer und Oberst der Schützpolizei
BORN: 26 June 1909
DIED: January 1945 (K.I.A.)
PARTY NUMBER: 5602263
SS NUMBER: 422156
AWARDS: 1939 Iron Cross Second Class, 14 June 1940; 1939 Iron Cross First Class, 19 June 1940; German Cross in Gold, 24 December 1941; Knight's Cross of the Iron Cross, 15 May 1942; Oakleaves,18 November 1944; Oakleaves with Swords, 4 February 1945; Infantry Assault Badge; SS Honour Ring.

Born in Mönchen-Gladbach, Rheinland, Dörner saw service on the Russian Front while serving as commanding officer of the 16th Panzer Reconnaissance Battalion, and in recognition of his bravery he was awarded the Knight's Cross of the Iron Cross. He commanded the 8th SS-Panzergrenadier Regiment and was awarded the Oakleaves, becoming the 650th recipient. He was killed in action near Budapest in January 1945, while serving as the commanding officer of the 4th Battle Group. He was posthumously awarded the Swords, becoming the 129th recipient.

DORR, Hans

RANK: SS-Obersturmbannführer
BORN: 7 April 1912
DIED: April 1945 (K.I.A.)
PARTY NUMBER: 4201019
SS NUMBER: 77360
AWARDS: 1939 Iron Cross Second Class; 1939 Iron Cross First Class, French Campaign; German Cross in Gold, 19 December 1941; Knight's Cross of the Iron Cross, 27 September 1942; Oakleaves, 13 November 1943; Swords, 9 July 1944; SS Honour Sword.

On 1 October 1934, Dorr joined the SS-Verfügungstruppe and fought in the Polish campaign and in France. The *Das Reich*

Division, which Dorr served in, had two infantry regiments, which later became panzergrenadier regiments. At the end of the French campaign they each comprised three battalions, each one having three companies. A company usually had nine machine guns, two anti-tank guns and three mortars. Attached to each battalion was a heavy weapons company with six heavy mortars and eight anti-tank weapons. There was also a dedicated motorised anti-tank company with 12 guns which was attached to each regiment. The division had the usual administrative and support units.

He was subsequently transferred to the Russian Front and commanded the 4th Company, SS-Panzergrenadier Regiment *Germania* where he won the Knight's Cross of the Iron Cross. While serving as commander of the first battalion of *Germania* he was awarded the Oakleaves, becoming the 327th recipient. Only six months later, while commanding the 9th SS-Panzergrenadier Regiment *Germania*, he was awarded the Swords for continued bravery, becoming the 77th recipient. After being fatally wounded he died in Burgenlan, Austria, in April 1945 and is buried in Judenburg cemetery, Styria, Austria.

DÜRR, Emil
RANK: SS-Unterscharführer
BORN: 11 June 1920
DIED: 27 June 1944 (K.I.A.)
PARTY NUMBER: —
SS NUMBER: —
AWARDS: 1939 Iron Cross Second Class, 23 June 1944; 1939 Iron Cross First Class, 24 June 1944; Knight's Cross of the Iron Cross, 23 August 1944 (posthumous).

Dürr was an assault gun leader in 4th Company (heavy), 26th SS-Panzergrenadier Regiment, 12th SS Panzer Division *Hitlerjugend*. An Allied flamethrowing tank threatened the lives of a number of men in his unit during the fierce and bloody fighting around Caen in Normandy. Despite being seriously wounded, he attempted to destroy the tank three times and finally succeeded. But he died in the process, and for his selfless bravery he was posthumously awarded the Knight's Cross of the Iron Cross.

DYCK, Anton van
RANK: SS-Untersturmführer
PARTY NUMBER: —
SS NUMBER: —
AWARDS: 1939 Iron Cross Second Class; War Merit Cross Second Class with Swords, 4 April 1942.

Van Dyck was born in Belgium, the son of a fervent Flemish nationalist. The Flemish equivalent of the German Allgemeine-SS was established in Antwerp in September 1940. Anton van Dyck was adjutant to Jef van der Wiele, leader of the Flemish SS, and served with the 1st Freiwilligen Legion *Flandern*. He was also adjutant to Jef François. He was leader of the Germanic SS in Flanders from 9 November 1943 to 15 September 1944. He was the first Fleming to be awarded the Iron Cross when he was only 20 years old. On 23 December 1943, he married Ingeborg Scharl in an SS wedding service that took place in the Hall of Pacification in Ghent. It is also reported that a further ceremony was held on the 20 May 1944 in Munich. One of his last missions was on 14 February 1945 to Bad Saran, looking for men to join the *Langemark* Regiment.

EBERSTEIN, (Friedrich) Karl von

RANK: SS-Obergruppenführer
BORN: 14 January 1894—
PARTY NUMBER: 15067
SS NUMBER: 1386
AWARDS: Golden Party Badge; 1914 Iron Cross Second Class; 1914 Iron Cross First Class; Cross of Honour 1914-1918 Combatants; War Merit Cross Second Class with Swords; War Merit Cross First Class with Swords; SS Honour Ring; SS Honour Sword.

Von Eberstein was an early member of the SS, joining in 1928. Lina von Osten enlisted his help to bring Heydrich (q.v.) to Himmler's (q.v.) notice, which he did on 14 June 1931. In 1934, he was the commander of the SS Higher Section for Dresden. At the time of the Röhm Purge, it appeared that Himmler was fermenting discord between the army and the SA in order to incite the two factions into rebelling against one another. To this end, he ordered Eberstein to muster his men in an army barracks and to keep contact with the military area command, thus strengthening Himmler's position against the SA. This worked to Himmler's advantage, in that the SS came through the 'Night of the Long Knives' as the dominant force and their loyalty endeared them to Hitler. The purge effectively emasculated the SA, and it appears that at least 1000 people lost their lives as a result of the action. The SA was commanded by Victor Lutze after Röhm's death, but he quickly became a minor Nazi Party figure. Eberstein himself became Higher SS and Police leader for Munich, and the spokesman for the SS at Nuremberg.

Left: The SS parades its banners at the Nuremberg Nazi Party rally in 1934. By this time the SA had been emasculated in the 'Night of the Long Knives'.

EGGELING, Joachim-Albrecht

RANK: SS-Obergruppenführer; Deputy Gauleiter of Magdeburg 1935-7; Gauleiter of Hall-Merseburg 1937-45
BORN: 30 November 1884
DIED: April 1945 (K.I.A.)
PARTY NUMBER: 11579
SS NUMBER: 186515
AWARDS: Golden Party Badge; 1914 Iron Cross Second Class; 1914 Iron Cross First Class; Cross of Honour 1914-1918 Combatants; 1914 Wound Badge Black Class; War Merit Cross Second Class without Swords; War Merit Cross First Class without Swords; SS Honour Ring; SS Honour Sword.

Born in Blankenburg, Harz, Eggeling served as a captain of a machine-gun unit during World War I. After the uprising in November 1918, he fought with the Goslar riflemen in Hanover

against the left-wing Spartacists. He joined the NSDAP in 1923 and was active as a political orator, working closely with Loeper (q.v.). During the Kampfzeit he was a leader in the Agrar political office. He was successful in building up the NSDAP in central Germany and became the leader of the farmers of Sachsen-Anhalt in 1933. He was Deputy Gauleiter of Magdeburg from 1935-1937 and was appointed to run the Gau after Loeper's death in 1935. In 1937 he was appointed Gauleiter of Hall-Merseburg. He was killed in action in April 1945, shortly before the fall of Hall.

EICHMANN, Adolf

RANK: SS-Obersturmbannführer
BORN: 19 March 1906
DIED: 31 May 1962 (E.A.)
PARTY NUMBER: 899895
SS NUMBER: 45326
AWARDS: War Merit Cross Second Class
    with Swords; SS Honour Ring.

Fanatically anti-Semitic, Eichmann was born in Solingen and educated in Linz, Austria. He became a travelling salesman and member of the Austrian Nazi party soon after leaving school. As a party activist he was forced to move to Germany in 1932. Here he wrote for *Der Stürmer*, an anti-Semitic newspaper, and afterwards joined the SD as a Jewish affairs expert. He visited Palestine in 1937 to meet Arab leaders, but the British mandate police deported him. Initially, he favoured the Zionists as a means of encouraging Jews to leave Europe, but this became totally impractical as immigration quotas for Palestine were vastly over-subscribed.

Eichmann was Head of Gestapo Section IV B6 in 1941, the department of Jewish affairs. At the Wannsee Conference on 12 January 1942, which introduced the 'Final Solution', the programme to eliminate all Jews, Eichmann pedantically took down the agenda. He obtained the final decree, signed by Bormann

(q.v.), which deprived Jews of all rights of appeal, on 1 July 1943. Eichmann organised the transportation to the camps and had gas chambers installed, as the most efficient method of killing. He viewed the extermination of the Jewish race as his chief ambition in life. In the spring and summer of 1944, for example, he took an avid part in the transportation of Hungarian Jews to Auschwitz, 400,000 of them dying there.

There were rumours that Eichmann had Jewish relations, even a Jewish mistress

There were rumours that Eichmann had Jewish relations, even a Jewish mistress when he lived in Vienna. His whereabouts at the end of the war and his escape from an American internment camp to South America, using a Vatican passport under the name of 'Ricardo Klement', are confused. His reported involvement with American and British intelligence is unsubstantiated, but highly probable. He settled in Buenos Aires in 1950 and it was here that he was discovered and kidnapped by Israeli agents in 1960. He stood trial in Israel, where his confession under intense interrogation was characteristically full and factual – ever the good bureaucrat – running to some 3500 pages. He was found guilty of crimes against humanity and hanged at Ramle on 31 May 1962.

EICKE, Theodor

RANK: SS-Obergruppenführer
    und General der Waffen-SS
BORN: 17 October 1892
DIED: 26 February 1943 (K.I.A.)
PARTY NUMBER: 114901
SS NUMBER: 2921
AWARDS: 1914 Iron Cross Second Class;
    Cross of Honour 1914-1918
    Combatants; 1939 Iron Cross Second
    Class Bar, 26 May 1940; 1939 Iron
    Cross First Class, 31 May 1940; Knight's
    Cross, 26 December 1941; Oakleaves,
    20 April 1942; SS Honour Ring;
    SS Honour Sword.

One of the most infamous Waffen-SS divisional commanders, Eicke was born in Huedingen, Alsace-Lorraine. He was an army paymaster in World War I, subsequently joining the Freikorps and fighting the Polish incursions on Germany's eastern borders. Employed by I. G. Farben as an industrial counter-espionage agent in 1923, he joined the police in 1927, but was dismissed the following year for his outspoken comments about the French occupying forces and the Weimar Republic. He joined the NSDAP as an SA man, transferring to the SS and rising to command an SS regiment in Rhein-Palatinate. He was sentenced to two years imprisonment in March 1932 for his part in bombing political opponents, but fled to Italy, returning the following year when Hitler assumed power.

Eicke formulated service regulations for both guards and prisoners

Eicke was a key figure in the liquidation of Röhm and his supporters, shooting Röhm at midday on 1 July 1934 in his cell at Stadelheim prison after Röhm had refused to shoot himself. In the summer of that year, and as a direct result of the Röhm Putsch, most of the unofficial camps were closed. The remaining SA camps were removed from the jurisdiction of the civil authorities and taken over by the SS. The first full-time SS concentration camp unit was recruited from members of the Allgemeine-SS and was entirely under the overall command of the SS district south, who made it a depository for its unwanted personnel. The conditions that the guards lived under were little better than the inmates. In June 1933, Eicke took command. He improved conditions, lifted the morale and discipline of his men and formulated service regulations for both guards and prisoners which remained virtually unchanged until the end of the war. In recognition Himmler, in 1934, appointed him Inspector of Concentration Camps and Head of the SS Totenkopf Verbände, the unit created specifically to guard the increasing numbers of concentration camp inmates.

By the end of 1938 Eicke's men had all received some basic military training. When World War II broke out, he formed a division from the Totenkopf units, undergoing further military training at Obermünsigen Württemberg during the winter of 1939. It saw action in northern France during the 1940 campaign, but

Eicke was unhappy that it was not properly deployed by army command. The *Totenkopf* Division fought in Russia, distinguishing itself and its leader at Demjansk. Fighting in the pocket was severe and losses were heavy on both sides. The *Totenkopf* lost 7000 men between December 1941 and mid-March 1942. What was worse, the division was held at the front until October 1942, continually trying to defeat the Russian attacks thrown against it. This it managed to do, but in the process being decimated. In one action, for example, the division lost over 1000 men in a matter of hours in the face of a furious Red Army assault. By the time of its withdrawal the *Totenkopf* numbered 6400 men.

On 26 February 1943, Eicke was on an inspection flight in a Fiesler Stork when he was shot down, crashing behind enemy lines. He was idolised by his men, who recovered his body with the loss of several lives. He was given a Viking-style burial at a divisional cemetery near Orelka, Russia.

EIGRUBER, August

RANK: SS-Obergruppenführer,
  Gauleiter of Upper Danube 1938-45
BORN: 16 April 1907
DIED: 28 May 1947 (E.A.)
PARTY NUMBER: 83432
SS NUMBER: 292778
AWARDS: Golden Party Badge; War Merit
  Cross Second Class without Swords;
  War Merit Cross First Class without
  Swords; SS Honour Ring; SS Honour
  Sword.

Born in Steyr, Austria, Eigruber founded the *Österreichische Beobachter* in 1936. He held a variety of posts in the Austrian Nazi Party prior to the Anschluss in 1938. Afterwards he became Gauleiter of Upper Danube, a position he held to the war's end when he was arrested and tried for war crimes. Indicted in connection with the atrocities at Mauthausen concentration camp, which was within his jurisdiction, he was sentenced to death and executed at Landsberg Prison by the Americans in 1949.

ENNSBERGER, Alois

RANK: SS-Hauptsturmführer
BORN: 26 October 1914
DIED: 7 April 1973 (D)
PARTY NUMBER: —
SS NUMBER: —
AWARDS: War Merit Cross Second Class
  with Swords; War Merit Cross First
  Class with Swords; Knight's Cross of
  the War Merit Cross with Swords,
  28 November 1943.

In November 1943 Ennsberger was technical maintenance officer of the first detachment in Panzer Regiment *Das Reich*, serving on the Russian Front. He and his men performed a magnificent service in the repair and maintenance of the division's equipment. In recognition of these services he was awarded the Knight's Cross of the War Merit Cross with Swords. He survived the war and died in Salzburg, Austria, in 1973.

ERBPRINZ ZU WALDECK UND PYRMONT, Josias

RANK: SS-Obergruppenführer
BORN: 13 May 1896
DIED: December 1967 (D)
PARTY NUMBER: 160025
SS NUMBER: 2139
AWARDS: Golden Party Badge; 1914 Iron
  Cross Second Class; 1914 Iron Cross
  First Class; Cross of Honour 1914-18
  Combatants; 1914 Wound Badge Black
  Class; 1939 Iron Cross Second Class
  Bar; 1939 Iron Cross First Class Bar;
  SS Honour Ring; SS Honour Sword.

Himmler's (q.v.) first 'blue-blooded' recruit joined the SS in 1928 and witnessed the executions of Röhm's supporters in Munich. Unlike Hitler, Himmler was not anti-royalist and made his attacks on the nobility begrudgingly; thus the prince remained in office as SS Police Leader in Kassel-Mainfranken until May 1945.

With jurisdiction over Buchenwald concentration camp, Waldeck was arrested at the end of the war, and on 11 April 1947 the trials of the Buchenwald staff opened at Dachau. Waldeck was one of the main defendants and the only member of a German princely house to be tried for war crimes. He was held responsible for the appalling conditions that had prevailed there, was found guilty and sentenced to life imprisonment – some would say a lenient sentence. Released in December 1960, he died seven years later in Schaumburg.

ERTEL, Karl-Heinz

RANK: SS-Hauptsturmführer
BORN: 26 November 1919
DIED: 25 January 1993 (D)
PARTY NUMBER: —
SS NUMBER: —
AWARDS: 1939 Iron Cross Second Class, 19 October 1942; 1939 Iron Cross First Class, 7 January 1943; Knight's Cross of the Iron Cross, 23 August 1944.

A Westphalian, Ertel was regimental adjutant of 49th SS-Freiwilligen Panzergrenadier Regiment *De Ruiter*, SS-Freiwilligen Panzergrenadier Brigade *Nederland*, III (Germ.) SS Panzer Corps. In 1944, the Russians threatened the Narva Bridgehead, and Collani (q.v.), his commander, was wounded. In the early hours of the morning of 27 June, the Russians attacked north of the town, threatening the main supply line to Narva. A successful counterattack was launched against the Soviets by the First Battalion of the 49th SS-Volunteers' Regiment commanded by Hans Meyer. In the process Hans Meyer was killed and Hans Collani was severely wounded, and died two days later in hospital. After his regimental commander, Collani, had been wounded, Ertel assembled soldiers from any available units to prevent the Soviets from making a sudden or surprise attempt at a breakthrough. The tactic worked, for the Russians were thrown back and Ertel effectively saved the crucial supply line to Narva. For his leadership in this action he was awarded the Knight's Cross of the Iron Cross. He died in 1993 in Lippstadt.

EULING, Karl-Heinz

RANK: SS-Hauptsturmführer
BORN: 16 August 1919—
PARTY NUMBER: —
SS NUMBER: —
AWARDS: 1939 Iron Cross Second Class, 21 December 1942; 1939 Iron Cross First Class, 14 September 1943; Knight's Cross of the Iron Cross, 15 October 1944.

Commanding officer of the 4th Battalion, 21st SS-Panzergrenadier Regiment, 10th SS Panzer Division *Frundsberg*, II SS Panzer Corps, in September 1944, Euling and his unit distinguished themselves during the fierce fighting surrounding the Allied airdrop at Arnhem. Before the landing Allied paratroopers were able to completely encircle his exposed battalion, Euling managed to extricate himself and his men, leading them back under heavy enemy fire to their own lines with the loss of only two casualties. For this leadership and bravery he was awarded the Knight's Cross of the Iron Cross.

EWERT, Walther

RANK: SS-Oberführer
BORN: 20 November 1903
DIED: 4 July 1976 (D)
PARTY NUMBER: 2564086
SS NUMBER: 265897
AWARDS: 1939 Iron Cross Second Class;
War Merit Cross Second Class with
Swords; War Merit Cross First Class
with Swords; German Cross in Silver;
Knights Cross of the War Merit Cross
with Swords, 26 December 1944;
SS Honour Ring; SS Honour Sword.

A professional soldier, Ewert was born in Zalesie, Schubin District, west Prussia. From 1921 until 1934 he served with the Reichswehr. He was in the chief training section until 1935, when he became quartermaster to the *Leibstandarte*. He was promoted again in 1943 to quartermaster of I SS Panzer Corps with a further promotion to quartermaster of the 6th SS Panzer Army, a position he held until the end of the war. Though titled SS, the 6th Army also contained army units. In I SS Panzer Corps were the elite *Leibstandarte* and *Hitlerjugend* Divisions. Army units included the 12th and 277th Volsgrenadier Divisions and the Luftwaffe's 3rd Paratroop Division. In 6th Army's II SS Panzer Corps were the *Das Reich* and *Hohenstaufen* Divisions. The 6th's LXVII Corps included the 272nd and 326th Volsgrenadier Divisions. In addition, there was a host of tank and assault gun detachments which were attached to the army. These included the powerful Tiger tank, which could knock out any Allied tank then in service with its 88mm gun.

For the offensive the German Army amassed 240,000 men, an incredible feat for this late stage of the war. However, by its end the Germans had achieved nothing strategically, but they had lost 130,000 men, of which 19,000 had been killed, and 600 priceless panzers. In addition, large supplies of ammunition had been exhausted: there were only five rounds of ammunition for each German gun along the whole of the Western Front in early 1945. In recognition of his services as a quartermaster, Ewert was awarded the Knight's Cross of the War Merit Cross with Swords. He survived the war and died in 1976.

FAULHABER Markus

RANK: SS-Sturmbannführer
BORN: 22 July 1914
DIED: 9 May 1945 (K.I.A.)
PARTY NUMBER: —
SS NUMBER: —
AWARDS: 1939 Iron Cross Second Class,
14 November 1939; 1939 Iron Cross
First Class, 14 July 1941; Knight's Cross
of the Iron Cross, 25 December 1942.

Faulhaber served as commanding officer of 3rd Company SS-Panzergrenadier Regiment *Germania*, SS Panzer Division *Wiking*, 1st Panzer Army, nicknamed the 'Iron Third'.

In July 1942 the Germans launched the summer offensive in Russia in the Kursk-Kharkov section, aiming for the Caucasian oil fields. Kleist's Panzer army broke through the Russian defences and poured into the Caucasus. Within six weeks the entire Don River region was in German hands with the SS-Division Wiking making one of the deepest penetrations. Wiking remained on the defensive in the Caucasus during the winter of 1942/43. It was for his leadership during this time that Faulhaber was awarded the Knight's Cross of the Iron Cross.

In 1945 the Americans ordered Faulhaber to persuade German soldiers hiding in the Austrian mountains to come down into the valley and surrender. Faulhaber, accompanied by his adjutant SS-Obersturmführer Christen Dall, drove into the mountains, although Faulhaber was wounded and had an arm bandaged. Their vehicle came off the road and fell into the swollen River Salzach. Dall managed to get clear but Faulhaber drowned.

FEGELEIN, Hermann Otto

RANK: SS-Gruppenführer und Generalleutnant der Waffen-SS
BORN: 30 October 1906
DIED: 29 April 1945 (E.R.)
PARTY NUMBER: 1200158
SS NUMBER: 66680
AWARDS: 1939 Iron Cross Second Class, 15 December 1940; 1939 Iron Cross First Class, 28 June 1941; Knight's Cross of the Iron Cross, 2 March 1942; Oakleaves, 25 December 1942; Oakleaves with Swords, 30 July 1944; 1939 Wound Badge Black Class; 1939 Wound Badge Silver Class; '20 July 1944' Wound Badge Silver Class; German Cross in Gold, 1 November 1943; Close Combat Bar in Silver, 5 December 1943; War Merit Cross Second Class Bronze with Swords; Medal for the Winter Campaign in Russia 1941-1942, 1 April 1942; German Horseman's Badge Gold; SS Honour Ring; SS Honour Sword.

A career soldier, Fegelein enlisted in the 17th Cavalry Regiment in 1925. He served briefly in the Freikorps Rossbach and also with the Bavarian State Police. On 1 March 1933, he joined the cavalry branch of the SS. He rode in professional competitions and represented Germany as a member of the equestrian team at the 1936 Olympics. On 12 January 1939, Hermann Fegelein, with other members of the SS show-jumping team, Temme-Waldemar, were inter-

viewed in front of German cameras with their horse Firster. Fegelein became an adjutant attached to the SS District South and eventually commanded the SS cavalry school at Munich. He formed the first Waffen-SS cavalry units from reinforced SS-Totenkopf Verbände in Warsaw.

Apart from serving in the Polish campaign in 1939, all Fegelein's service was on the Russian Front, where he was involved in actions against Red Army units and partisans. When Germany attacked the Soviet Union in June 1941, thousands of Russian soldiers managed to evade capture and fled into the swamps and dense forests. Operating from these refuges they began to threaten German supply lines and soon represented a formidable challenge to the German war effort. Army Group Centre formed special units to fight the partisans, consisting of the SS Cavalry Brigade, the 1st and 2nd SS Infantry Brigades, and some smaller army and police units. After several months of fierce and bloody fighting, during which both sides sustained heavy losses, the supply lines were made safe. Field Marshal Model awarded Fegelein and his unit a citation for actions in support of Army Group Centre, and Fegelein himself received the Knight's Cross of the Iron Cross.

Eva pleaded for her brother-in-law's life, pointing out her sister was pregnant

Wounded three times during these actions, Fegelein's most famous injury occurred during the attempted assassination of Hitler on 20 July 1944, when he was serving as Himmler's (q.v.) personal adjutant to Hitler. Fegelein had married Eva Braun's sister, Margarete, on 3 June 1944, just one month earlier. Afterwards he returned to the Russian Front in command of the 8th SS Kavallerie Division *Florian Geyer*, then returned to serve once again as SS-adjutant at Hitler's headquarters.

At the end of the war he was in the Berlin bunker with Hitler and his immediate entourage. On 27 April 1945, Fegelein vanished from the bunker; once aware of his absence, Hitler ordered a search. The Gestapo arrested him at his home in Berlin under suspicious circumstances: he was in civilian dress and had on his person a large amount of Swiss francs and jewellery. He was returned to the bunker and here Hitler, who had begun to doubt Himmler's loyalty, turned his vengeance upon Fegelein, who ardently protested his innocence. Eva pleaded for her brother-in-law's life, pointing out that her sister was pregnant. Hitler acquiesced to her request and spared him, after rebuking him for his lack of courage. A few hours later the BBC reported that Himmler had offered to surrender the German Army unconditionally to the Allies. Hitler became uncontrollable, had Fegelein court-martialled, found guilty, and condemned to death for his perceived part in Himmler's disloyalty. However, Fegelein's disloyalty was most likely to his wife, for there were rumours that he intended to run off with a beautiful Hungarian girl. To exacerbate the situation further, some of the jewellery found upon him was believed to be Eva's, so she remained silent as Fegelein was escorted by an SS squad into the Chancellery garden where they executed him on 28 April 1945.

FEGELEIN, Waldemar

RANK: SS-Standartenführer der Reserve
BORN: 9 January 1912—
PARTY NUMBER: 2942829
SS NUMBER: 229780
AWARDS: 1939 Iron Cross Second Class, 15 December 1940;1939 Iron Cross First Class, 10 July 1941; German Cross in Gold, 2 December 1944; Knight's Cross of the Iron Cross, 16 December 1943; Close Combat Clasp; SS Honour Ring; SS Honour Sword.

The younger brother of Hermann Fegelein (q.v.), Waldemar Fegelein was also an accomplished horseman and a member of  the SS show-jumping team. He was the commanding officer of the Second SS Cavalry Regiment, *Florian Geyer* Division. He won the Knight's Cross of the Iron Cross for his bravery on the Russian Front, which was awarded by Heinrich Himmler (q.v.) in person. His ultimate fate is unknown.

FELDMEIJER, Johannes Hendrik

RANK: SS-Standartenführer
BORN: 30 November 1910
DIED: 22 February 1945 (K.I.A.)
PARTY NUMBER: —
SS NUMBER: 440001
AWARDS: 1939 Iron Cross Second Class; 1939 Wound Badge Black Class; SS Honour Ring.

A Dutchman, Feldmeijer joined the NSB in 1932 and became director of NSB propaganda by 1936. The NSB (*Nationaal-Socialistische Beweging*) was founded on 14 December 1931 by civil engineer Anton Mussert, although clearly inspired by German example. It tried to stress its Dutch patriotism. In August 1939 Feldmeijer formed the 'Mussert Guard', the embryonic Dutch SS. In May 1940, together with other NSB leaders, he was arrested and imprisoned in France, but was freed after its fall. Feldmeijer was one of Mussert's principal lieutenants, and it was at his instigation that the Dutch formed their own SS.

The Nederländische-SS was formed on 11 September 1940 as the contemporary of the German Allgemeine-SS. It adopted the same black uniform and the same system of ranks, although Feldmeijer held the unique rank of Voorman which had no SS equivalent. In March 1943 this was changed to Standartenführer, however. No facilities existed for training, and initially the recruits were obliged to go to Germany for instruction. In May 1941 a training school was opened at Auegoor near Arnhem. On 1 November 1942, the title was changed to the more general term 'Germanic SS in Holland', thus loosening the ties between it and the NSB. It was now a part of a larger non-German Teutonic SS movement, which embraced all the so-called Nordic countries.

Feldmeijer worked with Rauter (q.v.,) to undermine the position of the Dutch Nazi leader, Mussert, but as Feldmeijer was neither forceful nor shrewd, Mussert survived relatively unscathed. Feldmeijer introduced the German SS concept of 'sponsoring members', i.e. civilians who paid a subscription of not less than 1 Florin per month, earning them the right to wear a badge of SS runes. By 1944 there were some 4000 sponsoring members.

Feldmeijer transferred to the Waffen-SS and saw service in the Balkans and Russia. He was killed in action on 22 February 1945.

FIEDLER, Johann

RANK: SS-Oberscharführer
BORN: 28 April 1922
DIED: 1985 (D)
PARTY NUMBER: —
SS NUMBER: —
AWARDS: 1939 Iron Cross Second Class, 3 June 1942; 1939 Iron Cross First Class, 14 October 1943; Knight's Cross of the Iron Cross, 16 June 1944; Medal for the Winter Campaign in Russia 1941-1942; Close Combat Clasp Silver Class; General Assault Badge; 1939 Wound Badge Silver Class; Demjansk Shield.

A Sudeten German, Fiedler was the son of a cobbler who became an apprentice locksmith. He applied to join the Waffen-SS in May 1941 and was called up in Prague, where he undertook basic training, passed and was then attached to the 3rd SS Panzer Division *Totenkopf*.

Fiedler was moved to the northern section of the Russian Front as part of Operation 'Barbarossa' and attached to SS-Totenkopf Regiment 3. He was wounded for the first time at Demjansk. After the encircled divisions broke out on 21 April 1942, the *Totenkopf* enjoyed a relatively quiet couple of months receiving much-needed rest and reinforcements. They were soon back in the line when elements of the regiment came under fire directed from Soviet concealed positions during a pitched battle near Pascani. Spotting the enemy, Fiedler realised that unless they were neutralised, his unit would be pinned down with disastrous effect. With total disregard for his safety, he stormed the Soviet positions, destroying them, taking 39 prisoners and capturing an anti-tank gun, five light and two heavy machine guns. All this was achieved despite being wounded and losing a large quantity of blood. For this action and the determination and bravery he showed, he was awarded the Knight's Cross of the Iron Cross.

Captured by Soviet troops in December 1944 near Frankfurt-on-Oder while serving with a combat group, he managed to escape and reached his own lines in January 1945. He finally went into American custody after the general surrender in May 1945. After the war, he returned to his trade as a locksmith and died in 1985 in Wechingen.

FORSTER, Albert

RANK: SS-Obergruppenführer, Gauleiter of Danzig
BORN: 26 July 1902
DIED: c.31 March 1954 (E.A.)
PARTY NUMBER: 1924
SS NUMBER: 158
AWARDS: Gau General Commemorative Badge 1923 or 1925; Gau Danzig Commemorative Badge; SS Honour Ring; SS Honour Sword.

Forster was born in Fürth, Bavaria, and as an apprentice he was drawn to the nascent NSDAP, subsequently forming a group in his home town. He maintained his beliefs in the party, even after losing his job for his political ideals. In October 1930, while working as a bank clerk, he was appointed Gauleiter of Danzig and also elected to the Reichstag, representing Franconia. He organised the secret preparations for the takeover of Danzig, enabling the German nationalists and pro-Nazi movement to gradually gain strength until, in June 1933, Danzig had a Nazi-dominated government. From then until its re-incorporation into the German Reich in September 1933, the free city closely modelled itself on Germany.

Forster was rewarded by being appointed governor just before the outbreak of World War II. Unique among the Nazi hierarchy, in his capacity of Gauleiter and governor-designate, Forster instituted a decoration known as the Danzig Cross on 31 August 1939 to reward meritorious service in building the Nazi Party within the free city. Most awards were made on 24 October 1939, and by the end of the year 88 awards of the first class and 253 of the second class had been conferred, making it one of the rarest awards of the Nazi period.

Noteworthy for committing numerous atrocities against the Poles, Forster fell into British captivity in 1945 and was extradited to Poland, where he was sentenced to death. Three accounts of his demise are reported: first, the Polish authorities informed his wife that he had died in 1952; second, he was executed on 31 March 1954; third, the German Red Cross states: 'he was executed just before Christmas 1955.'

FRANK, Karl Hermann

RANK: SS-Obergruppenführer
BORN: 24 January 1898
DIED: 22 May 1946 (E.A.)
PARTY NUMBER: 6600002
SS NUMBER: 310466
AWARDS: Golden Party Badge; War Merit Cross Second Class with Swords; War Merit Cross First Class with Swords; SS Honour Ring; SS Honour Sword.

Frank was a fanatical Sudeten-German Freikorps leader, as well as deputy leader of the Sudeten-German Party and adjutant to Henlein (q.v.). A close associate of Himmler (q.v.) during the Munich crisis of 1938, Frank was made head of the Czech police force after the German takeover as a reward for his loyalty, although this force was really a puppet of the SD. He became Higher SS and Police Leader, directly subordinate to Himmler, and was also a state secretary in the Ministry of the Interior. Following the assassination of Heydrich (q.v.), he was ordered to assume the functions of Protector, and it was in his name that the actions against the Czech people were carried out. He proclaimed martial law, arrested 3188 people and executed 1357, while a further 657 died under police interrogation. He also ordered the destruction of the villages of Lidice and Lezaky. Frank effectively continued to rule Bohemia and Moravia for the rest of the war, although Frick was nominally the protector. At the war's end he was arrested, tried by a Czech court and publicly hanged near Prague on 22 May 1946.

FREEMAN, Benson Railton Metcalf

RANK: SS-Untersturmführer
BORN: 6 October 1903—
PARTY NUMBER: —
SS NUMBER: —

An Englishman, Freeman was commissioned in August 1924 into the Kings Own Royal Regiment as a second lieutenant. He later qualified as a fighter pilot, transferring to the RAF. In 1931 he retired, taking up farming, which gave him time to develop his political views, and in 1937 he joined the BUF (British Union of Fascists), remaining a member until September 1939.

Despite the conflict of loyalties produced by his political beliefs, Freeman returned to the RAF, assuming that he would hold a non-combatant position. On 22 May 1940, however, he was ordered to fly to Merville in France, where on landing the planes were destroyed by enemy air action. Freeman, accompanied by other RAF personnel, ordered a DC3 for England, only to be forced down by ground fire and taken prisoner. He moved to a special camp established to extract information from newly captured air crew. However, it seems that his incarceration was due to his pro-Nazi views, and his position in the camp became increasingly uneasy; he was concerned to discover that air crews were being informed in briefings by MI9 that he was 'a German informer'. Eventually, after a number of heated disagreements with his fellow prisoners, he and a few others were asked to sign a document requesting their removal from the camp. He was eventually taken to Berlin to meet Rudolf Hess (q.v), who asked him if he was prepared to help in the 'promotion of peace and the frustration of Bolshevist plans'. Freeman agreed.

In June 1942 he became a propagandist and the next two years were a disaster for him and his employers. In September 1944 a chance meeting with d'Alquen (q.v.) at a social function in Berlin changed his resolve. Taking a liking to Freeman and holding similar views on the likelihood of the German defeat in the East, d'Alquen offered him a commission in the 'Kurt Eggers Regiment'. Freeman joined the Waffen-SS in October 1944, where he made a declaration that he was 'an Englishman of Aryan descent and has never, neither now nor previously, been a member of a freemasons lodge nor any other secret society.' He was not required to command troops, but to vet propaganda material.

By the end of April 1945 d'Alquen decided to evacuate his remaining staff from Berlin. With his deputy, Sturmbannführer Anton Kriegbaum (q.v.), American SS-Hauptsturmführer Ackermann and Freeman, he commandeered three Storch planes and flew to Lenggries in southwest Germany. Pressurised to fly to Switzerland, Freeman refused and subsequently surrendered to American forces on 9 May. He was court-martialled, receiving a sentence of 10 years.

FREITAG, Fritz

RANK: SS-Brigadeführer und Generalmajor der Waffen-SS und Polizei
BORN: 28 April 1894
DIED: 10 May 1945 (S)
PARTY NUMBER: 3052501
SS NUMBER: 393266
AWARDS: 1939 Iron Cross Second Class Bar, 5 February 1942; 1939 Iron Cross First Class Bar, 6 March 1942; German Cross in Gold, 30 April 1943; Knight's Cross of the Iron Cross, 30 September 1944; War Merit Cross Second Class with Swords; Gold Wound Badge; SS Honour Ring.

Freitag commanded the largely Ukrainian SS-Freiwilligen Division *Galizien* from 20 November 1943 until 27 April 1945. Formed on Himmler's (q.v.) orders, its first commander was SS-Brigadeführer und General Major der Waffen-SS Walter Schimana, who held the position until 19 November 1943. Schimana may have been replaced because he was more an administrator than a military commander (some 70,000 Ukrainians had volunteered for German service by March 1943).

Notwithstanding his views, he was awarded the Knight's Cross

An East Prussian, Freitag was unpopular among the Ukrainian soldiers; he was self-seeking and unpleasant, a petty bureaucrat who did not trust anyone. Freitag's unpopularity with the Ukrainians and their champion, Major Heika, stemmed from the fact that he saw the Ukrainian division merely as a means of commanding another formation in the Waffen-SS. He cared nothing for the political role the Ukrainians sought for their division, did not try to understand the psychology of the Ukrainian soldier and refused to allow Ukrainian officers to fill staff and command positions. In fact, he did his best to reserve even company and platoon commands for German personnel. Notwithstanding his views, and the poor leadership engendered by his attitude, he was awarded the Knight's Cross of the Iron Cross for accomplishments with the division. With its surrender, he committed suicide on 10 May 1945 in Austria.

FREY, Albert

RANK: SS-Standartenführer
BORN: 16 February 1913—
PARTY NUMBER: 4137086
SS NUMBER: 111913
AWARDS: 1939 Iron Cross Second Class,
   25 September 1939; 1939 Iron Cross
   First Class, 30 June 1940; German Cross
   in Gold, 17 November 1941; Knight's
   Cross of the Iron Cross, 3 March 1943;
   Oakleaves, 20 December 1943;
   SS Honour Ring; SS Honour Sword.

Born in Heidelberg, Frey joined the SS-Verfügungstruppe and was later transferred to the *Leibstandarte SS Adolf Hitler*. With the outbreak of war he saw action in Poland and in the French campaign of 1940. He then fought on the Russian Front during Operation 'Barbarossa' in 1941 and distinguished himself in a number of battles.

In early 1943 Frey's battalion came under fierce attack just north of Taganrog. His qualities of courage and leadership came to the fore, and he directed the defence for five hours until the Russians withdrew. There was no respite, and his bravery in the face of vastly superior forces eventually helped to win the battles of Donetz and Kharkov. In recognition of his bravery and outstanding leadership as commanding officer of the 1st Battalion, 1st SS-Panzergrenadier-Regiment, LSSAH, he was awarded the Knight's Cross of the Iron Cross.

He energetically directed the battle, and as night fell his force repulsed the enemy

The elite I SS Panzer Corps in early 1943 comprised the *Leibstandarte*, *Das Reich* and *Totenkopf* Divisions. Commanded by Hausser (q.v.), it had pulled out of Kharkov in mid-February, in contradiction of Hitler's orders. Then, in early March Hausser counterattacked. The Waffen-SS retook Kharkov in a stunning operation which ended on 15 March. The fighting for the city itself was particularly savage, with over 11,500 Waffen-SS soldiers being killed in action. Nevertheless, Soviet losses had been higher. During one operation, for example, the *Das Reich* and *Totenkopf* Divisions had destroyed two entire Russian armies, knocking out 600 enemy tanks, killing 23,000 Red Army troops and capturing a further 9000, as well as capturing 400 artillery pieces and 600 anti-tank guns.

Later in the same year, in Zhitomir, a region west of Kiev, he gathered the available forces to form a battle group to repulse the attacking Soviets. He sustained direct fire from tanks, assault guns, heavy artillery and fighter bombers, but nothing could dislodge him. His battle group was in the direct line of an advancing division and engaged the main force of an elite tank brigade employed as the advance guard for the division. He energetically directed the battle, and as night fell his beleaguered force repulsed the attacking enemy in hand-to-hand fighting, holding their ground and eventually winning the day. In recognition of this feat he was awarded the Oakleaves, becoming the 359th recipient.

FRÜHAUF, Carl-Heinz

RANK: SS-Sturmbannführer der Reserve
BORN: 14 February 1914
DIED: 18 April 1976 (D)
PARTY NUMBER:
SS NUMBER: 61349
AWARDS: 1939 Iron Cross Second Class,
10 November 1941; 1939 Iron Cross
First Class, 26 September 1941;
Knight's Cross of the Iron Cross, 4 June
1944; Close Combat Clasp Bronze
Class, 20 November 1944; Medal for
the Winter Campaign in Russia
1941-1942, 15 September 1942;
Commemorative Medal of 13 March
1938; Commemorative Medal of
1 October 1938; Prague Castle Bar;
1939 Wound Badge Silver Class.

Frühauf fought with distinction right through the war. He was born in Hamburg, the son of a master builder, and studied to become a mechanical engineer. During this period he also joined the NSDAP and SS, attending courses in police work given by the Hamburg police. After obtaining his degree he joined the SS-Verfügungstruppe from 1 April 1934 to March 1935. He was an instructor at the SS sports school at Sternberg/ Mecklenberg, and from November 1937 until June 1938 held various posts including primary marksmanship instructor and platoon leader in both first and third companies of the SS-Regiment *Germania*. Frühauf took part in the Polish campaign as platoon leader in the regiment's armoured reconnaissance squadron.

After demonstrating outstanding leadership qualities, Frühauf was selected to attend the officers' training school at Brünswick in February 1940. He completed the course in May 1940 and went on to the army cavalry school for armoured reconnaissance training in Krampnitz, completing the course in July 1940. He became adjutant to the 2nd Battalion SS-Regiment *Germania*, and on 1 March 1941 was transferred as an ordnance officer to the divisional staff of the newly formed *Wiking* Division, joining the regimental staff of SS-Infantry Regiment *Germania* at the beginning of Operation 'Barbarossa'. From September 1941, he was company commander of the 15th Motorcycle Reconnaissance Company, and in May 1942 he became regimental adjutant to the SS Supply and Service Regiment.

Frühauf was wounded in the neck on 18 September 1942 during the drive towards the Caucasus oil fields, and spent two months in hospital. After convalescence leave he became commander of an SS-Armoured Reconnaissance Company Training Centre at Ellwagen, a position he held from November 1942 to September 1943. He was reassigned to combat duty, and in January 1944 served as battalion commander of the 23rd Pioneer Battalion, SS-Panzergrenadier Regiment *Nederland*. On 13 March he became battalion commander of the SS-Panzergrenadier Regiment *De Ruiter*.

During March 1944, his battalion was engaged in the heavy fighting at the Narva Bridgehead, and the 5th Company's position was overrun. The battalion's reserve was already committed and the situation was desperate. Frühauf mustered every non-essential soldier and led a successful counterattack, throwing back the enemy to the former frontline after intensive hand-to-hand fighting. He was awarded the Knight's Cross of the Iron Cross for this action. On 27 July 1944, he was severely wounded by a tank high-explosive shell and transported back on the last hospital ship from Reval to Gotenhafen; he spent four months in the field hospital in Zappat, east Prussia.

On 9 November 1944, he was assigned to the First SS Armoured Reconnaissance Detachment (Training) at Sennelager, near Paderborn. After the American forces crossed the Rhine at Remagen in March 1945 he formed an SS tank brigade *Westfalen* and opposed the American breakout at the bridgehead, suffering hard counterattacks until the total disintegration of the unit. He became commander of a tank detachment attached to the 11th Army, and fought a retreating action until 18 April 1945 when, in the area of Elbingerode, he surrendered. He became an American POW at Attichy, St. Abold in France, and was then interned in Heilbronn and Darmstadt. He was employed in the building trade until de-Nazification. From 1952 he was a sales manager until 1974, when he became ill. He died in Hamburg in 1976.

GEBHARDT, Prof Dr Karl Franz

RANK: SS-Gruppenführer
   und Generalleutnant der Waffen-SS
BORN: 23 November 1897
DIED: 2 June 1948 (E.A.)
PARTY NUMBER: 1723317
SS NUMBER: 265894
AWARDS: 1914 Iron Cross Second Class;
   1914 Iron Cross First Class; Cross of
   Honour 1914-1918 Combatants; 1914
   Wound Badge Black Class; 1939 Iron
   Cross Second Class Bar; 1939 Iron
   Cross First Class Bar; German Cross in
   Silver, 20 April 1944; War Merit Cross
   Second Class; War Merit Cross First
   Class; Knight's Cross of the War Merit
   Cross with Swords, 31 May 1944;
   Knight's Cross of the War Merit Cross
   Second Class; Knight's Cross of the
   War Merit Cross First Class; 1939
   Wound Badge; SS Honour Ring;
   SS Honour Sword.

Gebhardt, a friend of Himmler (q.v.), became professor of orthopaedic surgery at Berlin University, the head of the medical department of the German Academy for Physical Education, Head of the Hohenlychen Hospital and chief consultant for the SS and police – he was one of the best-known surgeons in Germany. He was promoted to SS-Sturmbannführer on 20 April 1935, and to SS-Oberführer on 20 April 1938. He received the Iron Cross Bar and German Cross in Silver on attachment to *Das Reich*.

Left: SS panzergrenadiers of the Germania *Regiment,* Wiking *Division, search for the enemy as they drive east during the German 1942 summer offensive.*

Together with Hitler's doctor, he cared for SS-Obergruppenführer Heydrich (q.v.) after he was badly wounded in the assassination attempt. Heydrich died from gangrene and Gebhardt was relegated to performing fatal sulphonamide experiments on female concentration camp prisoners. Experiments on prisoners were also carried out in his clinic.

In 1946 he was tried at Nuremberg in the so-called medical trial, indicted and condemned to death. He was hanged at Landsberg Prison on 2 June 1948.

GILLE, Herbert

RANK: SS-Obergruppenführer
   und General der Waffen-SS
BORN: 8 March 1897
DIED: 27 December 1966 (D)
PARTY NUMBER: 537337
SS NUMBER: 39854
AWARDS: 1914 Iron Cross Second Class;
   1914 Iron Cross First Class; Cross of
   Honour 1914-1918 Combatants;
   Knight's Cross, 8 October 1942; Oak
   Leaves, 1 November 1943; Oakleaves
   with Swords, 20 February 1944;
   Oakleaves, Swords & Diamonds,
   19 April 1944; 1939 Iron Cross Second
   Class, Bar; 1939 Iron Cross First Class
   Bar; German Cross in Gold, 4 March
   1942; SS Honour Ring; SS Honour
   Sword; Finnish Cross with Swords.

A highly skilled soldier, Gille joined the army as a cadet, serving with distinction as an artillery officer in World War I. In 1934 he joined the SS-Verfügungstruppe, and on outbreak of World War II saw service in the Polish and Western campaigns and then on the Russian Front.

While commanding the SS-Artillery Regiment, *Wiking* Division, he was awarded the Knight's Cross of the Iron Cross, and subsequently went on to command the division itself. His unit suffered severe losses, and the nominal roll, on occasion, was down to a few hundred men. He begged for reinforcements, but received the Oakleaves instead, becoming the 315th recipient. Further pleadings for more men made him the 47th recipient of the Swords, an award he earned for conspicuous bravery while fighting, surrounded, on the Eastern Front. In less than two days, for example, his unit suffered more than 2000 casualties at the hands of the encircling Russians. Finally he was awarded the Diamonds, becoming the 12th recipient. He took command of IV SS Panzer Corps and continued to fight at the front with his men, seeing action in Hungary and finally in Austria.

When the war was over, he ran a small book shop and founded the veterans' magazine, *Wiking-Ruf*. He died in 1966 in Stemmen near Hanover.

GLOBOCNIK, Odilo
RANK: SS-Gruppenführer
BORN: 21 April 1904
DIED: 31 May 1945 (S)
PARTY NUMBER: 442939
SS NUMBER: 292776
AWARDS: Golden Party Badge; 1939 Iron Cross Second Class; 1939 Iron Cross First Class; War Merit Cross Second Class with Swords; War Merit Cross First Class with Swords; SS Honour Ring; SS Honour Sword.

A vicious character, Globocnik was born in Trieste, Italy, and emigrated to Austria in 1918. In 1922 he joined the NSDAP, holding a number of posts in the Austrian party. He joined the SS in 1933 and later that year was promoted to Deputy Gauleiter of Austria, despite his involvement in a murderous jewellery robbery in the suburbs of Favoriten. He contributed to the Anschluss and after Austria's absorption into the Reich, was rewarded by being appointed State Secretary. For a short time from 24 May 1938, he was Gauleiter of Vienna, but this position was short-lived: he was dismissed in January 1939 for personal corruption and illegal speculations in foreign exchange.

This blight on his character curtailed Globocnik's career in the NSDAP, but the SS seemed totally unconcerned, and in September 1939 he became SS and Police Leader in Lublin. Himmler (q.v.) selected him for the job of liquidator of the Polish Jews. He became, by default, head of the death camp organisation, Abteilung Reinhard, and founded the line of extermination camps along the Bug river. Unstable to the point that he terrorised his own camp commanders, he publicly plundered his victims, and Frank's (q.v.) civil administration had to put up with this drunken sadist for four years. Himmler transferred him to Trieste as SS and Police Leader for the Adriatic coast. After the war he was taken prisoner by the British and he committed suicide in Weissensee in Corinthia.

GLÜCKS, Richard
RANK: SS-Gruppenführer
BORN: 22 April 1889—
PARTY NUMBER: 214805
SS NUMBER: 58706
AWARDS: 1914 Iron Cross Second Class; 1914 Iron Cross First Class; Cross of Honour 1914-1918 Combatants; War Merit Cross Second Class with Swords; War Merit Cross First Class with Swords; SS Honour Ring; SS Honour Sword.

Glücks joined Theodor Eicke's (q.v.) staff in 1936 and was appointed to succeed him as inspector of concentration camps in 1939, a position he held until the war's end. He was last seen near the Danish border in May 1945 and thereafter vanished without trace. There is a story that Glücks ended up in a naval hospital working under a false name after the surrender.

GÖSTL, Erich
RANK: SS-Panzergrenadier
BORN: 17 April 1925
DIED: 27 October 1990 (D)
PARTY NUMBER: —
SS NUMBER: —
AWARDS: 1939 Iron Cross Second Class, 19 July 1944; 1939 Iron Cross First Class, 16 August 1944; Knight's Cross of the Iron Cross, 31 October 1944.

A brave man, Göstl was born in Vienna, Austria, in October 1944. He was a panzergrenadier with the 6th Company, 1st SS-Panzergrenadier Regiment, 1st SS Panzer Division *Leibstandarte SS Adolf Hitler*. In his capacity as a light machine-gunner during the June 1944 Normandy invasion, he defended his position against a British attack. He was blinded in one eye but continued to return fire. He was hit in the other eye, but despite these wounds he continued to fire his weapon until the British attack was repulsed. Erich Göstl's characteristics were fittingly described as 'heroism without exaggerated pathos, a man of deeds rather than words', and he was awarded the Knight's Cross of the Iron Cross. He survived the war and returned to Vienna where his physical handicap did not stand in the way of him obtaining a doctorate of law. He died in 1990 in Vienna.

GOTTBERG, Curt von
RANK: SS-Obergruppenführer
BORN: 11 February 1896
DIED: 9 May 1945 (S)
PARTY NUMBER: 948753
SS NUMBER: 45923
AWARDS: 1914 Iron Cross First and Second Classes; Cross of Honour 1914-1918 Combatants; 1939 Iron Cross Second Class Bar, 6 December 1942; 1939 Iron Cross First Class Bar, 20 February 1943; German Cross in Gold, 7 August 1943; Knight's Cross, 30 June 1944; SS Honour Ring, SS Honour Sword.

Having fought in World War I, von Gottberg joined the police and later the SS-Verfügungstruppe. While serving with this unit he lost a leg in an accident prior to the war, but nevertheless saw service on the Russian Front from 1942.

In the summer of 1944 he was the commanding offer of Battle Group V Gottberg, Army Group Centre, a unit composed of police and Waffen-SS personnel. During the retreat of German forces of Army Group Centre, his men sacrificed themselves, providing an escape route for numerous units to cross the Beresina and Niemen rivers, and averting a calamity. Von Gottberg was delegated to take over command of the newly formed XII SS Army Corps, but he was well aware of his military inadequacies and relinquished his command to General of the Army Blumentritt.

Von Gottberg was a brave commander who held the respect of his men, as well as their devotion. It was for these qualities that he was awarded the Knight's Cross of the Iron Cross. At the end of the war he committed suicide at Leutznöft in the district of Flensburg, on 9 May 1945.

GOTTKE, Heinrich
RANK: SS-Oberscharführer
BORN: 7 July 1921—
PARTY NUMBER: —
SS NUMBER: —
AWARDS: 1939 Iron Cross Second Class, 20 July 1941; 1939 Iron Cross First Class, 14 December 1944; Knight's Cross of the Iron Cross, 17 December 1944.

Gottke was a forward observer 3rd Battery, 17th SS-Anti-Aircraft Detachment, 17th SS Panzergrenadier Division *Götz von Berlichingen*, XIII SS Army Corps, and fought in Russia from 1941, and on the Western Front during the severe winter of 1944-45. Stationed near the Blies river at Erfweiler, between Saarbrücken

and Smargemünd, Gottke saw a concentration of American infantry and tanks moving up and so directed artillery fire onto them, driving them back. On 16 December 1944, the thinly manned German defence position was attacked again by American infantry supported by tanks and other armoured vehicles, with the result that the German position had to be evacuated. Gottke's observation post was situated in front of his own line and from this vantage point he could see the tanks. He called the 17th SS-Artillery Regiment, as well as an anti-aircraft detachment, to lay down a barrage of fire on the advancing infantry and armour, recklessly using his own position as the target. His radio message 'fire on the hermit' remained a legend with his division. The concentrated barrage halted the American advance. Gottke was awarded the Knight's Cross of the Iron Cross for his bravery.

GRAF, Ulrich
RANK: SS-Brigadeführer
BORN: 6 July 1878
DIED: 3 March 1950 (D)
PARTY NUMBER: 8
SS NUMBER: 26
AWARDS: Golden Party Badge; Coburg Badge 14 October 1932; Blood Order No 21; SS Honour Ring; SS Honour Sword.

Graf was born in Pachhagel, Dillingen-Donau, the son of a small farmer. He joined the army before his 18th birthday and served for several years. A roughneck and amateur wrestler, he held several jobs including one for the Munich council. He left his job as a butcher to become Hitler's personal bodyguard, afterwards forming the Stosstrupp with eight others. He was on the Coburg expedition that broke the communist hold on the city, which provided the impetus for the 1923 Putsch. He was at Hitler's side when the police opened fire, and he jumped in front of him, stopping five bullets that left him critically wounded, but undoubtedly saving Hitler's life. From 1 January 1925 until it was dissolved in 1933, he was a Munich town councillor. He was made a freeman of his home town in 1934, and in 1935 Hitler appointed him Munich Alderman. In 1936 he was elected to the Reichstag.

After the war he served five years in a labour camp, a sentence his daughter thought unfair, blaming it for his death in 1950.

GRAWITZ, Prof Dr Ernst-Robert
RANK: SS-Obergruppenführer
BORN: 8 June 1899
DIED: April 1945 (S)
PARTY NUMBER: 1102844
SS NUMBER: 27483
AWARDS: 1914 Iron Cross Second Class; Cross of Honour 1914-1918 Combatants; 1939 Iron Cross Second Class Bar; War Merit Cross Second Class with Swords; War Merit Cross First Class with Swords; SS Honour Ring; SS Honour Sword.

Head of the SS medical services from 1936 until the end of the war, and controller of the German Red Cross, Grawitz worked with Dr Herbert Linden of the health ministry, and under Brandt (q.v.) and Bouhler (q.v.), to choose doctors for leadership roles. Their criteria included the closeness of these doctors to the regime, high recognition in the profession and known sympathy for euthanasia or a radical approach to it.

Despite a rift with Himmler (q.v.), when his favourite general Bach-Zelewski (q.v.) suffered a nervous breakdown after his experience with the killings in Russia, Grawitz remained a trusted adviser. He recommended the use of gas chambers as the most efficient method of mass killing. The methods of selection for work or death in the camps were largely laid down by Grawitz, who held the view that only those Jews completely fit and able to work should be selected for employment. The weak, the old and those who were only relatively robust would quickly become incapable, causing a further deterioration in their health and an unnecessary need for an increase in hospital accommodation. Further medical personnel and medicines would be required, all for no purpose, since the Jews would have to be killed in the end. Grawitz committed suicide in April 1945.

GREISER, Arthur
RANK: SS-Obergruppenführer,
   Gauleiter of Warthegau 1939-45
BORN: 22 January 1897
DIED: 21 July 1946 (E.A.)
PARTY NUMBER: 166635
SS NUMBER: 10795
AWARDS: 1914 Iron Cross Second Class;
   1914 Iron Cross First Class; Cross of
   Honour 1914-1918 Combatants; 1914
   Wound Badge Black Class; Golden
   Party Badge; SS Honour Ring;
   SS Honour Sword.

Greiser was a pilot during World War I and co-founded the Stahlhem, the war veterans' organisation in Danzig. In 1929, he joined the NSDAP and became president of the Danzig senate. With the absorption of Danzig into Greater Germany in September 1939, and the invasion of Poland, he was rewarded by being appointed Gauleiter of the new Gau Warthegau, which was renamed Wartheland in 1940. He held this position until the war's end. On the 25 May 1945, SS-Obergruppenführer Heinz Reinefarth (q.v.) and Arthur Greiser surrendered to the Americans in Austria, probably thinking they would be treated less harshly. He was extradited to Poland, where he was tried, found guilty of war crimes and hanged at Poznan.

GRESE, Irma
RANK: SS-Helferinnen
BORN: 7 October 1923
DIED: 13 December 1945 (E.A.)

Having joined the SS when she was 18, Grese's first appointment was to supervise women prisoners at the Auschwitz concentration camp. A 19-year-old sadist, she was promoted to control blocks of women prisoners. She was known there as the 'angel of Birkenau'. It has been reported that she was lover to both Mengele and SS-Sturmbannfuhrer Karl Mummenthey. When Auschwitz closed, she was transferred to Bergen-Belsen to oversee the female quarters. When the camp was liberated in April 1945 she was captured and charged with war crimes. A British military court sat between 17 September and 17 November, trying 45 former staff members; 14 were acquitted, 19 sentenced to varying terms of imprisonment and 11 executed. Grese was numbered nine during the trial and found guilty. She fervently denied up to the end that she had ever ill-treated detainees, all to no avail. She was hanged on the 12 December 1945.

GRIMMINGER, Jakob
RANK: SS-Standartenführer
BORN: 25 April 1892
DIED: 28 January 1969 (D)
PARTY NUMBER: 759
SS NUMBER: 135
AWARDS: 1914 Iron Cross Second Class;
   Cross of Honour 1914-1918
   Combatants; Golden Party Badge;
   Coburg Badge 14 October 1932; Blood
   Order No 714, 9 November 1923;
   Turkey Iron Half Moon First Class;
   SS Honour Ring; SS Honour Sword.

Grimminger served honourably in World War I and joined the NSDAP soon after, becoming an early party member. He took part in the 1923 Putsch and was in 10 Company, SA Regiment *Munich*. He was appointed standard-bearer of the hallowed blood flag which had been carried on the march and was spattered with the

Above: Jakob Grimminger with the hallowed blood flag, which was carried during the 1923 Munich Beer Hall Putsch and was revered ever after by the Nazis.

GROSS, Martin

RANK: SS-Obersturmbannführer
BORN: 15 April 1911
DIED: 1 March 1984 (D)
PARTY NUMBER: 454840
SS NUMBER: 6684
AWARDS: 1939 Iron Cross Second Class, 1 October 1939; 1939 Iron Cross First Class, 20 July 1940; German Cross in Gold, 28 March 1943; Knight's Cross of the Iron Cross, 22 July 1943; 1939 Wound Badge Black Class; Commemorative Medal of 13 March 1938; Commemorative Medal of 1 October 1938; SS Honour Ring; SS Honour Sword.

Born in Frankfurt-am-Main, the son of a railway official, Gross joined the SS in May 1933 and was attached to the *Leibstandarte*. He took part in the occupation of Austria and the Sudetenland, and was a platoon commander in the *Leibstandarte* in Poland in 1939, and in the campaign in the West.

In 1941 he was seriously wounded at Rostov while in command of the 5th company. After recovering, he was posted to a staff position and then to command the 1st Panzer Regiment of the *Leibstandarte*. Gross was with his unit near Bielgorod on the morning of 12 July 1943, when the Soviets attacked his position. Despite their superiority in numbers, the attackers were repulsed, encircled and then crushed. Ninety Soviet tanks, most of them T-34s, were destroyed during three hours of intense fighting; a further 30 tanks damaged in close-quarter fighting were attributed to the grenadiers. Gross was awarded the Knight's Cross of the Iron Cross and remained on the Eastern Front when the *Leibstandarte* was transferred to Normandy in the summer of 1944. He commanded a panzer brigade and was involved in continuous actions around Riga and in Lithuania.

As commander of the 12th Panzer Regiment in the *Hitlerjugend* in November 1944, Gross was later in action in the Ardennes. He moved to Hungary and fought a rearguard action to Austria, where the division, consisting of only 455 men, surrendered to the Americans in May 1945. He died in Luer in 1984.

blood of the fallen. About 2000 took part in the march to the centre of Munich, but they were stopped by police, who blocked their path. The police opened fire and both Hitler and Göring were wounded. All in all it was a rather feeble and ill-planned attempt to take control in Bavaria and Germany. However, it did provide the Nazis with publicity. The flag became the spiritual icon of the Nazi Party, and each new standard was consecrated by being ritually touched by the blood flag at the presentation ceremony. Grimminger became a Munich city councillor, but after the war he faded into obscurity and died in Munich in poverty.

GROTHMANN, Werner
RANK: SS Obersturmbannführer
BORN: 23 August 1915—
PARTY NUMBER: —
SS NUMBER: 181334
AWARDS: 1939 Iron Cross Second Class; 1939 Iron Cross First Class; SS Honour Ring; SS Honour Sword.

Grothmann succeeded Karl Wolff (q.v.) as Himmler's (q.v.) military adjutant in 1943. Grothmann could best be described as an 'old hand at court'. He was with Himmler when he tried to escape in an ill-conceived disguise, and was apprehended on 23 May 1945 by the British authorities. Why Himmler revealed himself to the British is still a mystery, but one theory is that Grothmann and Himmler's secretary, perceiving the futility of Himmler's plans, were going to turn him in anyway.

GRÜNEWALD, Adam
RANK: SS-Sturmbannführer
BORN: 20 October 1902
DIED: January 1945 (K.I.A.)
PARTY NUMBER: 536404
SS NUMBER: 253631
AWARDS: SS Honour Ring; SS Honour Sword.

Before the war Grünewald served as commander of the Dachau detention centre and was an administrative officer in the Totenkopfverbande. He was transferred to the new SS-TK at the beginning of the war and was appointed to command the bakery company. He executed this assignment well enough to be promoted to command the division's procurement service, and remained with the *Totenkopf* Division from November 1939 until October 1942. He was reassigned to camp duty as commander of the detention centre at Oranienburg, a post he held until January 1943, when he was moved up to the larger assignment of commandant of the huge concentration camp and deportation centre in Vught in occupied Holland.

Grünewald's stewardship of Vught became unusually notorious, and in early 1944 an SS investigation revealed that he had sanctioned especially brutal treatment of prisoners, allowing such overcrowding in the camp's detention cells that the unsanitary conditions killed a number of women political detainees. Grünewald was removed from his command and court-martialled at Himmler's express order. As punishment he was demoted to the rank of SS private and sentenced in April 1944 to an indefinite term of combat with the *Totenkopf* Division. While fighting with the division in Hungary in January 1945, Grünewald was killed in action fighting the Russians.

GÜNSCHE, Otto
RANK: SS-Sturmbannführer
BORN: 1917—
PARTY NUMBER: —
SS NUMBER: 257773
AWARDS: 1939 Iron Cross Second Class; 1939 Iron Cross First Class; War Merit Cross Second Class with Swords; Wound Badge '20 July 1944' Black Class; Army Long Service Medal 4 Years' Service; Golden Hitler Youth Honour Badge; Commemorative Medal of 13 March 1938; Commemorative Medal of 1 October 1938; Prague Castle Bar; Commemorative Medal For The Return Of The Memel Region; German Defence Medal; Infantry Assault Badge.

Günsche joined the SS Begleit-Kommando on 1 May 1936, the unit tasked with protecting Hitler. From 1940 until 1941, he was employed as an SS ordnance officer, followed by training and active service. In January 1943, he was appointed personal adjutant and served with Fritz Darges (q.v.) until August of that year, when he returned to active service. Appointed as Hitler's personal adjutant in March 1944, he was injured in the 20 July Bomb Plot, suffering lacerations to his head and seared eyebrows. Notwithstanding his own state, he helped Hitler to stumble from the shattered building.

Günsche remained in this job until the end of the war, and one of his last duties was, on Hitler's express orders, to see to the

Above: Otto Günsche and the man he was sworn to protect, his beloved Führer. It was Günsche who helped burn Hitler's body following his suicide.

Right: Waffen-SS soldiers of the Das Reich *Division on the outskirts of a burning Russian village during the early stages of Operation 'Barbarossa', July 1941.*

destruction of the couple's bodies. Hitler had informed him that he and Eva were committing suicide and told him to 'be sure to burn our bodies. I don't want to be put on display in some Russian waxworks.' Günsche was the first person to see his body and helped to incinerate it. He attempted to escape Berlin, but was arrested by the Soviets and imprisoned for 10 years.

GUSTAVSSON, Karl-Heinz

RANK: SS-Hauptsturmführer
BORN: 10 February 1915—
PARTY NUMBER: —
SS NUMBER: —
AWARDS: 1939 Iron Cross Second Class; 1939 Iron Cross First Class; Knight's Cross of the Iron Cross, 3 March 1945; Knight's Cross of the War Merit Cross Second Class with Swords; Close Combat Clasp in Silver; Infantry Assault Badge Silver Class; Medal for the Winter Campaign in Russia 1941-1942; 1939 Wound Badge Silver Class.

Gustavsson joined the police in his hometown of Hamburg on 1 April 1934. He joined the army in 1935 and was promoted to Unteroffizier on 2 October 1938.

He transferred to the armed SS on 5 September 1939 and fought in Poland. In the Russian campaign he was the company commander of the 2nd SS Brigade, later to become SS-Sturmbrigade *Langemark*. He attended the SS-Junkerschule at Bad Tölz from 1 March until 31 May 1942. From 1943 he become battery commander of the SS-Sturmbrigade *Langemark*.

On 15 September 1944, he was attached to *Das Reich* in the Ardennes Offensive. He was then at Remagen when the Americans managed to capture the bridge across the Rhine. Here, Gustavsson formed a Kampfgruppe and succeeded in blocking the advancing American armour, being credited with 13 tanks destroyed. In action on 13 March 1945 he suffered his fourth wound, the severity of which led to the amputation of his right leg in 1949. For his bravery he was awarded the Knight's Cross.

HANKE, Karl

RANK: SS-Obergruppenführer,
Gauleiter of Lower Silesia 1940-45
BORN: 24 August 1903
DIED: 1945 (M)
PARTY NUMBER: 102606
SS NUMBER: 203013
AWARDS: German Order, 12 April 1945;
SS Honour Ring; SS Honour Sword.

Hanke's first key position in the NSDAP was as personal adjutant to Göbbels in the Propaganda Ministry. He paid court to Magda, Göbbels' wife, while his boss was having a liaison with Lida Baarova, a Czech film star, although both affairs were broken off at Hitler's insistence. Promoted to State Secretary in the Propaganda Ministry, Hanke joined the army at the beginning of the war.

He was attached to Erwin Rommel's staff in the French campaign of 1940, and although not a career soldier, fought courageously enough. He was recommended for the Knight's Cross of the Iron Cross by Rommel himself, but this recommendation was subsequently withdrawn because of some unpleasant remarks Hanke had made. He was released from military service at the end of 1940.

Still not in favour in Berlin, Hanke was appointed Gauleiter of Niedersachsen, Lower Silesia, a position he held until the end of the war. In the closing weeks of the war he conducted the defence of Breslau, and on 12 April 1945 was awarded the party's and state's highest decoration, the German Order, referred to in the announcement as the 'Golden Cross of the German Order'.

Soon after he flew from besieged Breslau, ostensibly to take up his appointment with Dönitz in Flensburg, as he had been nominated in Hitler's will to succeed Himmler (q.v.) as Reichsführer-SS and head of the police. In fact, he flew by helicopter to find refuge at Field Marshal Schörner's headquarters at Kronenberg, and there to disguise himself. Three ends have been promulgated for him: first, that he was shot by Czech partisans while escaping from arrest soon after the capitulation in May 1945; second, that he was beaten to death by them; third, that he was executed by the Poles. No one knows for certain.

HANSEN, Max

RANK: SS-Standartenführer
BORN: 31 July 1908
DIED: 7 March 1990 (D)
PARTY NUMBER: 478376
SS NUMBER: 27813
AWARDS: 1939 Iron Cross Second Class;
1939 Iron Cross First Class; German
Cross in Gold, 29 December 1942;
Knight's Cross of the Iron Cross,
28 March 1943; Oakleaves 28 March
1945; SS Honour Ring; SS Honour Sword.

One of the *Leibstandarte*'s most accomplished officers, Hansen was born in Niebüll Holstein. He joined the Waffen-SS and fought in Poland and France in 1940. As commanding officer of the 2nd Battalion, 1st SS-Panzergrenadier Regiment *Leibstandarte* in Army Group South, he was awarded the Knight's Cross of the Iron Cross for his part in retaking Kharkov in early 1943 during Manstein's counterattack. He was transferred to the West in 1944 with his regiment, subsequently fighting in the Battle of the Bulge and later in Hungary. He was awarded the Oakleaves, becoming the 812th recipient, in recognition of his daring leadership. He died in his home town of Niebüll in early 1990.

HARMEL, Heinz

RANK: SS-Brigadeführer —
BORN: 29 June 1906—
PARTY NUMBER: —
SS NUMBER: 278276
AWARDS: 1939 Iron Cross Second Class,
30 May 1940; 1939 Iron Cross First
Class, 1 June 1940; Knight's Cross,
31 March 1942; Oakleaves, 7
September 1943; Oakleaves with
Swords, 28 November 1944; German
Cross in Gold, 29 November 1941;
SS Honour Ring; SS Honour Sword.

The son of a high-ranking military surgeon, Harmel was employed as a farm administrator prior to Hitler's assumption of power. He joined the SS-Verfügungstruppe, and in January 1938 was attached to the 3rd Battalion *Der Führer* in Klagenfurt, Styria. He saw action during the campaign in France before being transferred to the Russian Front where he commanded the SS-Panzergrenadier Regiment *Deutschland*. Awarded the Knight's Cross of the Iron Cross in 1942, he became the 296th recipient of the Oakleaves in 1944.

Harmel was trusted by his command and disliked unnecessary red tape. He was severely reprimanded for giving permission to a young SS-Rottenführer to marry his Dutch girlfriend who was expecting his child. Himmler (q.v.) personally reserved that right, and recommendation of suitability had to be obtained from RSHA. Himmler bitterly complained to Paul Hausser (q.v.) and Georg Keppler (q.v.) about Harmel's insubordination, and Harmel was transferred to the Western Front in April 1944.

Given command of the 10th SS Panzer Division *Frundsberg*, Harmel fought at Arnhem and in the heavy battles that raged in Normandy, Alsace, Pomerania, and Saxony. He was relieved of his command by Field Marshal Schörner's chief of staff, General von Natzmer, towards the end of April 1945 for failing to obey Hitler's orders to deploy *Frundsberg* for a last stand. He was transferred to the south. Here he was ordered by the gauleiter in his role as Reich Defence Commissioner to build up a defensive front in the Carinthian area. Harmel managed to halt the British with badly equipped and trained units until the capitulation.

HARTJENSTEIN, Friedrich

RANK: SS-Sturmbannführer
BORN: 3 July 1905
DIED: 1954 (D)
PARTY NUMBER: —
SS NUMBER: 327350
AWARDS: 1939 Iron Cross Second Class;
1939 Iron Cross First Class; SS Honour
Ring; SS Honour Sword.

Having seen extensive duty in the reserve Totenkopf regiments, Hartjenstein was transferred in March 1940 to the *Totenkopf* Division where, by October 1941, he had served successively as a company commander and staff officer. The *Totenkopf* Division's officer corps was depleted during the first summer of the Russian campaign, leading Eicke (q.v.) to give Hartjenstein command of the 1st Battalion of Infantry Regiment 3. The results were disastrous, and Hartjenstein proved totally unfit to command an infantry battalion. His incompetence led to the severe mauling of his unit during the spring of 1942. Eicke had no option but to relieve him of his command in late August and transfer him to camp duties.

On 10 March 1943 he was promoted to commandant of Birkenau

Hartjenstein was given command of the SS guard detachment at Auschwitz, where he evidently redeemed himself, as on 10 March 1943 he was promoted to commandant of Birkenau extermination camp, the main liquidation centre within the Auschwitz complex. Birkenau had a railway siding disguised as a railway station – though in every sense it was the end of the line. It started operations in 1941 as a speedily built camp for the extermination of Russian prisoners of war. Hartjenstein held this position until May 1944, when Himmler (q.v.) transferred him to command the large slave labour camp of Natzweiler in Alsace in recognition of his outstanding service. He was captured by the French in 1945 and a military tribunal found him guilty of mass murder of prisoners in Natzweiler. He was condemned to death, but while this sentence was under appeal in 1954 he died of a heart attack in prison in Metz.

HARZER, Walter

RANK: SS-Standartenführer
BORN: 29 September 1912
DIED: 29 May 1982 (D)
PARTY NUMBER: 477371
SS NUMBER: 23101
AWARDS: 1939 Iron Cross Second Class, 29 September 1939; 1939 Iron Cross First Class, 26 October 1941; German Cross in Gold, 19 August 1944; Knight's Cross of the Iron Cross, 21 September 1944; SS Honour Ring; SS Honour Sword.

Harzer served in the Polish campaign and on the Russian Front as part of Operation 'Barbarossa', and was the first divisional staff officer of the 9th SS Panzer Division *Hohenstaufen*. While the division was refitting in northern Ukraine in preparation for a new offensive near Kovel, the Allies landed in Normandy. On 11 June 1944 Hitler cancelled the planned offensive in the East and ordered the transfer of II SS Panzer Corps to France. *Hohenstaufen* fought continuously and without replacement in Normandy from its arrival in late June until its withdrawal on 12 August 1944.

On 10 September remnants of the division were ordered to Germany for a complete refit, handing over their equipment to their sister division, *Frundsberg*, at Arnhem. On 17 September the men were on the point of departing when the 1st British Airborne Division landed near Nijmegen, taking the Germans totally by surprise. Under Model's orders, SS Battle Group *Harzer* was formed from the remnants of the *Hohenstaufen* Division. It moved on Arnhem and engaged the Guards Armoured Division behind Eindhoven. The battle of Arnhem raged for eight days, and on 29 September the Allies surrendered. This was seen as a great victory for *Hohenstaufen*, and in particular for the commander of Battle Group *Harzer*. In recognition of his achievements, Harzer was awarded the Knight's Cross of the Iron Cross (after Arnhem *Hohenstaufen* was pulled back to Germany to prepare for the Ardennes Offensive at the end of 1944). His last posting was as commander of the 4th SS Panzergrenadier Division *SS-Polizei*, which he held from the 28 November 1944 until May 1945. He died in Stuttgart in 1982.

HAUSSER, Paul

RANK: SS-Oberstgruppenführer und Generaloberst der Waffen-SS
BORN: 7 October 1880
DIED: 21 December 1972 (D)
PARTY NUMBER: 4158779
SS NUMBER: 239795
AWARDS: 1914 Iron Cross Second Class; 1914 Iron Cross First Class; Cross of Honour 1914-1918 Combatants; 1939 Iron Cross Second Class Bar, September 1939; 1939 Iron Cross First Class Bar, 17 May 1940; Knight's Cross, 8 August 1941; Oakleaves, 28 July 1943; Oakleaves with Swords, 26 August 1944; 1939 Wound Badge Silver; SS Honour Ring; SS Honour Sword.

Hausser entered military service as a cadet, and was commissioned prior to the outbreak of World War I, when he served as a line and staff officer. In 1932 he retired from the Reichswehr as a major-general, only to be reactivated in 1934 when he joined the SS-Verfügungstruppe. He was made inspector of that organisation in 1936, bringing outstanding qualities of leadership to the job, and formulating the directives and codes of practice it was to use. Known as 'Papa' Hausser by his men, Paul Hausser made a remarkable impact on the SS.

Hitler ordered Hausser to hold the city at all costs, but he abandoned it

Hausser was engaged in combat from the start in Poland and France. The *Das Reich* Division was transferred to the Russian Front where, as a Generalleutnant of the Waffen-SS attached to Army Group Centre, he earned the Knight's Cross of the Iron Cross. He was severely wounded two months later, losing his eye; the black eye patch he sported afterwards became his trademark on and off the battlefield. His military endeavours were remarkable. The Russian offensive of early 1943 took Kursk and threatened Kharkov. Hitler ordered Hausser, in command of II SS Panzer Corps, to hold the city at all costs. However, Hausser realised that to get trapped inside the city would mean annihilation. On 15 February, therefore, he abandoned the city, but in a brilliant counterattack he retook it in March. His actions undoubtedly saved the Waffen-SS corps and inflicted a massive defeat on the Red Army. It was also a badly needed morale booster following the debacle at Stalingrad. For actions such as these on the Russian Front, and while serving as II SS Panzer Corps commander, he was awarded the Oakleaves, becoming the 216th recipient (though Hitler did delay four months before eventually including him in the Kharkov medal winners).

When German forces were threatened with encirclement by the Allies in the Falaise Gap in 1944, Hausser effectively led the breakout, and he was again severely wounded. His bravery earned him the Oakleaves with Swords, of which he was the 90th recipient. During the closing months of the war he commanded Army Group G until his capture in April 1945. He died at Ludwigsburg in December 1972.

HEIN, Willi
RANK: SS-Hauptsturmführer
BORN: 26 April 1917—
PARTY NUMBER: —
SS NUMBER: —
AWARDS: 1939 Iron Cross Second Class, 26 July 1942; 1939 Iron Cross First Class, 20 January 1943; German Cross in Gold, 30 December 1943; Knight's Cross of the Iron Cross, 4 March 1944; Army Honour Roll Clasp, 7 November 1943.

The son of a decorator from Holstein, Hein served in the Reichsarbeitsdienst from April to October 1939 and then volunteered for the Waffen-SS, being attached to the Freiwilligen Grenadier Regiment *Nordland*. He was sent to the SS-Junkerschule at Bad Tölz in 1942, and upon graduating was attached as a troop commander to 5th SS-Panzer Regiment *Wiking* on the Eastern Front.

In August 1943 he was involved in the fierce fighting around Kharkov, and for his service received a Führer-Commendation. The SS Division *Wiking* had been committed to the battle in the Cherkassy cauldron in the summer of 1944. Strong Soviet forces had overrun the divisional supply lines at Olschana. With only two hastily repaired assault guns, accompanied by a mere two dozen men, Hein was given the job of counterattacking. Despite his pitifully inadequate force he duly set off into the night and succeeded in repulsing the Soviets, destroying three T-34 tanks and capturing over 200 prisoners. His bravery earned him the Knight's Cross of the Iron Cross. He was seriously wounded in action during the defence of Budapest (in December 1944 the *Wiking* and *Totenkopf* Divisions tried in vain to relieve the besieged city, losing heavily and being repulsed). Hein ended the war in hospital.

HEISSMEYER, August
RANK: SS-Obergruppenführer
BORN: 11 January 1897—
PARTY NUMBER: 21573
SS NUMBER: 4370
AWARDS: Golden Party Badge; 1914 Iron
Cross Second Class; 1914 Iron Cross
First Class; Cross of Honour 1914-1918
Combatants; 1914 Wound Badge Black
Class; War Merit Cross Second Class
with Swords; War Merit Cross First
Class with Swords; SS Honour Ring;
SS Honour Sword.

Married to Gertrud Scholtz-
Klink, the Nazi women's leader,
Heissmeyer became head of the
SS district Rhine in 1934. From
1935 to 1940 he controlled the
SS main office (SS-Hauptamt).
In 1943 he became the controlling authority for all political
education institutions. He
opposed the links between the
police and the SS, but was overruled by his chief, Himmler (q.v.).

HELLDORF,
(Wolf Heinrich) Graf von
RANK: SS-Oberstgruppenführer,
General der Ordnungspolizei,
Polizeipräsident von Berlin
BORN: 14 October 1896
DIED: 15 August 1944 (E.R.)
PARTY NUMBER: —
SS NUMBER: —
AWARDS: 1914 Iron Cross Second Class;
1914 Iron Cross First Class; Saxon
Order of the White Falcon Second
Class with Swords; Knight's Cross
with Swords, 10 February 1944.

Graf Helldorf entered the Thüringische Husaren-Regiment Nr. 12
as an officer cadet and was promoted to leutnant on 22 March
1915. Having enjoyed a distinguished career during World War
I, he was discharged as part of the army reductions in December
1919. Like many other disillusioned soldiers, he joined various
Freikorps, such as Lützow and Rossbach, but following his partic-
ipation in the Kapp Putsch in 1920 as leader of the Offizier-
Stosstrupp des Freikorps-Rossbach, he went into exile in Italy.
He returned in 1924, becoming involved in another right-wing
organisation. Following Röhm's execution, von Helldorf took
over the leadership of Frontbann Nord, the successor to the
banned SA. In the same year he joined the NSDAP, and was an
elected representative in the Prussian local government. His
appointment as Führer of Berlin-Brandenburg followed in 1931.

Von Helldorf was promoted to SA-Obergruppenführer in
1933. In March 1933, he successfully seized the Karl-Liebknecht-
Haus in Berlin, the KPD-Polizeizentrale. From March until July
1933, he was Kommissarische Polizeipräsident of Potsdam, and
later the Polizeipräsident of Berlin. He belonged to the Reichstag
from 12 November 1933, and in an interview with the *Völkischer
Beobachter*, the NSDAP's main voice, he spoke of the need for the
'cleansing of Berlin of anti-state elements'.

A loyal party member, von Helldorf's job principally entailed
the 'struggle against Jews' in Berlin, as well as the 'struggle against

communists and reactionary crises'; he was also instructed to take action against political catholicism. Von Helldorf somehow avoided being implicated in the murder of Hannussen, a Jewish clairvoyant par excellence, from whom he had borrowed large sums of money. Hannussen had a hold over von Helldorf, and was in a strong position to blackmail him. After von Helldorf was appointed Polizeipräsident, Hannussen was murdered, and no records about the exchanges were ever recovered. From November 1938, Graf Helldorf was the Verbindungsführer der SA zur Deutschen Polizei.

At the presentation of von Helldorf's *Ritterkreuz*, Göbbels gave a speech, in which he said, among other things: 'It is party member Graf von Helldorf who organised the police and fire brigade with great energy and determination, to combat the sweeping fires on the nights of bombing with ever greater success.' He was damned with such faint praise, and six months later was one of the 20 July 1944 conspirators. He was arrested and convicted by the Peoples' Court, finally to be hanged on 15 August 1944.

HENLEIN, Konrad (Dr honoris causa)

RANK: SS-Obergruppenführer
BORN: 6 May 1898
DIED: 10 May 1945 (S)
PARTY NUMBER: 6600001
SS NUMBER: 310307
AWARDS: Golden Party Badge; Cross of Honour 1914-1918 Combatants; 1914 Wound Badge Black Class; War Merit Cross Second Class without Swords; War Merit Cross First Class without Swords; SS Honour Ring; SS Honour Sword.

A Bohemian who served in the Austrian Army during World War I, Henlein began his career as a bank clerk. In 1919 he became a gymnastics teacher in the recently formed Deutsche Turnerbund in the Sudetenland. It was to be as much a political and nationalist force as a physical training group, and he became its head in 1923. The Treaty of Versailles had reconstructed Europe creating new states and realigned borders, among which was

Czechoslovakia. However, considerable numbers of ethnic Germans were left within the confines of the new country. These minorities were not always happy to accept their new national status, and their reluctance turned to militancy within neighbouring Germany during Hitler's rise to power. Discontent was deliberately encouraged as part of long-term Nazi strategy. Hitler saw the chance to expand into the region, enlarging his Empire and enriching it with all the important armaments and vehicle works that the region held. By 1933, Henlein had founded the Sudeten-German Party with an ideology and organisation based on that of the NSDAP.

Funded by the German Foreign Office, Henlein was used to ferment the crisis of 1938, visiting Germany between March and September for instructions. From July 1938, the German Army ran weekly, five-day courses Monday to Saturday at Neuhammer for Freiwilliger Schutzdienst men who secretly slipped out of and back into Czechoslovakia under the guise of holiday makers or travelling businessmen. In Germany they were instructed in the military arts. Each course comprised some 50 trainees, who at its conclusion took an oath of loyalty to Hitler. When the Czech Government offered to accede to all Sudeten German demands, Henlein broke off negotiations with them on a minor pretext (his group was used to foment the Sudeten crisis). Hitler made speeches threatening violence (a peaceful solution would not suit his aims), Sudeten leaders rose against the Czech Government, martial law was declared and Henlein fled to Germany. A Sudeten Freikorps was raised and supported by SS detachments, who occupied two frontier towns: the Sudeten uprising had begun. This was prevented only by the shameful 'Munich Agreement', by which Britain and France, without consulting or even informing the Czechs, turned over the entire Sudetenland to Hitler. Henlein was rewarded with the post of gauleiter after Hitler marched into Czechoslovakia in March 1939.

In early May 1945, he was captured by the US Seventh Army, and later committed suicide in an Allied internment camp at Pilsen, by slashing his wrists with a concealed razor blade.

HESS, Rudolf

RANK: SS-Obergruppenführer
BORN: 26 April 1894
DIED: 17 August 1987 (S)
PARTY NUMBER: 16
AWARDS: 1914 Iron Cross Second Class;
     Cross of Honour 1914-1918
     Combatants; 1914 Wound Badge Black
     Class, 12 June 1916; Blood Order No
     29, November 1923; SS Honour Ring.

Hess was born in Alexandria, Egypt, the son of a German merchant, and was educated in Switzerland and Hamburg. He served in the same regiment as Hitler during World War I. Later, he transferred to the Imperial Air Force as a lieutenant. With the end of the war he served in der Ritter von Epp in the Freikorps. Hess came under the influence of the geopolitical Professor Karl Haushofer while at university at Munich. His right-wing views, already formed, were seduced by the oratory of Hitler and he joined the NSDAP in 1920. He marched with Hitler in the 1923 Putsch and was imprisoned at Landsberg. The closeness of the two men occurred during this period, with Hitler dictating *Mein Kampf* to Hess.

On his release, Hess played a leading part in the reformation of the NSDAP. By 1932 he had been appointed chairman of the central political commission of the party. When Hitler assumed power Hess became Deputy Leader, and in June 1933 Reich Minister without Portfolio. In 1935 Hess was a selector of all senior Nazi officials. He was appointed a ministerial member for the defence of the Reich in 1939. For a man of very modest intellectual ability it was a meteoric rise in power.

By 1939, however, Hess had been eclipsed by the generals and admirals on one hand, and Göring and Himmler on the other. Hess felt himself estranged from Hitler and excluded from the centre of power. His loyalty to Hitler prompted his flight to Britain on 10 May 1941, and he hoped, ultimately, to recover his position with the Führer. Hess believed a diplomatic coup was possible if he could have an audience with George VI, whom he might persuade to dismiss Churchill. Peace could then be made between the two countries and they could act in concert against a common enemy: Russia. Hess flew himself to Britain. On landing he gave his name as Captain Horn and asked to be escorted to the Duke of Hamilton, whom he had met at the 1936 Berlin Olympic Games.

He was incarcerated until 1945 and then tried at Nuremberg. Sentenced to life at Spandau, Hess committed suicide in 1987.

HEWEL, Walther

RANK: SS-Brigadeführer
BORN: 25 March 1904
DIED: 2 May 1945 (K.I.A.)
PARTY NUMBER: 3280789
SS NUMBER: 283985
AWARDS: Golden Party Badge; Blood Order No 90; Stosstrupp Adolf Hitler; 20 July Wound Badge Black Class; SS Honour Ring; SS Honour Sword.

Hewel's father was a wealthy conserves manufacturer whose business was ruined in the currency collapse after World War I. Hewel was an early Nazi member, taking part in the 1923 Putsch, after which he was jailed in Landsberg, where he is reputed to have corrected the final text of *Mein Kampf*. His part as a young student in the Putsch was conveniently forgotten for many years and he settled down as a planter in Sumatra, but he eventually succumbed to Hitler's appeals for his return.

By the beginning of the war Hewel's popularity with Hitler as a court entertainer had induced Ribbentrop (q.v.) to negotiate for his services, and he became Ribbentrop's foreign ministry representative at the Führer's headquarters. Although Hewel was far too timid to use his intimacy with the Führer to become another Bormann (q.v.), he had no scruples about advising Hitler without Ribbentrop's approval and Ribbentrop had to accept this unsatisfactory situation.

Hewel discovered that Himmler's Abwehr advisers had a better knowledge of Eastern European affairs than the foreign office. Hewel's recommendation for autonomy in the Baltic states, which had Himmler's (q.v.) approval, was rejected by Hitler. A right-wing coup had put Hungary under the quasi-fascist rule of Admiral Nicholas Horthy. In 1920, when he was appointed Regent, he had taken the Hungarians, albeit without great popular enthusiasm, into Hitler's 'crusade' against communism. His enthusiasm for the cause was wavering in 1944. Undaunted, Hewel put forward another SS proposal, this time with success, luring Admiral Horthy to Hitler's guest castle at Klessheim and there, with the threat of kidnapping, forcing him to accept a German occupational force in Hungary, consisting of Plenipotentiary Edmund Veesenmayer, (q.v.) a Higher SS Police Leader, a police force and garrison in

the capital. The elderly regent agreed, appointing a pro-German cabinet and dismissing a number of generals.

Hewel was wounded with Hitler in the 20 July Bomb Plot. He probably died trying to escape from the bunker in May 1945, a fact confirmed by his wife, but his death is unsubstantiated.

HEYDE, Dr Werner

RANK: SS-Obersturmbannführer
BORN: 25 April 1902
DIED: 1961 (S)
PARTY NUMBER: 3068165
SS NUMBER: 276656
AWARDS: SS Honour Ring

Born in Lausitz, the son of a textile manufacturer, Heyde enlisted in the army at sixteen during the last months of World War I. At 18 he participated in the Kapp Putsch and then in a long series of organisations and events connected with radical nationalism and National Socialism. His early scholastic achievements did not continue when he attended Hoche's psychiatric lectures as a medical student during the early 1920s, but he developed into a competent, though unremarkable, psychiatrist.

He was involved in secret acticities, which probably involved advice on torture

Originally a ward physician, and eventually a clinical chief doctor in a psychiatric hospital, he joined the NSDAP on 1 May 1933. In 1935, he became leader of the Würzburg Office of Racial Politics and was appointed a full professor at Würzburg in 1939. His SS career really began when he formed a close relationship with one of his patients, Theodore Eicke (q.v.), who persuaded Heyde to join the party and, in 1936, to join the SS.

One of Heyde's assignments was the establishment of neuropsychiatric research and supervising psychiatric, neurological and heredity research on concentration camp prisoners. He was also a consulting neuropsychiatric expert for the Gestapo. In this capacity he was involved in secret activities, which probably included advice on torture methods used to induce prisoners to provide information, as well as psychiatric evaluations useful to the Gestapo. He was a central figure in the extermination programme, the structure of the deception of prisoners and the overall killing procedures.

After the war he was arrested but escaped, obtaining false papers, and had a number of jobs. Finally, using the alias 'Sawade', he obtained a position as a sports physician in a school near Kiel. He lived a flamboyant lifestyle and was subsequently exposed. He was arrested, but committed suicide in his cell in 1961 before the trial began.

HEYDRICH, Reinhard

RANK: SS-Obergruppenführer
BORN: 7 March 1904
DIED: 4 June 1942 (K.I.A.)
PARTY NUMBER: 544916
SS NUMBER: 10120
AWARDS: German Order (Posthumous), 9 June 1942; Blood Order No ? (Posthumous), 4 June 1942; Golden Party Badge; German Olympic Games Decoration First Class; German Social Welfare Decoration First Class; 1939 Iron Cross Second Class; 1939 Iron Cross First Class; Danzig Cross First Class; Pilot's Badge; Luftwaffe Reconnaissance, Air, Sea Rescue & Meteorological Clasp; Police Long Service Cross 18 years' service; NSDAP Long Service Medal 10 Years; Commemorative Medal of 13 March 1938; Commemorative Medal of 1 October 1938; Prague Castle Bar; Commemorative Medal for the Return of the Memel Region; German Defence Medal; Wound Badge; SS Honour Ring; SS Honour Sword.

A man of exceptional skills and talents, Heydrich was born in Halle, Saxony, the son of the founder of the Halle Conservatory.

He inherited his musical ability from his father and could play the violin to concert pitch. With singular intellectual ability, he was also an accomplished sportsman, especially in the fields of fencing, sailing and swimming. In 1922, he joined the navy as a cadet and was under the orders and tutelage of Admiral Canaris. In April 1931, however, after allegations of dishonourable conduct towards a young lady who declared that he had impregnated her, he was brought before an honour-court, presided over by Canaris, which found him guilty and dismissed him from the service. Heydrich became engaged to Lina von Osten, who was to convert him to Nazism and he joined the NSDAP in 1931. Lina enlisted the help of Friedrich Karl von Eberstein (q.v.) to bring him to Himmler's (q.v.) notice. Himmler found him appealing; the interview on 14 June 1931 was short and he came straight to the point: 'I want to set up a security and information service within the SS and I need a specialist. If you think you can do this management job, will you please write down on paper how you think you would tackle it, I'll give you 20 minutes.'

Heydrich's father's real name was described as Süss, of Jewish connotations

Heydrich's considerable organisational abilities, his total ruthlessness, the intensity of his anti-Semitism and his Nordic appearance were self-evident or were soon to be so. Himmler perhaps perceived the perverse view that Heydrich's fear of being considered Jewish, or partly Jewish, would be a means of controlling his talented associate. Heydrich's ancestry was, in SS terms, questionable; in the *Lexicon of Music and Musicians*, Heydrich's father's real name was described as Süss, a name with distinctly Jewish connotations. Later investigations tended to indicate that the family was not, in fact, Jewish, but Heydrich was rather sensitive about the issue and had gone so far as to erase the name Sarah from his mother's gravestone.

On 5 October 1931 Heydrich became a member of the SS, and after a short spell at the Brown House decided to set up the SD in another location, away from enquiring eyes. Certainly from this time Heydrich experienced a meteoric rise, becoming the second most powerful man in the RSHA. By 1941 he was head of the SD, he had contrived numerous espionage plans, become head of the SS security police and organised the Einsatzgruppen. In July 1941 Göring ordered Heydrich to submit a comprehensive draft for the achievement of the 'final solution of the Jewish problem'. It was his hand which drafted the protocol, endorsed by the Wannsee Conference in January 1942, and led to the systematic murder of European Jews in the extermination camps in the East from 1942 to 1944 (the conference was held in the SS RHSA at Wannsee in Berlin; Heydrich chaired the conference).

Perhaps in reward for his efforts, certainly in recognition of his considerable talents, he was appointed to succeed von Neurath as Protector of Bohemia and Moravia in September 1941. His administration of the territory was masterful. It began in brutality, but within months adroitly combined stick and carrot. Czech industrial production began to rise. Fuelled with this success, he issued additional ration cards on a productivity basis. The message was unequivocal: collaborate and prosper, or resist and perish. Heydrich was shown the crown jewels of Czechoslovakia by

President Hacha, who told him of an intriguing legend that surrounded them: any person who was not the true heir who put the crown on his head is sure to die. It seems that Heydrich laughed and tried it on.

A plan was implemented in London for the assassination of Heydrich. This decision has always caused speculation, as he was the only Nazi leader thus targeted. The decision to assassinate Heydrich was taken by the British Government because of his policies in Czechoslovakia. London knew subsequent reprisals would shatter any cooperation between the Czechs and their German rulers, a cooperation which London feared could be transferred to other conquered countries.

In late spring 1942, a section of Czech soldiers flew from England and were dropped outside Prague. The assassination team struck on 27 May 1942. Heydrich, possibly through bravado, rode in an open-topped, unprotected car on his way from his residence to the palace. It was machine-gunned on the Kirchmayer Boulevard. He was injured and drew his pistol. The assassin's Sten gun jammed. Heydrich was about to pursue him when a grenade, thrown by another member, Kubis, exploded, impregnating him with horsehair stuffing and pieces of metal springs from the car seat. He died painfully from septicaemia on 4 June in a Prague hospital.

It was well known that Heydrich kept files on all the leading Nazis, even Hitler

Heydrich's coffin lay in state in the main courtyard of Hradcany Castle and the people of Prague filed by in resemblance of homage, some giving the Nazi salute. At 1500 hours on 8 June 1942, Heydrich's coffin was carried into the courtyard of the Reich Chancellery for the state funeral. Hitler bestowed upon him the German Order, the highest party and state award. Heydrich was the archetypal Nazi: cold, ruthless and cunning. It was well known, for example, that he kept files on all the leading Nazis, even on Hitler himself, and many inside and outside the party were secretly relieved to see him dead. Himmler's first act after he had recovered from the shock of hearing about Heydrich's death, was to locate the key to the safe in which Reinhard Heydrich kept all his 'personal' files.

HILDEBRANDT, Friedrich

RANK: SS-Obergruppenführer,
     Gauleiter of Mecklenburg 1925-45
BORN: 19 September 1898
DIED: 5 November 1948 (E.A)
PARTY NUMBER: 3653
SS NUMBER: 128802
AWARDS: Golden Party Badge; 1914 Iron
     Cross Second Class; 1914 Iron Cross
     First Class; Cross of Honour 1914-1918
     Combatants; 1914 Wound Badge in
     Silver; War Merit Cross Second Class
     with Swords; War Merit Cross First
     Class with Swords; Gau General
     Commemorative Badge 1923 or 1925;
     SS Honour Ring; SS Honour Sword.

Hildebrandt was born in Mecklenburg, where he was a farm worker before serving in World War I and sustaining several wounds. He joined a department of the security police in Halle in 1920, but he was quickly dismissed because of the excessive use of brutality. By 1923, he had joined the NSDAP and in 1925 was appointed Gauleiter of Mecklenburg, a position he held until the war's end. With his appointment he laid the foundations for the party organisation, and in July 1932 the party took power in his district. After the war he was tried for crimes against humanity and found guilty, sentenced to death and executed at Landsberg Prison by the Americans in 1948.

HILDEBRANDT, Richard

RANK: SS-Obergruppenführer
BORN: 13 March 1897
DIED: 1953 (S)
PARTY NUMBER: 89221
SS NUMBER: 7088
AWARDS: Golden Party Badge; 1914 Iron
     Cross Second Class; Cross of Honour
     1914-1918 Combatants; 1939 Iron
     Cross First Class; 1939 Iron Cross
     Second Class Bar; War Merit Cross
     Second Class with Swords; War Merit
     Cross First Class with Swords;
     SS Honour Ring; SS Honour Sword.

The SS police leader in Danzig-West Preussen from 1939 to 1943, Hildebrandt became the head of RuSHA, the race and settlement office of the SS, a position he held until the end of the war. RuSHA had been the SS marriage office, looking at the suitability of both partners since 1931. Under Darré (q.v.) it was also concerned with research on racial Germans living abroad.

Hildebrandt gave the researches a different orientation. In the name of racial selection and the detection of Nordic blood, RuSHA kidnapped children to be brought up as Germans, decided who should be deported from desirable resettlement areas, those to be deprived of their property, those to be conscripted for slave labour and the execution of those guilty of miscegenation with Germans. RuSHA was at the disposition of the executive police of the SS in all of those matters. After the war Hildebrandt was tried for war crimes and sentenced on 10 March 1948 to 25 years' imprisonment. He died in 1953 in Landsberg Prison.

HILGENFELDT, Erich

RANK: SS-Gruppenführer
BORN: 2 July 1897
DIED: 1945
PARTY NUMBER: 143642
SS NUMBER: 289225
AWARDS: 1914 Iron Cross Second Class; 1914 Iron Cross First Class; Cross of Honour 1914-1918 Combatants; War Merit Cross Second Class without Swords; War Merit Cross First Class without Swords; Commemorative Medal of 13 March 1938; Commemorative Medal of 1 October 1938; Golden Party Badge; Danzig Cross First Class; Imperial Army Observer's Badge; SS Honour Ring; SS Honour Sword.

After service in World War I, Hilgenfeldt became an economic statistician. In 1929 he joined the NSDAP and subsequently headed the party run annual winter relief programme and became chief of the Office of People's Welfare and a member of the Reichstag.

HIMMLER, Heinrich

RANK: Reichsführer-SS und Chef der Deutschen Polizei
BORN: 7 October 1900
DIED: 23 May 1945 (S)
PARTY NUMBER: 14303
SS NUMBER: 168
AWARDS: Combined Pilot and Observer Badge in Gold with Diamonds July 1942; Blood Order No 3, 9 November 1923; Golden Party Badge; Golden Hitler Youth Honour Badge with Oakleaves; German Olympic Games Decoration, First Class; Gau General Commemorative Badge 1923 or 1925; Nuremberg Party Day Badge of 1929, 15 August 1929; SS Long Service Cross 12 Years' Service; NSDAP Long Service Medal 15 Years; NSDAP Long Service Medal 10 Years; Commemorative Medal of 13 March 1938; Commemorative Medal of 1 October 1938; Prague Castle Bar; Commemorative Medal For The Return Of The Memel Region; German Defence Medal; SS Honour Ring; SS Honour Sword.

Himmler was born in Landshut, Bavaria, into a solid respectable middle-class family. His father was a headmaster, who was conservative in outlook and staunchly monarchist. Heinrich was named after his godfather, Prince Heinrich of Bavaria, to whom his father was tutor. As well as being a sickly child, young Heinrich had to endure the discomfiture of attending his father's school.

Heinrich welcomed the outbreak of World War I enthusiastically, but it was not until January 1918 that he was able to report for duty as an officer cadet in the 11th Bavarian Infantry Regiment. He was discharged on 17 December 1918, and returned to school in Landshut. He attended the Munich Technical High School where he studied for a degree in agriculture. He became embroiled in right-wing politics, first joining the Freikorps Oberland and then the Reichskriegsflagge. He joined the NSDAP in August 1923 and

Above: Reichsführer-SS Heinrich Himmler. He devoted his life to the expansion of his elite SS, which by 1934 alone had 200,000 members and was still growing.

carried the imperial war flag during the Beer Hall Putsch, leading the column as it marched through the streets of Munich. The coup ended in a complete fiasco: the rank and file surrendered their weapons, identified themselves to the police and returned home, while the leaders were arrested. He returned to Landshut where he sold advertising space in the *Völkischer Beobachter*. He acted as general secretary to Gregor Strasser, who, in February 1925, agreed to disband his party and assimilate it into the reformed NSDAP.

Himmler now found himself a local party official with command over the tiny SS in his district. Strasser was appointed Reich Propaganda Leader of the NSDAP in September 1926, and Himmler accompanied him to party headquarters as his secretary. However, his party career still allowed him time to run a chicken smallholding where he carried out breeding experiments. He married Margarete Bodern, the daughter of a German landowner from Conerzewo, west Prussia, on 3 July 1928. Known as Marge, she was eight years older than Himmler and specialised in homeopathy and herbs. It was in fact her money that enabled Himmler to buy the smallholding.

Himmler's organisational ability did not go unnoticed and he was appointed Deputy SS Leader and then National Leader in January 1929 when he commanded approximately 1000 men, while the SS was still part of the SA. He gradually asserted the separation of the SS from the SA, and quickly won approval for a recruiting system designed to create a truly elite body. The army, which perceived Röhm and the SA as a rival, took a fairly favourable view of the SS as a force, regarding it simply as a bodyguard.

Himmler devoted his life to the expansion of the SS. By 1934, it was 200,000 strong and Himmler had added many refinements to the recruiting process, such as biological criteria and the concept of racial purity in order to select the finest troops from the large number of applicants who ranged from ex-Freikorps to unemployed bourgeois volunteers. Himmler became Polizeipräsident of Munich after Hitler became Chancellor in January 1933. This modest post enabled him to gradually gain control of the German police network except in Prussia, where Göring was Minister of the Interior. But he finally achieved complete control in 1936.

Himmler expanded the SS far beyond the bounds of any other military force; he was responsible for the ideological and mystical ceremonies, and for acquiring funding for the socio-historical research organisation, the Ahnenerbe. The castle of Wewelsburg was rebuilt at immense expense as a shrine to Germanic civilisation. Here, the Hold Order of the SS was founded and, from 1934, ceremonies were held several times a year. Karl Wolff (q.v.) ushered each SS leader into a monastic cell, where he steeped himself in Germanic mysticism surrounded by treasures from ancient Germany. Beneath their mock medieval coats of arms, the leading 12 'High' SS officers were assigned places around an Arthurian table.

Himmler took over the Gestapo and made it a Europe-wide organisation

Himmler also started the Allach ceramics works in Dachau which produced fine porcelain and earthenware. A Damascus smithy was also established. Himmler concerned himself with the perfecting of a future German elite through the SS. Not only would they be of guaranteed Aryan stock, but would be encouraged to form the new 'master race' through the large Lebensborn network of maternity homes.

Himmler took over the Gestapo and made it a Europe-wide organisation. Through Heydrich and the SD he formed an intelligence service that covered internal and external German operations. His involvement in the 'Night of the Long Knives' eliminated the power of the SA and closed their 'wild man camps', leading to the formation of the concentration camp system. In 1943, he became Minister of the Interior as well.

Himmler was appointed Chief of the Home Army in 1944, and a week before Hitler's suicide he made an effort to negotiate the surrender of Germany. Hitler, having heard of Himmler's treachery, dismissed him from all posts. The final Dönitz government saw him as a liability. He tried to escape at 1700 hours on 22 May 1945, a miserable-looking and shabbily dressed man with two rather more military looking companions, and was stopped by a British bridge control detail at Bremervorde in northern Germany. The identity papers in the name of Heinrich Hizinger and the black eye patch could not conceal his true identity. Himmler revealed himself. As a doctor made an oral inspection, he bit on a cyanide phial and was dead within seconds.

HINZ, Bruno

RANK: SS-Hauptsturmführer
BORN: 25 August 1915
DIED: 28 February 1968 (D)
PARTY NUMBER: —
SS NUMBER: —
AWARDS: 1939 Iron Cross Second Class, 16 June 1940; 1939 Iron Cross First Class, 2 December 1941; German Cross in Gold, 15 April 1943; Knight's Cross of the Iron Cross, 2 December 1943; Oakleaves, 23 August 1944; Medal for the Winter Campaign in Russia 1941-1942; Close Combat Clasp Silver Class; Army Long Service Medal Four Years; Commemorative Medal of 13 March 1938; Commemorative Medal of 1 October 1938.

As SS-Untersturmführer in the Second Company, SS-Panzergrenadier Regiment *Westland*, SS Panzer Division *Wiking*, 8th Army, Army Group South, on the Russian Front, he was awarded the Knight's Cross of the Iron Cross for his bravery and leadership.

He showed the same qualities in August 1944, when he was the company commanding officer of a battle group from the 17th SS Panzergrenadier Division *Götz von Berlichingen* and was awarded the Oakleaves, becoming the 559th recipient. He survived the war and lived in Munich, where he died in 1968.

HIRNING, Hans

RANK: SS-Oberscharführer
BORN: 14 November 1922
DIED: 30 April 1945 (K.I.A.)
PARTY NUMBER: —
SS NUMBER: —
AWARDS: 1939 Iron Cross Second Class, 24 October 1941; 1939 Iron Cross First Class, 14 July 1942; Knight's Cross of the Iron Cross, 23 October 1942.

Hirning fought on the Russian Front from 1941, and in October 1942 was with the *Totenkopf* Division, against Soviet forces who had been attempting for weeks to penetrate the thin German lines in his sector. A Soviet breakthrough would have had a disastrous effect on the German supply route. Hirning and his small band of man represented the last strongpoint. The Soviets deployed an anti-tank gun in front of his position. He attempted to destroy it with a demolition charge, but this failed. Undeterred, and assisted by a comrade, he succeeded in his second attempt, saving his position. For this bravery he was awarded the Knight's Cross of the Iron Cross. He continued to fight with the division into 1945 and was killed in action in the closing days of the war near Dürnholz in Czechoslovakia.

HIRT, Professor Dr August
RANK: SS-Sturmbannführer
BORN: 29 April 1898—
PARTY NUMBER: 4012784
SS NUMBER: 100414
AWARDS: 1914 Iron Cross Second Class;
   Cross of Honour 1914-1918
   Combatants; 1914 Wound Badge
   Silver Class.

Professor Hirt occupied the chair of anatomy at the University of Strasbourg, where SS students were particularly numerous. He was a member of the Ahnenerbe, which was set up with the object of studying and researching Germanic antiquity for the purpose of supporting National Socialist beliefs with scientific proof. Himmler was willingly seduced by the fascination of an idea that lay so close to his preoccupation, and the society was accordingly set up in 1935, with the status of a learned society. Hirt was one of the most alarming individuals among the researchers. With Himmler's support he brought together at the concentration camp in Auschwitz a collection of skulls for the purpose of making anthropomorphic measurements. Hirt had 'far-reaching perspectives', and he stated: 'we have large collections of skulls of almost all races and peoples at our disposal. Of the Jewish race, however, only very few specimens of skulls are available. The war in the East now presents us with the opportunity to overcome this deficiency. By procuring the skulls of the Jewish-Bolshevik Commissars, who represent the prototype of the repulsive, but characteristic, subhuman, we have the chance now to obtain scientific material.'

Following the induced death of the victim, the head would be severed from the body

He did not want the heads of the already dead. He proposed that the heads of person's first be measured while alive. Then following the induced death of the victim, taking care not to damage it, the doctor would sever the head from the body and would forward it in a hermetically sealed tin can to Strasbourg.

He went personally to the front to study the behaviour of combatants in relation to their racial category. Hirt wished to study skeletons, and by June 1943 SS-Standartenführer Wolfram Sievers had collected at Auschwitz the men and women who were to furnish the skeletons for the 'scientific measurements'. A total of 115 victims – 79 Jews, 30 Jewesses, four Asiatics and two Poles – were processed. Joseph Krammer undertook the killings with gas supplied by Hirt. The bodies were sent to Strasbourg, where he assembled the skeleton collection which was previously nonexistent. But time was fast running out for him. The advancing American and French troops were approaching Strasbourg and Hirt asked for a directive as to what was to be done with the collection. The order was obtained to dispose of the evidence. But the Allies found evidence both physical and written of the enterprise. Hirt disappeared and as he left Strasbourg he was heard boasting that no one would ever take him alive. It seems no one has, alive or dead.

HOPPE, Paul-Werner
RANK: SS-Sturmbannführer
BORN: 28 February 1910—
PARTY NUMBER: 1596491
SS NUMBER: 116695
AWARDS: SS Honour Ring; SS Honour Sword.

In February 1933 Hoppe joined the SS, and by the beginning of the war had become a key member of Eicke's (q.v.) staff in the inspectorate of concentration camps. In September 1939 he was among the group of SS officers selected to help Eicke plan the organisation of the *Totenkopf* Division. The following month he was transferred to the new SSTK as Eicke's adjutant.

In April 1941 he was rewarded with the command of an infantry company. Wounded in the leg during the heavy fighting near Lake Ilmen in the spring of 1942, Hoppe was forced to take convalescent leave, and after recovering was transferred to the concentration camp system as commander of an SS guard detachment in Auschwitz in July 1942. In a transfer letter, Richard Glücks (q.v.), Eicke's wartime successor as inspector of concentration camps, wrote that Hoppe's wound had allowed the camp system to acquire the services of a man with unique knowledge of the entire concentration camp network, citing Hoppe's pre-war experiences in the camp inspectorate. In late July 1942, Glücks suggested that Hoppe be appointed commandant of the Stutthof concentration camp near Danzig, and Hoppe moved there in September 1942, remaining until the end of the war.

In April 1945, Hoppe was arrested by the British in Holstein and while in their custody awaiting extradition to Poland, he escaped and went into hiding. He remained free for the next seven years, living under various aliases in Switzerland and West Germany. He was finally arrested on 17 April 1953 by the German authorities at Witten in the Ruhr. The disposition of his case dragged on for four years until finally, on 4 June 1957, Hoppe was sentenced to a mere nine years in prison.

HÖSS, Rudolf

RANK: SS-Obersturmbannführer
BORN: 22 November 1900
DIED: 2 April 1947 (E.A.)
PARTY NUMBER: —
SS NUMBER: 193616
AWARDS: 1914 Iron Cross Second Class; 1914 Iron Cross First Class; 1914 Wound Badge Silver Class; War Merit Cross Second Class with Swords; War Merit Cross First Class with Swords; SS Honour Ring; SS Honour Sword.

In a strong field of contenders, Rudolf Höss was one of the most dedicated concentration camp commandants, pursuing his contemptible work with a missionary zeal. He was born in Baden-Baden, the son of a shopkeeper who had hoped to become a Catholic priest. He joined the army and saw service in World War I at a very tender age. He was wounded several times. After the war he joined the Freikorps and was arrested with Bormann (q.v.) for the murder of Walther Kado, a teacher who was suspected of informing on Freikorps members to the French occupational forces in the Ruhr. They were found guilty and sentenced to life imprisonment in 1923. He was released five years later, and promptly joined the SS.

In 1940 he became the camp commandant of Auschwitz, then only a detention camp. Höss enlisted the aid of German firms to construct gas chambers, informing them that he wanted the capacity to liquidate 2000 prisoners at one time. On a fact-finding mission to Treblinka, he was disgusted by the smell of the gas chambers, the unreliable carbon dioxide pipes from old captured engines and the slow process of burning the bodies. He decided to have crematoria at Auschwitz. He had six gas chambers constructed, two large, accommodating 2000 people, and four smaller, taking 1500 each. There were five furnaces that utilised body fat as fuel. The furnaces could only dispose of 2000 corpses, while the chambers could liquidate 10,000. Höss complained at his trial that 2000 could be killed in half an hour, but the cremation was more time-consuming.

Höss had discovered a deadly chemical, Zyklon B, which satisfied his quest for a more efficient means of murder. He tried it experimentally in, and was happy to discover that the occupants died in 10 minutes. Höss set up a subsidiary camp at Birkenau, and was known as the 'death camp king'. He became the Deputy Inspector of concentration camps in 1944. Questioned in Nuremberg about his feelings, Höss admitted that he never had close friends and felt more comfortable alone. He also admitted sex was never an important factor to him (after his wife knew of his work they rarely had intercourse). He stated, however, that he was completely normal. He was hanged at Auschwitz in 1947.

HÖSSLER, Franz

RANK: SS-Obersturmführer
BORN: unknown
DIED: 1945 (E.A.)
PARTY NUMBER: —
SS NUMBER: —

Commandant of the women's camp at Auschwitz-Birkenau, Franz Hössler was later transferred to Bergen-Belsen, where he was apprehended in April 1945 by the British. He was tried for war crimes by a British tribunal, found guilty and sentenced to death and subsequently hanged.

HÖTTL, Dr Wilhelm

RANK: SS-Sturmbannführer
BORN: 19 March 1915—
PARTY NUMBER: 6309616
SS NUMBER: 309510
AWARDS: War Merit Cross Second Class with Swords; War Merit Cross First Class with Swords; SS Honour Ring.

An Austrian and a member of the SD after the Anschluss of 1938, Höttl kept a brief on the leaders of the SS. He had personal dealings only once on the phone with Himmler (q.v.) and only recorded what he gleaned from colleagues. This could be far from reliable. For example, he concluded that Himmler was no more than a rubber stamp man who owed his position to the intrigues of Heydrich (q.v.), who meant to supplant him. He was doubtless impressed by Heydrich's drive and ambition. Heydrich also drove those working for him hard – he viewed himself and his subordinates as missionaries. He was also impressed by Heydrich's total contempt for his fellow man – something Himmler had only in small quantities. His investigations into Heydrich led him to believe that Heydrich was, indeed, half-Jewish, and had been blackmailed by Admiral Canaris.

Höttl became the director of intelligence for the SS in southeast Europe and Italy in 1943. After the war he was a defence witness for Kaltenbrunner (q.v.). He also wrote his memoirs, which give an insight into the SS and its procedures.

HUBER, Franz Josef

RANK: SS-Brigadeführer
BORN: 22 January 1902—
PARTY NUMBER: 4583151
SS NUMBER: 107099
AWARDS: War Merit Cross Second Class with Swords; War Merit Cross First Class with Swords; SS Honour Ring; SS Honour Sword.

Huber was the Vienna Gestapo chief and was engaged in top-level security meetings with Himmler (q.v.). One such occasion was in November 1939 at the Burgerbrau Bierkeller, where he was in the company of Artur Nebe (q.v.), Chief of Criminal Police, Heinrich Himmler, Reinhard Heydrich (q.v.) and Heinrich Müller (q.v.), chief of the Gestapo. Müller spent practically all his time in his office, on account of his unpleasant conditions at home. Most of his social life was spent with officials such as Hüber.

HUPPENKOTHEN, Walter

RANK: SS-Standartenführer
BORN: 31 December 1907—
PARTY NUMBER: 1950150
SS NUMBER: 126785
AWARDS: 1939 Iron Cross Second Class; War Merit Cross Second Class without Swords; SS Honour Ring; SS Honour Sword.

The Criminal Commissar of the Gestapo, Huppenkothen was ordered by Himmler (q.v.) to investigate Göring's connection with the resistance circle that was responsible for the attempt on Hitler's life in the 20 July Bomb Plot. No evidence of any collusion on Göring's part was discovered.

The conspirators were ill-prepared and were apprehended or chose to commit suicide. One of the main conspirators was Admiral Canaris, who headed the Abwehr. It seems that Keitel, who was always singularly loyal to him, contrived to halt the Volksgericht trial where he was to be arraigned for his involvement in the plot. This was to have followed Canaris's expulsion from the Wehrmacht. Hitler immediately ordered Himmler to convene a summary court with the former inspector of the SS judicial section, SS-Sturmbannführer Dr Otto Thorbeck, as judge and Huppenkothen acting as the Gestapo prosecutor.

This secret trial was somehow delayed until 9 April 1945, when it took place in Flossenbürg concentration camp. Canaris was tried along with Hans Oster, Pastor Bonhöffer, Judge Advocate Carl Sack and the Abwehr officers Strünck and Gehre, all being the last indicted conspirators. They were all found guilty and condemned to death. All the condemned men were led to the gallows naked. It could be argued that they were the 'lucky' ones. Those executed in early August 1944 were hanged with a wire noose, the hangman laughing and joking as he went about his grisly work. The victims' death throes were recorded on camera, the film then being speedily developed and rushed over to Hitler's residence for his amusement and private satisfaction.

Huppenkothen was tried in Munich in February 1951 for being an accessory

Neither Huppenkothen or Thorbeck supposedly attended the executions held in April 1945; they claimed, rather dubiously, that they did not even know whether Hitler had confirmed their findings or whether the sentences had been carried out.

Huppenkothen was tried in Munich in February 1951 for being an accessory to the murder of the five men. The charges were dismissed, but he was found guilty of 'extorting evidence and causing bodily harm' and sentenced to three and a half years of imprisonment. This case was reviewed by the West German Federal Supreme Court in Karlsruhe, which quashed the sentence but ordered a second trial. In November 1952 the Munich court upheld the original verdict, but indicted Thorbeck as a second defendant. The case continued to drag on. In October 1955 a third trial was held at Augsburg; new witnesses stated that they had seen Walter Huppenkothen attend the executions which took place on 9 April 1945. Thorbeck was sentenced to four years' and Huppenkothen to seven years' imprisonment. Another trial on 19 June 1956 in Karlsruhe dismissed Huppenkothen's appeal; Thorbeck's, on the other hand, was allowed without hearing any fresh evidence.

HUSS, Fritz
RANK: SS-Obersturmbannführer
BORN: 22 April 1912
DIED: 4 September 1944 (K.I.A.)
PARTY NUMBER: —
SS NUMBER: —
AWARDS: War Merit Cross Second Class with Swords; War Merit Cross First Class with Swords; Knight's Cross of the War Merit Cross with Swords (posthumous) 10 November 1944; DRL Sports Badge; SA Sports Badge.

Huss served as a technical maintenance officer and was the commanding officer in the 2nd SS-Maintenance Company, 2nd SS Panzer Division *Das Reich*. He was killed near Liège, Belgium, on 4 September 1944. In recognition of his vital work in maintaining the division's equipment he was awarded posthumously the Knight's Cross of the War Merit Cross with Swords. It is presumed that the award relates to the time in late August 1944 when the division retreated across the lower Seine near Rouen, across France to St Vith and then across the German frontier, before taking defensive positions behind the West Wall in the area of Schnee-Eifel in September 1944. The division had fought particularly hard during the battles in the Falaise Pocket in early August, when it had secured the southern end of the gap between Falaise and Argentan. This gap was only 32km (20 miles) wide, but it was the only escape route for 24 German divisions trapped inside the pocket. Eventually over 20,000 trapped German soldiers were able to escape, though 50,000 more went into Allied captivity and the Germans lost over 5000 armoured vehicles destroyed. All the Waffen-SS divisions involved in the fighting suffered enormously; the *Hitlerjugend*, for example, had entered the Normandy battles with a strength of 21,300 men. By the time the battles in and around the Falaise Pocket had ended it had been reduced to 300 men and 10 tanks.

In the few months after the Falaise battles, the *Das Reich* Division was newly refitted and incorporated into the formidable 6th SS Panzer Army under the command of 'Sepp' Dietrich (q.v.) and was chosen to lead the Ardennes Offensive, which was launched at the end of 1944.

JECKELN, Friedrich
RANK: SS-Obergruppenführer
und General der Polizei
BORN: 2 February 1895
DIED: 3 February 1946 (E.A)
PARTY NUMBER: 163348
SS NUMBER: 4367
AWARDS: 1914 Iron Cross Second Class;
1939 Iron Cross Second Class Bar,
October 1941; German Cross in Gold,
19 December 1943; Knight's Cross
of the Iron Cross, 27 August 1944;
Oakleaves, 8 March 1945; SS Honour
Ring; SS Honour Sword.

A resolute member of the SS, Jeckeln was born in Hormberg, Baden. After serving in the 76th Field Artillery Regiment during World War I, he joined the Border Protection Force East, and subsequently the police.

With the invasion of Russia in 1941, Jeckeln was appointed Higher SS and Police Leader with his headquarters in Riga, Latvia. Officially he had responsibility for the protection of German installations against partisan attacks; in reality, he headed an Einsatzgruppe designated to exterminate Jews in Kiev. In 1941, with great zeal, he performed his task of liquidation, reporting 44,125 executions, mainly of Jews, in the month of August alone. In February and March 1942 he initi-

Left: A member of Jeckeln's Einsatzgruppe stands over another of the thousands of Jews and others who were murdered in and around Kiev after June 1941.

ated an operation entitled 'Action March Fever'; when completed he reported 8350 Jews liquidated, 1274 persons shot on suspicion and 389 partisans killed.

In mid-August 1944, strong Soviet forces attempted a breakthrough southwest of Lake Plesaku, which posed a grave threat to Latvian territory. Jeckeln commanded a combined battle group of poorly armed German and Latvian police forces in the 18th Army, Army Group North, and won the Knight's Cross of the Iron Cross for his efforts.

After the war he was tried by the Russians as a major war criminal. His responsibility for security, together with his cooperation with the Latvian puppet government, were used as his indictment. He was found guilty and executed in Riga in 1946.

JOST, Heinz
RANK: SS-Brigadeführer
BORN: 9 July 1904—
PARTY NUMBER: 75946
SS NUMBER: 36243
AWARDS: Golden Party Badge; SS Honour
Ring; SS Honour Sword.

Jost joined the NSDAP in 1928 and was a member of the SD from 1934. Having worked in Spain during the Civil War, he was made head of the foreign intelligence section of the SS in 1938.

This intelligence service, later known as Amt VI SD-Ausland, was responsible for investigations abroad and included Heydrich's (q.v.) military intelligence service. It was successfully led by Jost until 1941 when Schellenberg (q.v.) took over, although he was nominally Jost's deputy, until the beginning of 1942.

Jost worked with the occupying forces in Czechoslovakia. When Heydrich planned an elaborate subterfuge to give credence to the German invasion of Poland in 1939 by staging a mock Polish invasion on the German radio station at Gleiwitz, it fell to Jost to inform Admiral Canaris (head of the army intelligence service, the Abwehr), that Hitler had ordered the Abwehr to assist the SD. Jost gave him a list of requirements that included 150 Polish Army uniforms, side-arms, pay books and 364 men to be placed on temporary duty with the SD.

Heydrich got rid of Jost by giving him command of an Einsatzgruppe in Russia, an offer which he dared not refuse. He was the original commander of Einsatzgruppe A, but managed to discover a loophole in the assignment and found another position prior to the start of the killings. He entered the Ostministerium under Alfred Rosenberg, as liaison officer at Ewald von Kleist's Southern Army Group headquarters in South Russia. Himmler did not discover him until May 1944, when he succeeded in transferring him to the Waffen-SS as a lowly SS-Untersturmführer.

After the war Jost was tried as a war criminal and sentenced to life imprisonment, although the sentence was commuted and he was released in December 1951. One report, however, stated that he was one of the last war criminals to be hanged at Landsberg in 1951 by the American forces.

JURY, Dr Hugo

RANK: SS-Obergruppenführer,
　　Gauleiter of Lower Danube 1938-45
BORN: 13 July 1887
DIED: 8 May 1945 (S)
PARTY NUMBER: 410338
SS NUMBER: 292777
AWARDS: Golden Party Badge; SS Honour
　　Ring; SS Honour Sword.

A doctor specialising in tuberculosis, Jury was a key member of the Austrian Nazi Party, becoming deputy leader to Seyss-Inquart (q.v.). In 1934, Austrian Nazis had murdered Chancellor Dollfuss in an attempted coup. However, government forces led by Kurt

Schuschnigg defeated the Nazis. He was also a prime mover in the Austrian Anschluss of 1938, and held the post of Minister of Social Administration in Seyss-Inquart's extremely short-lived government. He was appointed Gauleiter of Lower Danube in 1938, a post he held until he committed suicide on the day Germany surrendered.

JÜTTNER, Hans

RANK: SS-Obergruppenführer
　　und General der Waffen-SS
BORN: 2 March 1894
DIED: 24 May 1965 (D)
PARTY NUMBER: 541163
SS NUMBER: 264497
AWARDS: 1914 Iron Cross Second Class;
　　1914 Iron Cross First Class; Cross of
　　Honour 1914-1918 Combatants; Order
　　of the Zähringer Lion with Swords;
　　1939 Iron Cross Second Class Bar; 1939
　　Iron Cross First Class Bar; Order of the
　　Zähringer Lion with Swords; War Merit
　　Cross Second Class; War Merit Cross
　　First Class; Knight's Cross of the War
　　Merit Cross with Swords, 30 October
　　1944; German Cross in Silver, 1 July
　　1943 (approx); SS Honour Ring;
　　SS Honour Sword.

After serving in World War I, Jüttner joined the NSDAP and SA in 1931. In 1935 he transferred to the SS-Verfügungstruppe, and in 1936 he was employed as a consultant in its inspectorate.

In 1939 he was made leader of the inspectorate of the Verfügungstruppe-Ersatztruppen, renamed Kommandoamt SS-VT in 1940, and in August 1940 he was appointed the chief of staff of the SS-Führungshauptamt (SSFHA). Appointed chief of the SSFHA in 1943, Jüttner controlled all Waffen-SS field troops, training and reserve units, schools, command garrisons and accompanying headquarters.

From 21 July 1944 he was, as Himmler's permanent representative, both commander of the reserve army and chief of military armaments.

In 1945 he was arrested by the British and sentenced in 1948 to 10 years' imprisonment, reduced to four years. He died in 1965.

KAINDLE, Anton
RANK: SS-Standartenführer
BORN: 14 July 1902
DIED: 1951 (D)
PARTY NUMBER: 4390500
SS NUMBER: 241248
AWARDS: 1939 Iron Cross Second Class;
War Merit Cross Second Class with
Swords; War Merit Cross First Class
with Swords; SS Honour Ring;
SS Honour Sword.

A competent administrative officer, Kaindle served on the staff of the inspectorate of concentration camps before the war, moving with Eicke (q.v.) to the *Totenkopf* Division in October 1939 as the division's personnel officer. He remained a member of Eicke's staff until October 1941, when Himmler moved him back to the inspectorate of concentration camps, as chief paymaster of the camp guard units.

Kaindle was transferred from the *Totenkopf* Division because of his obvious administrative qualifications at a time when the casualties of the SS field divisions were draining personnel from the camp administrative system (the war in Russia was consuming human and material resources at an alarming rate). However, Heinrich Himmler desperately needed SS officers with Kaindle's competence and experience nearer to home. His second term with the camp inspectorate, however, was brief. In August 1942, Kaindle was appointed to untangle a complicated financial scandal involving the commandant at Sachsenhausen. Himmler sent the honest and reliable Kaindle to serve as commandant of Sachsenhausen until the end of the war, where he gained a reputation among his superiors as a scrupulously correct, thoroughly reliable camp commander.

Kaindle was tried as a war criminal by the Russians in 1947 and sentenced to life imprisonment, where he died in 1951.

KAISER, Vincenz
RANK: SS-Obersturmbannführer
BORN: 28 February 1904
DIED: 20 April 1945 (M.I.A.)
PARTY NUMBER: 54828
SS NUMBER: 17127
AWARDS: Golden Party Badge; German
Cross in Gold, 29 October 1941; 1939
Iron Cross Second Class; 1939 Iron
Cross First Class, 24 August 1941; 1939
Wound Badge Silver Class; Knight's
Cross, 6 April 1943; Oakleaves; four
Silver Tank Destruction Strips; Infantry
Assault Badge.

Kaiser was born in Judenberg, Austria. He saw service on the Russian Front with the *Das Reich* Division, when he was awarded the Knight's Cross of the Iron Cross. Kaiser next went on to command a battle group from *Götz von Berlichingen*. On 20 April 1945, he was missing in action in the vicinity of Nuremberg.

KALTENBRUNNER, Dr Ernst

RANK: SS-Obergruppenführer
    und General der Polizei
BORN: 4 October 1903
DIED: 16 October 1946 (E.A.)
PARTY NUMBER: 300179
SS NUMBER: 13039
AWARDS: Golden Party Badge; Blood Order,
    6 May 1942; Knight's Cross of the War
    Merit Cross with Swords, 15 November
    1944; War Merit Cross with Swords
    Second Class; War Merit Cross First
    Class with Swords; SS Honour Ring;
    SS Honour Sword.

Kaltenbrunner was born in Ried in Innkreis, not far from Branau am Inn, Hitler's birthplace. After receiving his law doctorate at the early age of 23, Kaltenbrunner spent two years with a lawyer in Salzburg, before setting himself up in practice in Linz in 1928.

During this time he began his political activities as a member of the Independent Movement for a Free Austria. He joined the Austrian National Socialists in 1932 and a year later he entered the SS, where he founded the Sturmbann with Adolf Eichmann (q.v.) and was a party speaker in north Austria. Still in the first year of his membership, Kaltenbrunner was commissioned as the leader of the SS-Standarte 37, and in April 1935 as the leader of the whole Austrian SS. In January 1936, he was arrested and committed to the Dollfuss concentration camp at Kaisersteinbruch for being involved in anti-government activities; he was released in 1937.

Through the Austrian Bundeskanzler, Dr Seyss-Inquart (q.v.), Kaltenbrunner was appointed State Secretary of Security on 11 March 1938 and a day later was promoted to SS-Brigadeführer and appointed to the deployment of the SS-Oberabschnitts Öster-reich. Kaltenbrunner advised Himmler on the legal grounds for the reunification of Austria with Germany. In September 1938 Kaltenbrunner was promoted to SS-Gruppenführer and appointed to higher SS and Police Chief of Vienna, Upper and Lower Donau. One month earlier he had joined the Grossdeutschen Reichstag. In April 1942, he was promoted to Generalleutnant der Polizei, on 21 June 1943 to SS-Obergruppenführer and General der Polizei. After Heydrich's (q.v.) death, Himmler appointed Kaltenbrunner as his successor, after eight months of doing the job himself. Later on Himmler said of Kaltenbrunner: 'Presumably he is only in a drunk state to be able to think clearly.' This clearly illustrates Himmler's views on Kaltenbrunner's typical state.

The bestowal of the Knight's Cross of the War Merit Cross with Swords followed Kaltenbrunner's completion of the preliminary proceedings against the chief of the Abwehr, Canaris, with the proof of his involvement in the 20 July Bomb Plot. He received the Golden Party Badge (Honour Award) on 20 July 1944, having become an honourary holder of the Blood Order in May 1942.

At Nuremberg he was charged by the International Military Tribunal and condemned to death on 1 October 1946. He was executed 15 days later.

KAMINISKI, Bronislav Vladislavovich

RANK: SS-Brigadeführer
BORN: unknown
DIED: September 1944 (E.R.)
PARTY NUMBER: —
SS NUMBER: —
AWARDS: 1939 Iron Cross Second Class;
    1939 Iron Cross First Class.

Born in St Petersburg, the son of a Polish father and German mother, Kaminiski was a chemical engineer who had no reason to love the Soviets. Under suspicion as a 'foreigner', bourgeois intellectual and potential dissident, he spent five years in one of Stalin's labour camps, and was released only a few months prior to the German invasion. He was a brilliant if autocratic organiser, spoke German fluently and threw himself wholeheartedly behind the German cause. He tried, unsuccessfully, to form a Russian Nazi Party, but apart from this one failure his record was one of unqualified success.

In January 1942, the town of Lokot fell under the jurisdiction of the Second Panzer Army. It stood on the edge of the Bryanask Forest, about halfway between Orec and Kursk in central Russia. It became a model of self-sufficiency under his guidance, having its own newspapers, hospitals, banks and even its own tax system devised by Kaminiski. The stipulated food supplies never failed to be delivered to the Wehrmacht on time, and the Germans found it necessary to maintain only a minimum liaison staff. The original defence force of 500 men was expanded into a small private army, which by September 1943 had grown into a brigade of some 10,000 men organised in five infantry regiments, supported by its own artillery of 36 field guns, and armour comprising 24 captured Soviet T-34 tanks, as well as various engineer, signals and medical units. This force went under the grandiose title of the 'Russian People's Liberation Army', or RONA.

He was shot by an SS firing squad for the offence of looting

RONA fought several successful actions against the partisans of Bryanask and even induced some of them to change sides. Kaminiski was dubbed, 'the War Lord of the Bryanask Forest'. By the autumn of 1943, the Germans were in continuous retreat in Russia, and it was not long before Lokot had to be evacuated in the face of the Red Army's relentless advance. Kaminiski and his RONA, which now comprised some 15,000 men, were removed to Ratibor on the Polish-Czech border, prompting an exodus accompanied by 10,500 civilians and 1500 cows.

In March 1944 the RONA was renamed a 'Volksheer Brigade' (People's Brigade). In July it was accepted into the Waffen-SS as SS Assault Brigade RONA. Kaminiski was granted a commission as a Waffen-Brigadeführer. His men were not, as yet, deemed fit for frontline service and were sent for further training to Hungary. When the Polish Home Army began its abortive uprising in Warsaw

in August 1944, one regiment of around 1700 men under Vrolov was detached from the brigade and sent to the Polish capital to assist in the suppression of the revolt. It arrived on 5 August, but was withdrawn three weeks later on the orders of Erich von dem Bach-Zelewski (q.v.) because of its atrocious conduct and general lack of discipline. Kaminiski himself was in Warsaw for only about 10 days. Later, he was arrested by the SS in Lodz and charged with looting, an offence punishable by death. He was shot by an SS firing squad on being found guilty. His death, was officially attributed to a Polish partisan ambush on the road to Lodz.

KAMMLER, Dr Hans
RANK: SS-Gruppenführer
BORN: 26 August 1901
DIED: May 1945 (K.I.A.)
PARTY NUMBER: 1011855
SS NUMBER: 113619
AWARDS: 1939 Iron Cross Second Class; 1939 Iron Cross First Class; War Merit Cross Second Class with Swords; War Merit Cross First Class with Swords; Knight's Cross of the War Merit Cross with Swords 1945; SS Honour Ring; SS Honour Sword.

Kammler worked in the Reich Aeronautical Ministry until the end of 1941. He joined the Allgemeine-SS in 1938, transferring to the SS Economic Administration Department in the autumn of 1941. He was appointed chief of Amtsgruppe C, overseeing the Reich's building and construction industry, as well as that the SS. Under his leadership the SS-Baustäbe was created, which employed thousands of concentration camp prisoners as builders between 1943 and 1943, on military projects such as the Atlantic Wall, as well as in clearance operations in bombed-out German towns and cities. He may have been in charge of the

construction of the gas chambers at Auschwitz, although this has never been proved.

Kammler's ascent into the administrative hierarchy of the Reich began on 26 August 1943, when the SS succeeded in establishing production of the V-bombs. An agreement between Kammler, Armaments Minister Speer and General Dornberger proposed the installation and operation of the 'A4' underground factory by the SS. Two days later, the first prisoner transport arrived at Camp Dora, 5km (three miles) northwest of Nordhausen. Kammler was then set up, carrying out all subsequent building work for the Armaments Ministry. Approximately 60,000 prisoners arrived and cleared away an underground surface area of eight million square metres; 13,000 of them did not survive. In January 1944 the first A4 (renamed the Vergeltungswaffe 2 or V-2) left the production line, and from August the plant was producing about 600 missiles a month. In 15 months about 6000 missiles were produced, of which 3500 were shot down.

'Don't concern yourself with the human victims. The work must be done'

From 1943 Sonderstab Kammler employed skilled workers from all sections of the Wehrmacht, being assigned increasing numbers of special weapon projects. Himmler (q.v.) personally appointed Kammler to run the 'Jägerprogram', the scheme implementing the transfer of the aeroplane industry into underground plants: he led 15 projects and also started the production of the 'Volksjäger' He 162 jet fighter shortly before the 'ultimate victory'. From May 1944 he was involved with the Geilenberg Programme, transferring fuel production into underground factories.

In August 1944 Hitler appointed Kammler Plenipotentiary for the V-2 project, involving him with the preparation for their launching, and in September he took command of the division. In December 1944 he was promoted to commander general of the AK, in this capacity receiving orders directly from Hitler for the employment of the V-2. On 31 January 1945, all sections involved in the deployment of the V-1 and V-2, personnel and materials, were put under the control of the Waffen-SS under Kammler's command. Shortly before this Reichsmarschall Göring had appointed him special emissary for ensuring advancement of

development and testing of rocket-propelled weapons, answerable to the Reichsmarschall, as well as inspector of the equipment of all Luftwaffe units equipped with rocket-propelled weapons.

On 27 March 1945, as the Reich collapsed, Kammler was designated the Führer's Plenipotentiary for jet planes. All sections of the Wehrmacht, the NSDAP and the Reich would be affected by Kammler's orders from this day. A truly incredible career of a man who had not served a single day in the army!

Kammler's indisputable successes were made possible by strictly following his motto, as expressed to SS leaders: 'Don't concern yourselves with the human victims. The work must be done, and in the shortest possible time.' A few weeks before the end of the war he was transferred to the defence of Harz against the advancing Allies. His ultimate fate is unclear, but he probably died in the Battle of Berlin.

KÄMPFE, Helmut
RANK: SS-Obersturmbannführer der Reserve
BORN: 31 July 1909
DIED: 10 June 1944 (K.I.A.)
PARTY NUMBER: —
SS NUMBER: —
AWARDS: 1939 Iron Cross Second Class, 26 August 1941; 1939 Iron Cross First Class, 7 November 1941; German Cross in Gold, 11 March 1943; Knight's Cross of the Iron Cross, 10 December 1943; Medal for the Winter Campaign in Russia 1941-1942; Commemorative Medal of 13 March 1938; Prague Castle Bar; Close Combat Clasp Silver Class; General Assault Badge; 1939 Wound Badge Silver Class.

Kämpfe was born in Jena, Thüringen. He saw service on the Russian Front and was the commanding officer of the 3rd Battalion, 4th SS-Panzergrenadier Regiment *Der Führer*, *Das Reich* Division. Kämpfe was awarded the Knight's Cross of the Iron Cross for bravery demonstrated by himself and his battalion during the fighting east of Zhitomir, Russia.

Most of the division was withdrawn from Russia at the beginning of March 1944 for refitting with men and materials in southern France, near Montauban. In June 1944 it was transferred via Brives, Tulle, Limoges, Poitiers, Tours and Laval to the area around Chaumont and Villedien. There were bloody encounters with the French Resistance during the transfer, and individual units suffered heavy casualties in the battle against the 'invisible enemy'. In one of these attacks on 9 June 1944, Kämpfe was kidnapped with his driver. He was apparently executed by his captors on 10 June 1944 near Limoges. This triggered a reprisal action against the village of Oradour-sur-Glane; the entire village of 642 inhabitants was exterminated. The women were separated from the men and were mown down with 207 children by machine guns in the church. Two days later, the bodies of 15 children were found packed behind the altar.

KAPPLER, Herbert

RANK: SS-Obersturmbannführer
BORN: 29 September 1907—
PARTY NUMBER: 594899
SS NUMBER: 55211
AWARDS: SS Honour Ring; SS Honour Sword.

Heydrich (q.v.) chose to appoint Herbert Kappler, a typical Gestapo man. as security police commander for Rome. Höttl (q.v.) described his colleague as 'an intelligent Schwabian'. Kappler held the position from 1941 until 1944, during which time he was expected to be an intelligence officer as well as a butcher, the normal combination of skills expected by Heydrich. This was in contradiction to Hitler's edicts, for he forbade the use of secret agents on Italy's friendly soil.

In March 1944, in retaliation for the killing of German soldiers by the partisans, Kappler ordered 335 Italian civilians into the Ardeatine tunnel, where they were executed. After the war he was sentenced in 1947 in Rome to life imprisonment for this action.

In 1980, 33 years later, having been in hospital for several months undergoing treatment for stomach cancer, he appealed for release on humanitarian grounds, but this was denied by the Italian High Court. The fraternity of ex-SS men decided to rectify the matter and a bizarre plan was devised. Kappler was held on the fourth floor of the military hospital in Rome. His wife Annalise visited him almost daily, and on 15 August she visited with a large suitcase, explaining to the guards that it was to take his dirty clothes away in. She stayed until 0100 hours the following morning, and when she left she was dragging the heavy case. One of the guards generously offered to help but she refused, saying that she had help outside. The case containing Kappler, who now weighed only 100 pounds, was placed in a Fiat and his escape was not discovered until the following day. His fate after this hilarious incident is unknown.

KAUFMANN, Karl

RANK: SS-Obergruppenführer, Gauleiter of Rheinland-North 27 September 1925–7 March 1926, joint Gauleiter of the Ruhr (with Göbbels and von Pfeiffer) 7 March–20 June 1926, Gauleiter of the Ruhr 20 June 1926–1 October 1928, Gauleiter of Hamburg 15 April 1929–8 May 1945
BORN: 10 October 1900
DIED: 1969 (D)
PARTY NUMBER: 95
SS NUMBER: 119495
AWARDS: Golden Party Badge; SS Honour Ring; SS Honour Sword.

After serving in World War I, Kaufmann joined the Peoples' Defence Union, the Capp Putsch and the Erhardt Brigade. In 1921 he became a member of the NSDAP, joining the Munich group. He took part in the 1923 Putsch and was arrested. He escaped, and while evading rearrest worked as a labourer in upper Bavaria.

A steady Nazi civil servant, he became Gauleiter of Rheinland-North from September 1925 to March 1926, Gauleiter of the

Ruhr with Göbbels and von Pfeiffer until June 1926, Gauleiter of the Ruhr alone to 1 October 1928, and Gauleiter of Hamburg from April 1929 until the war's end. He and General Busch, in direct contradiction to Dönitz's orders, declared Hamburg an open city in 1945, effectively inviting the British into Schleswig-Holstein.

KEHRL, Hans
RANK: SS-Brigadeführer und Generalmajor der Polizei
BORN: 6 August 1892
DIED: 26 April 1984 (D)
PARTY NUMBER: 498187
SS NUMBER: 278247
AWARDS: Knight's Cross of the War Merit Cross with Swords, 27 November 1944 (23 September 1944); SS Honour Ring; SS Honour Sword.

Under Dr Frick, the Home Secretary of Germany's first National Socialist parliament in Thüringen, the dour Kehrl was appointed the Polizeidirektor in 1930. In 1932 he was entrusted with the leadership of the police division of the Thüringen home office. From

1934 he was the assistant secretary with the leadership of department IIIB in the home office. In January 1937, at Himmler's (q.v.) own request, he became Kommisarischen police chief of Hamburg under Frick, and in conjunction with Gauleiter K. Kaufmann (q.v.), a position he held until Hamburg fell to the advancing Allies on 3 May 1945.

KEHRL, Hans
RANK: SS-Brigadeführer
BORN: 8 September 1900
DIED: 26 April 1984 (D)
PARTY NUMBER: 1878921
SS NUMBER: 276899
AWARDS: War Merit Cross Second Class without Swords; War Merit Cross First Class without Swords; Knight's Cross of the War Merit Cross with Swords, 27 November 1944; SS Honour Ring; SS Honour Sword.

Born in Brandenburg/Havel, Kehrl was a leading textile manufacturer and consultant. He studied industrial textile technology in Reutlingen and at the weaving school in Aachen. He worked in the USA from 1921 to 1923 in different positions and factories. In 1923 he entered his father's factory, which he took over in 1926. One year later he had a position as the President of Industry and Chamber of Commerce in Cottbus.

Having joined the NSDAP, Kehrl was appointed as Gau-Wirkschaftsberater (business consultant for the area) in 1933, as well as an adviser for textile and cellulose questions. On 13 September 1936 he joined the SS with the rank of SS-Untersturmführer; he was promoted on 24 April 1938 to SS-Oberführer and to SS-Brigadeführer on 21 January 1941. Afterwards he was the main consultant and leader of the IV/2 department in the same area until January 1938. From 1 February 1938 until November 1942, Kehrl was the leader of the textile division in the Reichswirtschaftsministerium, as well as general consultant for special problems. In this capacity he was the inventor of clothes coupons. On 1 February 1943, Kehrl was the leader of the Hauptabteilung II (main division).

On 22 September 1943, Rüstungsminister Speer (Armaments Minister) appointed Kehrl the leader of representatives of the four-year plan of general plenipotentiaries of the established planning areas. He was also in charge of the raw materials and commodities areas.

He belonged to the RFSS circle of friends from 1942. After the war he was sentenced to 15 years' imprisonment as a war criminal by an American Military Tribunal.

KEMPKA, Erich
RANK: SS-Sturmbannführer
BORN: 16 October 1910
DIED: 24 January 1975 (D)
PARTY NUMBER: 225639
SS NUMBER: 2803
AWARDS: Golden Party Badge; SS Honour Ring; SS Honour Sword.

Kempka became Josef Turboven's chauffeur, transferring on 1 March 1932 to Hitler's staff as a member of his bodyguard, and acting as his chauffeur after the death of Julius Schreck (q.v.) in 1936.

Kempka's position gave him an intimate perception of Hitler's inner circle. He described Eva Braun as 'the unhappiest woman in Germany'. In the last days of the war, Hitler told Günsche (q.v.) that he and Eva were going to commit suicide and that he was to be sure that he burned their bodies so that they did not fall into Russian hands. Günsche ordered Kempka to forage for the fuel necessary to incinerate the corpses.

The corpses were doused with fuel and ignited by Bormann

Finding only 160 litres (42.21 gallons US) in the Reich Chancellery garage, Kempka 'borrowed' another 20 litres (5.27 gallons US) from the Chancellery's chief technician, Hentschel. It fell to Kempka, after the suicide pact, to carry Eva's body out to the garden; he carried her halfway up the stairs leading from the bunker to the garden, only to be relieved by Günsche, who carried her the rest of the way, placing her body next to Hitler's. The corpses were doused with the fuel and ignited by Bormann (q.v.) in a Viking-like funeral pyre, in accordance with Adolf Hitler's last orders.

KEPPLER, Georg
RANK: SS-Obergruppenführer und General der Waffen-SS
BORN: 7 May 1894
DIED: 16 June 1966 (D)
PARTY NUMBER: 338211
SS NUMBER: 273799
AWARDS: 1914 Iron Cross Second Class; 1914 Iron Cross First Class; Cross of Honour 1914-1918 Combatants; Iron Cross 1939 Second Class Bar, 13 May 1940; Iron Cross 1939 First Class Bar, 13 May 1940; Knight's Cross of the Iron Cross, 15 August 1940; SS Honour Ring; SS Honour Sword.

Born in Mainz, Keppler fought in World War I. Afterwards he joined the uniformed security police, the Sipo, and in 1933 was in charge of the Thüringian police in Gotha. In 1935 he joined the SS-Verfügungstruppe and served in the SS-Standarte *Deutschland*. He went on to help form the SS-Standarte *Der Führer* in 1938.

Keppler fought in Holland in 1940, where he broke through the Dutch Grebbe and Yssel Lines, for which he was awarded the Knight's Cross. In 1942 he commanded *Das Reich*, and was temporarily in command of I SS Panzer Corps in 1944 and then XVIII SS Corps on the Upper Rhine Front and the Black Forest, from January 1945 until the war's end. He died in Hamburg in 1966.

KEPPLER, Wilhelm

RANK: SS-Obergruppenführer
BORN: 14 December 1882
DIED: 13 June 1960 (D)
PARTY NUMBER: 62424
SS NUMBER: 50816
AWARDS: Golden Party Badge; War Merit Cross Second Class without Swords; War Merit Cross First Class without Swords; SS Honour Ring; SS Honour Sword.

Keppler became a member of the NSDAP in the 1920s. He was an engineer and industrialist who was a useful intermediary with the bankers and anti-Schleicher conservatives. In 1931 he brought together a group known as the 'Keppler circle' to support and fund the party. He was elected to the Reichstag, becoming a Commissioner for Economic Affairs in 1933. He was Hitler's economic adviser from 1932 to 1936, after which he was appointed adviser to Göring on the Four Year Plan.

During the war he was employed in the Ministry of Foreign Affairs

Attached to the German Embassy in Vienna as embassy secretary, Keppler helped to engineer the Anschluss, and subsequently became Reich Commissioner to Austria from March until June 1938. During the war he was employed in the Ministry of Foreign Affairs and became chairman of many SS businesses. He continued to run the Keppler Bureau in the Ministry of Economics and liaised with Himmler (q.v.). After the war he was sentenced to 10 years' imprisonment for his part in war crimes. He was released from Landsberg Prison in January 1951. Keppler was heavily involved before the war in trying to reduce the amount of imports to Germany by increasing the production of synthetic products.

Left: A battle-weary Norwegian NCO of the Wiking *Division on the Russian Front, February 1944. Note his distinctive German 'potato masher' grenade.*

KLEFFNER, Franz

RANK: SS-Obersturmbannführer
BORN: 2 June 1907
DIED: 16 March 1945 (K.I.A.)
PARTY NUMBER: 401687
SS NUMBER: 7939
AWARDS: Knight's Cross of the Iron Cross, February 1942; 1939 Iron Cross Second Class, 1 June 1940; 1939 Iron Cross First Class, 13 July 1941; Medal for the Winter Campaign in Russia 1941-1942; Commemorative Medal of 1 October 1938; Prague Castle Bar; Demjansk Shield; SS Honour Ring; SS Honour Sword.

A responsible, outspoken officer from Westphalia, Kleffner joined the SS-Totenkopfverbände in 1933, and in 1938 he was attached to the 4th SS-Totenkopf Standarte *Ostmark*.

Sent to the Russian Front in 1941, Kleffner was horrified by the attrition of soldiers, and gained a reputation for heavy drinking. Himmler (q.v.) is credited with reprimanding Kleffner for his excessive consumption of alcohol. Jost Schneider provides an explanation in his book *Verleihung Genehmigt!*: 'If one considers the situation, the disastrous winter of 1941-42, the heavy German losses, a temperature of -30°C for weeks on end, insufficient ammunition and supplies, it seems quite understandable that a man such as Kleffner, who had a deep sense of responsibility, very nearly became sick over the losses suffered by his battalion. Furthermore, Kleffner possessed the courage to tell the Reichsführer-SS how he felt about such matters of responsibility and the capacity for leadership. As a result he was reprimanded and even placed under temporary house arrest by Himmler.' Kleffner's combat experience and Himmler's expectations of his forces provide a salutary insight into the vast difference between actually experiencing battle and directing the conflict.

Kleffner was commander of the motorcycle battalion of the *Totenkopf* Division, and in late February 1942, with Karl Ullrich (q.v.), commander of the SS-TK engineer battalion, received the Knight's Cross of the Iron Cross for heroism in the Demjansk Pocket. The confirmation of the awards was made by radio from Hitler's headquarters.

Kleffner's frankness prevented his promotion: he was relieved as commanding officer of the SS Panzer Training and Replacement Regiment and was assigned to IV SS Panzer Corps. When Karl Ullrich became commanding officer of the *Wiking* Division on 9 October 1944, Kleffner took command of the SS-Panzergrenadier Regiment 6 *Theodor Eicke*. This brave soldier was killed in action on 16 March 1945 in the bitter fighting near Sakarestico in Hungary.

KLEINHEISTERKAMP, Matthias

RANK: SS-Obergruppenführer
und General der Waffen-SS
BORN: 22 June 1893
DIED: 8 May 1945 (S)
PARTY NUMBER: 4158838
SS NUMBER: 132399
AWARDS: 1914 Iron Cross Second
Class;1914 Iron Cross First Class;
Cross of Honour 1914-1918
Combatants; 1939 Iron Cross Second
Class Bar, 13 September 1939; 1939
Iron Cross First Class Bar, 2 October
1942; Knight's Cross of the Iron Cross,
31 March 1942; Oakleaves, 9 May 1945;
SS Honour Ring; SS Honour Sword;
Finnish Freedom Cross with Swords.

Born in Elberfeld, Rheinland, Kleinheisterkamp served throughout World War I and afterwards, as was usual with many German veterans of the war, was a member of several Freikorp units, finally joining the Reichswehr in 1921. In 1927 he became a first lieutenant with the 17th Infantry Regiment. In 1938 he joined the SS-Standarte *Deutschland*, becoming a staff officer commanding the 3rd Battalion.

Kleinheisterkamp fought in France in 1940 and took over command of the 3rd SS-Totenkopf Infantry Regiment when SS-Obersturmbannführer Goetze was killed in May 1940. He was transferred to the Russian Front with this unit, and when Theodore Eicke (q.v.) was wounded he took over the command of the division until Eicke's return. On 1 January 1942, he was given command of the *Das Reich* Division and was awarded the Knight's Cross of the Iron Cross. He went on the command the 6th SS Mountain Division *Nord* from April 1942 to the middle of December 1943 (this division was raised in Austria in 1940). He served as commanding general in VII SS Corps and finally in the same position with XI SS Army Corps. It was in this role that he received by telex the bestowal of the Oakleaves, becoming the 871st recipient. This award was made on 9 May 1945, but on 8 May he had already committed suicide on the Eastern Front near Halbe, Germany.

KLINGENBERG, Fritz

RANK: SS Obersturmbannführer
BORN: 17 December 1912
DIED: 22 March 1945 (K.I.A.)
PARTY NUMBER: 851328
SS NUMBER: 51487
AWARDS: 1939 Iron Cross Second Class,
    23 June 1940; 1939 Iron Cross First
    Class, 24 June 1940; German Cross in
    Gold, 28 April 1944; Knight's Cross
    of the Iron Cross, 14 May 1941;
    SS Honour Sword; SS Honour Ring.

Klingenberg volunteered for the SS-Verfügungstruppe in 1934, and went to the officers' training school at Bad Tölz in 1935. He was a company commander in the SS-Standarte *Germania* and subsequently served on the staff of the inspectorate of the SS-Verfügungstruppe. After the fall of France he assumed command of a newly-raised motorcycle battalion of *Das Reich*.

On 11 April 1941, determined to reach Belgrade before any other German troops, Klingenberg crossed the River Danube at Belgrade with barely a dozen men, and marched unopposed into the Yugoslav capital to accept the mayor's surrender. At the conclusion of the campaign Klingenberg was received by Hitler, who personally awarded him the Knight's Cross of the Iron Cross.

In 1942 he joined the staff of the SS-Officers' school Bad Tölz and specialised in the instruction of non-German officer candidates. In January 1945 he took command of the 17th SS Panzergrenadier

Division *Götz von Berlichingen*. He was killed in action not far from Herxheim in the Palatinate in March 1945. His remains have never been located.

KNIEP, Walter

RANK: SS-Sturmbannführer
BORN: 13 December 1909
DIED: 22 April 1944 (A)
PARTY NUMBER: —
SS NUMBER: —
AWARDS: 1939 Iron Cross Second Class,
    3 June 1940; 1939 Iron Cross First
    Class, 22 July 1940; Knight's Cross of
    the Iron Cross, 14 August 1943.

Kniep was one of the most successful assault gun officers in the Waffen-SS. Born in Lorenzen, East Prussia, he saw service on the Western Front in June 1940. He was transferred to the Russian Front where he commanded the SS-Assault Gun Detachment of the *Das Reich* Division. Assault guns were used in the Soviet campaign as in infantry support weapon, but later they played a greater role as tank destroyers. Surprisingly, the German Army lagged behind its opponents with regard to anti-tank weapons at the beginning of the Russian campaign. The standard German anti-tank piece was the 37mm gun, which could only knock out a T-34, with its sloped and thick armour, at point-blank range

Between 5 July 1943 and 17 January 1944, official reports credited Kniep's detachment with 129 Soviet tanks destroyed for only two German casualties, a record which earned Kniep the Knight's Cross of the Iron Cross.

Attached to the 17th SS Panzergrenadier Division *Götz von Berlichingen* at Thouars in France, Kniep was fatally wounded after firing practice when a soldier accidentally discharged his pistol while unloading it.

KNITTEL, Gustav

RANK: SS-Obersturmbannführer
BORN: 27 November 1914
DIED: 30 June 1976 (D)
PARTY NUMBER: 2242615
SS NUMBER: 111507
AWARDS: 1939 Iron Cross Second Class;
    1939 Iron Cross First Class,
    14 September 1941; Knight's Cross of
    the Iron Cross, 4 June 1944; German
    Cross in Gold, 23 January 1944; 1939
    Wound Badge Silver Class; SS Honour
    Ring; SS Honour Sword.

Knittel was born in Neu-Ulm, Danube. He took command of the 1st SS-Panzer Reconnaissance Detachment, LSSAH, on 16 June 1944 when 'Panzer' Meyer (q.v.) was transferred.

For bravery displayed in Russia he was awarded the Knight's Cross. Transferred to the West, he was involved in the Ardennes Offensive. After the war he was tried at Dachau in 1946 and given 15 years' imprisonment. He was released at Christmas 1953.

KNOCHEN, Dr Helmut

RANK: SS-Standartenführer
BORN: 14 March 1910
DIED: July 1956 (E.A.).
PARTY NUMBER: 1430331
SS NUMBER: 280350
AWARDS: 1914 Iron Cross Second
    Class;1914 Iron Cross First Class; Cross
    of Honour 1914-1918 Combatants;
    SS Honour Ring; SS Honour Sword.

Knochen was commander of the security police in Paris from 1940 to 1944. He was an appointee of Heydrich (q.v.), who wanted to dictate his own procedure and could countenance no other secret police but his own in any part of Europe.

Heydrich's new campaign opened with a farcical incident to blow up two Paris synagogues. Knochen reported to Stülpnagel, the military governor of France, that Eugé Delonche, the former leader of the ultra-right fascist 'Cagoulrds', was suspected by the French police of the bombings. Knochen had conveniently over-looked the fact that he had arrested a member of his own staff, SS-Obersturmführer Sommer. Stülpnagel discovered, quite by accident, that Sommer, during a court of enquiry, had admitted that he had provided the explosives on Knochen's order. It is unclear if Sommer was arrested in order to conceal Knochen's involvement in the bombings, or if he had been arrested for other infringements, and his providing of the bombs had been coinci-dentally discovered during the course of his enquiries. Stülpnagel was incensed and complained to Keitel that the Gestapo were intensifying his difficulties with the French, which the 'necessary shooting of hostages had already made bad enough'.

Keitel wrote to Heydrich on 22 October, requesting the recall of Max Thomas (q.v.) and Knochen from France. Thomas was transferred to an Einsatzgruppe in Russia, but Knochen remained. Stülpnagel withdrew his complaint against Knochen on 5 February because he expressed his willingness to cooperate.

Knochen was responsible for the execution of captured Allied airmen, and after the war he was tried by the British court at Wuppertal and sentenced in June 1946 to life imprisonment. He was subsequently sentenced to death, but this was commuted to 20 years' forced labour. He died during his prison term.

KNÖCHLEIN, Fritz

RANK: SS-Obersturmbannführer
BORN: 27 May 1911
DIED: 21 January 1949 (E.A.).
PARTY NUMBER: 157016
SS NUMBER: 87881
AWARDS: 1939 Iron Cross Second Class,
    31 May 1940; 1939 Iron Cross First
    Class, 15 June 1940; German Cross in
    Gold, 12 November 1941; Knight's
    Cross of the Iron Cross, 16 November
    1944; SS Honour Ring; SS Honour Sword.

Knöchlein was the officer responsible for the infamous murder of 100 British prisoners of war during the Allied retreat to Dunkirk in 1940. On 27 May 1940, during the French campaign near the village of Le Paradis, some 100 men of the Second Royal Norfolk Regiment barricaded themselves inside a farmhouse to slow the advance of the *Totenkopf* soldiers. They pinned down Knöchlein's company for nearly an hour with accurate rifle and machine-gun fire, killing and wounding several of his men. The defenders ran out of ammunition and decided to surrender. They showed a white flag, laid their weapons down and marched out, hands raised.

Knöchlein lined them up against a wall and cut them down with gunfire

Knöchlein had them searched, then marched them across the road into a barnyard, lined them up against a wall and cut them down in a withering crossfire from two heavy machine guns. The gunners continued until all cries were extinguished. Knöchlein then detailed a squad to bayonet and shoot in the head any who still showed signs of life. After an hour he was satisfied all were dead and ordered his company onward.

Miraculously, Privates Albert Pooley and William O'Callaghan survived. They evaded capture until the severity of Pooley's wounds forced them to give themselves up. Pooley was eventually repatriated to England in 1943, where he made a full report. Once the incident became known, both the *Totenkopf* Division and the German Army, to which it was subordinated, instituted investigations. It was claimed that the fighting had been particularly bitter and 'evidence' was presented that the Norfolks had used 'Dumm-Dumm' rounds. After the war the graves were discovered, and autopsies and the testimony of French witnesses clarified the situation. Knöchlein was tried by a British court, found guilty and sentenced to death. He was hanged in 1949 in Hameln, Weser, a British-controlled penitentiary.

KOCH, Karl-Otto

RANK: SS-Standartenführer
BORN: 2 August 1897
DIED: 1945 (E.R.)
PARTY NUMBER: 475586
SS NUMBER: 14830
AWARDS: 1914 Iron Cross Second Class;
    Cross of Honour 1914-1918
    Combatants; 1914 Wound Badge Black
    Class; Badge of the SA Rally at
    Brunswick 1931; SS Honour Ring;
    SS Honour Sword.

Koch became commandant of Esterwegen concentration camp. In an open-air wedding ceremony in 1936 he married Ilse and they both went to Buchenwald in 1939, he as camp commandant and she as an SS assistant. Despite Himmler's (q.v.) continuous preaching about SS honour and integrity, Koch and others like him grew exceedingly rich from the concentration camp system, but he went too far, even by the apppalling standards of the time. While commandant of the camp at Lublin, by an irony of SS practice, Koch was judged to be criminally involved by his SS peers. The investigation of an SS court conducted by Dr Morgan (q.v.) found him guilty of embezzlement and the illegal killing of two prisoners, Krämer and Peix. The SS court sentenced him to death and he was hanged by his SS colleagues.

KOCH, Ilse
RANK: SS-Helferinnen
BORN: 22 September 1906
DIED: 2 September 1967 (S)

Having married Karl Koch (q.v.), whom she referred to as 'Karli', in 1936, Ilse Koch accompanied her husband to Buchenwald as an SS-Helferinnen in 1939. She soon gained a reputation of having an unrestrained sexual appetite, and her extreme sadism is undoubtedly best illustrated by her collection of lampshades, gloves and wallets made from the tattooed skin of camp inmates, whom she had personally selected for execution. When the supply of prisoners bearing artistic tattoos was low, she had others decorated. She became known as the 'bitch of Buchenwald'.

She was judged to be a 'perverted, nymphomaniacal, power-mad demon'

While her husband was hanged by the SS, she continued her work at the camp until it was liberated in 1945 by US forces. Himmler took a curious attitude towards his concentration camp person-

nel. He believed corruption destroyed the SS's ideology and sadism undermined discipline. Surprisingly, sadists and criminals formed only a small percentage of the personnel involved in the mass extermination programme. Chillingly, most of those who took part were 'normal' people who were just 'doing their job'.

In 1947, at her first trial, Ilse was found guilty of murder and sentenced to life imprisonment. General Lucius Clay, reviewing the case, reduced her sentence to four years. On 17 October 1949 she was released from American captivity only to be immediately re-arrested for incitement to murder. A Senate investigation committee in 1948 had also reviewed her practices. She was brought to trial again in 1951, where she was once more sentenced to life imprisonment and judged to be a 'perverted, nymphomaniacal, power-mad demon'. While in prison she seduced an American Army warder and had his baby. She hanged herself in her cell in Aibach prison in September 1967.

KORRENG, August
RANK: SS-Brigadeführer
    und Generalmajor der Polizei
BORN: 1 May 1878
DIED: 7 June 1945 (S)
PARTY NUMBER: 449807
SS NUMBER: 29625
AWARDS: 1914 Iron Cross Second Class;
    1914 Iron Cross First Class; Cross of
    Honour 1914-1918 Combatants; War
    Merit Cross Second Class without
    Swords; War Merit Cross First Class
    without Swords; Knight's Cross of
    the War Merit Cross with Swords,
    25 February 1945; SS Honour Ring;
    SS Honour Sword.

A World War I veteran, Korreng joined the SS on 31 July 1933 with the rank of Untersturmführer. He was the police president of Düsseldorf and for his services was awarded the Knight's Cross of the War Merit Cross with Swords. The reason for the award of this prodigious honour is not known. Korreng committed suicide in Plettenberg, Westphalia, on 7 June 1945.

KRAAS, Hugo

RANK: SS-Brigadeführer
und Generalmajor der Waffen-SS
BORN: 25 January 1911
DIED: 20 February 1980 (D)
PARTY NUMBER: 2204561
SS NUMBER: 289633
AWARDS: 1939 Iron Cross Second Class,
16 October 1939; 1939 Iron Cross First
Class, 25 May 1940; German Cross in
Gold, 29 December 1941; Knight's
Cross of the Iron Cross, 28 March
1943; Oakleaves, 24 January 1944;
Army Long Service Medal, four years;
Commemorative Medal for the
13 March 1938; Commemorative Medal
of 1 October 1938; Prague Castle Bar;
Commemorative Medal for the return
of the Memel Region; SS Honour Ring;
SS Honour Sword.

Following his military service, Kraas joined the SS-Verfügungstruppe in 1935. He was a platoon leader in Poland, and in the French campaign in 1940 commanded a company in the LSSAH. He had a short spell in Italy before being employed in Operation 'Barbarossa', serving as commanding officer of the 1st Battalion, 2nd SS-Panzergrenadier Regiment, *Leibstandarte* Division.

In 1943 Kraas and his battalion played a major role in retaking Kharkov from the Soviets. In recognition of his leadership he was awarded the Knight's Cross of the Iron Cross. He went on to command the 2nd SS-Panzergrenadier-Regiment, 1st SS Panzer Division. In June 1944, in an area near Zhitomir, the regiment came under heavy attack. They undertook a successful defence against substantial numbers of Russian tanks; 95 were destroyed, turning the tide of the battle. For this and continued actions on the Eastern Front he was awarded the Oakleaves, becoming the 375th recipient. In November 1944 he became the last divisional commander of the 12th SS Panzer Division *Hitlerjugend*. He died in Schleswig in 1980.

KRAG, Ernst-August

RANK: SS-Sturmbannführer
BORN: 20 February 1915
DIED: 1985 (D)
PARTY NUMBER: 2403770
SS NUMBER: 70385
AWARDS: Knight's Cross of the Iron Cross,
23 October 1944; German Cross in
Gold, 20 April 1943; 1939 Iron Cross
Second Class, 25 July 1940; 1939 Iron
Cross First Class, 27 July 1941; 1939
Wound Badge Silver Class; Army Long
Service Medal four years; Medal for the
Winter Campaign in Russia 1941-1942;
Commemorative Medal of 13 March
1938; Close Combat Clasp Bronze
Class; Silver Tank Battle Badge '25';
SS Honour Ring.

Ernst Krag was born in Wiesbaden-Erbenheim Hersen. In May 1935, he joined the SS and was attached to 5 Kompanie of the *Germania* Standarte in Arolsen. He attended the paratroop training school at Stendal, qualifying and becoming one of Germany's first paratroopers. His next posting was to the SS-Junkerschule at Bad Tölz in 1938, and after graduating in 1939 he attended the artillery school in Jüterberg. He was posted as battery observation officer, *Das Reich*. During the Normandy campaign he led his unit with great skill and won the Knight's Cross. He fought in the Ardennes Offensive where he won the Oakleaves, becoming the 755th recipient. He died in Niederhausen in 1985.

KRAMER, Josef

RANK: SS-Hauptsturmführer
BORN: 10 November 1906
DIED: 13 December 1945 (E.A.)
PARTY NUMBER: 32217
SS NUMBER: 733597
AWARDS: War Merit Cross Second Class,
     spring 1943; War Merit Cross First
     Class, January 1945.

Kramer was an early participant in the concentration camp service, from 1934. He served in Natzweiler camp, where he was rewarded with the War Merit Cross First Class in the spring of 1943 for his efficiency in running the camp. He commanded the extermination centre at Auschwitz in the last months of its existence, before being transferred in November 1944 to Bergen-Belsen.

Bergen-Belsen was established in 1943 as an 'exchange camp' for Jews living in Germany and was originally perceived as a special 'privileged transit camp' for Jews with relatives in Palestine, Paraguay and Honduras, Jewish diamond workers and those decorated with the Iron Cross. By a grisly irony it was also clas-sified as a 'Krankenlager' – a reception centre for sick prisoners. Jews who had paid an individual ransom were forwarded from Strasshof to the camp. Meanwhile, Jewish international charities found 20 million Swiss francs to 'buy' Jews, and 1684, mainly from the former Romanian town of Cluj, were moved from Bergen-Belsen and released in Switzerland in two train loads on 21 August and 6 December 1944. But during late 1944 they were replaced by prisoners from camps evacuated from Eastern Europe, mere disease-ridden skeletons who were dying at the rate of 2-300 a day from spotted typhus.

From November 1944 conditions in Belsen deteriorated rapidly, ironically coincidental with Kramer's appointment. Evidence offered at his trial suggested he was responsible for selling off food supplies, but it is more likely that the desperate food shortage was the result of the increase in prisoner numbers from 15,000 to almost 50,000.

The horrific newsreels showed him to the world in 1945 as being stocky and well-fed among the dying inmates, his cheek scarred beneath the stubble, a man neither shocked nor stricken by conscience, a man simply awaiting new orders. Kramer was found guilty of war crimes and executed on 13 December 1945.

KRAUSE, Karl Wilhelm

RANK: SS-Hauptsturmführer
BORN: 5 March 1911—
PARTY NUMBER: —
SS NUMBER: —
AWARDS: German Cross in Gold; 1939 Iron Cross Second Class; 1939 Iron Cross First Class; Commemorative Medal of 13 March 1938; Commemorative Medal of 1 October 1938; Prague Castle Bar; Commemorative Medal for the return of the Memel Region; Destroyer's War Badge; Narvik Shield in Gold; DRL Sports Badge.

Born in Michelau, West Prussia, near Danzig, Krause studied cabinet making and architecture, before joining the navy in 1931. Hitler chose Krause to be his personal orderly in 1934, impressed by his tall, 'Nordic' appearance. Although he was not a Nazi, Krause was entrusted with the most important role of protecting the Führer from assault or assassination, which involved walking directly behind him on tours and at public appearances. Hitler often jokingly referred to him as 'shadow', as he had the ability of appearing to blend with Hitler's shadow, becoming unseen.

Krause was constantly with Hitler between 1934 and 1939. On Christmas Eve 1937, Hitler managed to elude the SS guards, and crept out, accompanied by Krause, on an incognito jaunt through Berlin, where they had an exciting midnight stroll. Himmler (q.v.) reprimanded Krause the next day for allowing Hitler to expose himself to nocturnal dangers. In September 1939, after a petty squabble over some 'spring water', Hitler dismissed Krause. He served in the navy, then as an ordnance aide in the Reich Chancellery. Finally, he joined the Waffen-SS and served in a flak unit, which was credited with shooting down 45 aircraft. He escaped from the Soviets and went into American custody. After various interrogations he was fined seven marks and released.

KRIEGBAUM, Anton

RANK: SS-Sturmbannführer
BORN: 20 November 1912—
PARTY NUMBER: —
SS NUMBER: 161609
AWARDS: 1939 Iron Cross Second Class; 1939 Iron Cross First Class.

Kriegbaum was d'Alquen's (q.v.) deputy who commanded the 'Kurt Eggers' regiment, responsible for providing Waffen-SS war correspondents and also for the implementation of tactical psychological operations on the frontline, including the 'Scorpion Ost' and 'Scorpion West' plans. Towards the end of April 1945, d'Alquen decided to evacuate his remaining staff from Berlin, and Kriegbaum, an American, SS-Hauptsturmführer Ackerman and an Englishman, Benson Freeman (q.v.), accompanied d'Alquen to an airfield at Potsdam, where they commandeered three aircraft to fly them to the southeast. Kriegbaum then disappeared.

KRON, Otto-Wilhelm

RANK: SS-Obersturmbannführer
BORN: 28 February 1911
DIED: 9 August 1951 (D)
PARTY NUMBER: 3061726
SS NUMBER: 31441
AWARDS: 1939 Iron Cross Second Class, 22 June 1940; 1939 Iron Cross First Class, 19 December 1941; Knight's Cross of the Iron Cross, 28 June 1942; Medal for the Winter Campaign in Russia 1941-1942; Commemorative Medal of 13 March 1938; Commemorative Medal of 10 October 1938; Prague Castle Bar; SS Honour Ring; SS Honour Sword.

Otto Kron was born in Speyer, Rhine-Palatinate, the son of a police officer. He studied law at Würzburg University and in 1931 joined the Allgemeine-SS. He was attached to the 1st SS-Totenkopf Standarte *Oberbayern* in 1938. He served on the Russian Front

and was the commanding officer of the flak detachment of the *Totenkopf* Division when, with some hurriedly assembled troops, he launched a counterattack against Soviet troops in June 1942. He succeeded in repulsing the enemy. For his bravery he won the Knight's Cross. He survived the war and died in Dachau in 1951.

KRÜGER, Friedrich Wilhelm

RANK: SS-Obergruppenführer
BORN: 8 May 1894
DIED: May 1945 (S)
PARTY NUMBER: 171191
SS NUMBER: 6123
AWARDS: Golden Party Badge; 1914 Iron Cross Second Class; 1914 Iron Cross First Class; Cross of Honour 1914-1918 Combatants; 1914 Wound Badge Silver Class; 1939 Iron Cross Second Class Bar, July 1943; 1939 Iron Cross First Class Bar, May 1944; Knight's Cross, 30 September 1944; War Merit Cross Second Class; War Merit Cross First Class; SS Honour Ring; SS Honour Sword.

The son of an army officer, Strasbourg-born Krüger served in World War I. He was the younger brother of Walter Krüger (q.v.) and, like him, joined the SS-Verfügungstruppe.

From 1939-44, he held the position of higher SS police leader in Poland, with his headquarters at Cracow. He took command of the the 6th SS Mountain Division *Nord* in Finland for three months in 1944. Following Arthur Phleps' death in February 1945, he took command of the 5th SS Mountain Corps in Yugoslavia until March 1945 when he was replaced by SS-Obergruppenführer und General der Waffen-SS und Polizei Friedrich Jeckeln (q.v.). Like his brother, he committed suicide in May 1945 in Austria.

KRÜGER, Walter

RANK: SS-Obergruppenführer
BORN: 27 February 1890
DIED: 20 May 1945 (S)
PARTY NUMBER: 3995130
SS NUMBER: 266184
AWARDS: 1914 Iron Cross Second Class; 1914 Iron Cross First Class; Cross of Honour 1914-1918 Combatants; 1914 Wound Badge Black Class; Knight's Cross, 13 December 1941; Oakleaves, 31 August 1943; Swords, 1 February 1945; SS Honour Ring; SS Honour Sword.

Born in Strassbourg, Alsace, the son of an army officer, Walter Krüger attended cadet school. As a young second lieutenant, he joined the 110th Fusilier Regiment, serving with distinction during World War I. He subsequently joined the Freikorps and fought in the Baltic region during 1919. He joined the Reichswehr and also spent some years in industry. In 1933, when Hitler gained power, Krüger worked in the Reichswehr and Wehrmacht training department. In 1935, he joined the SS-Verfügungstruppe where he formed the SS-Standarte *Germania*. He went on to serve as instructor at the SS-officers' school at Bad Tölz. In 1941 he took over command of the police division which fought on the Leningrad Front between Luga and Krassnowardeisk and took part in the siege itself, earning the Knight's Cross of the Iron Cross.

Krüger assumed command of the SS Division *Das Reich* in March 1943 and became the 286th recipient of the Oakleaves. He subsequently went on to act as inspector general of the infantry troops of the Waffen-SS. He assumed command of the newly formed VI (Latvian) SS Corps, consisting of the 15th and 19th Latvian volunteer divisions where he was awarded the Swords and was the 120th recipient. Only the strong resistance of the Wehrmacht and the corps in the autumn of 1944 prevented the total collapse of the German northeastern sector of front by the end of that year. Krüger committed suicide on the Baltic Front on 20 May 1945.

KRYSSING, P. C.
RANK: Legions-Obersturmbannführer
PARTY NUMBER: —
SS NUMBER: —

Freikorps *Danmark* was an officially sponsored body, and on 3 July 1941 Lieutenant-Colonel P. C. Kryssing of the 5th Artillery Regiment of the Danish Army was to be given command of the new unit. The Freikorps was part of the Waffen-SS from the start, but Himmler (q.v.) was displeased by the slow progress in training. The Danes, it transpired, suffered from inefficient leadership and poor coordination with their German instructors. Furthermore, Kryssing disliked what he considered to be German interference with his handling of the corps. He deliberately allowed the training programme to fall behind schedule, with the result that Himmler dismissed him from his command on 8 February 1942. Kryssing was then moved to an administration post on the grounds that an artillery man could not be expected to command an infantry battalion. He recommended as his replacement Captain Schock, but, as he was a freemason, he was deemed unacceptable to the SS.

KUBE, Wilhelm-Richard Paul
RANK: SS-Gruppenführer
    Gauleiter of Ostmark 1928-33;
    Gauleiter of Kurmark 1933-6
BORN: 13 November 1887
DIED: 22 September 1943 (K.I.A.)
PARTY NUMBER: 71682
SS NUMBER: 114771
AWARDS: War Merit Cross Second Class
    with Swords; War Merit Cross First
    Class with Swords; Knight's Cross of
    the War Merit Cross with Swords
    (Posthumous), 27 September 1943.

Wilhelm Kube was born in Glogau, the son of a Prussian sergeant. In 1928 he joined the NSDAP and the members of the DNVP enrolled in the NSDAP.

In recognition he was appointed, in 1928, Gauleiter of Ostmark and in 1933 Kurmark. A particularly nasty character, he was removed from office in 1936 on the grounds that he had apparently attributed Jewish ancestry to Major Walter Buch. The real basis for his dismissal, however, was undoubtedly corruption; considering who he had supposedly slandered, it is remarkable that he was still permitted to use the title Gauleiter (he was lucky to retain his freedom).

On 16 July 1941 Hitler proposed him for the position of Kommissar of Moscow (in expectation of another easy Blitzkrieg victory), but Göring and Rosenberg strongly opposed this posting and Kube was made the generalkommissariat of Belorussia. Although not hostile to the population of his territory and protesting against anti-Jewish measures, he was ineffective in resisting the atrocities, strangely taking the credit for 50,000 Jewish deaths in 1942. The real hallmark of Kube's regime was the introduction of corruption on a grand scale. He did argue that the Belorussians should be treated better and permitted self-government of some type, though no doubt he hoped to profit out of any such situation. He met a strange and grisly end, having a bomb planted under his bed by a servant girl, which blew him to pieces on 22 September 1943.

KUHBANDER, Eric

RANK: SS-Obersturmführer
BORN: 21 October 1921
DIED: 1985? (D)
PARTY NUMBER: —
SS NUMBER: 421069 (V)
AWARDS: 1939 Iron Cross Second Class; 1939 Iron Cross First Class, 17 March 1944; Anti-Partisan War Badge Gold Class, 15 February 1945; Infantry Assault Badge Bronze Class; 1939 Wound Badge Black Class, 14 October 1941; Golden Hitler Youth Honour Badge.

Kuhbander joined the Hitler Youth on 1 May 1931 and remained active in it until 15 September 1939, when he volunteered to join the SS and was attached to the *Deutschland* Regiment. Having fought in Holland and France from 11 May until 2 July 1940, he attended the SS-Junkerschule at Bad Tölz from 1 May until 15 September 1941.

On 9 November 1941 he was transferred to the SS Division *Das Reich* and served in Russia where he was wounded and returned to hospital in Rosenheim to recover. On 9 September Kuhbander was sent to the northern Italian area for anti-partisan operations. He was transferred to Dachau on 15 August 1944,

Kuhbander was in action near Villach in Austria as late as 6 May 1945

but returned to the 3rd battalion of the Karot Mountain Light Infantry Regiment of the SS No 1 Adriatic Coast in November 1944. He was awarded the Anti-Partisan War Badge in gold personally by Himmler on 15 February 1945 for having participated with bravery in 100 days of combat action against the partisans. Kuhbander was transferred to the *Prinz Eugen* Division on 7 February 1945 and was in action near Villach in Austria as late as 6 May 1945. He managed to get to British lines at the war's end, and ended up in a POW camp in England. He died in Rosenheim, the town of his birth.

KUMM, Otto

RANK: SS-Brigadeführer
   und Generalmajor der Waffen-SS
BORN: 1 October 1909—
PARTY NUMBER: 421230
SS NUMBER: 18727
AWARDS: 1939 Iron Cross Second Class,
   30 May 1940; 1939 Iron Cross First
   Class, 3 June 1940; Knight's Cross,
   16 February 1942; Oakleaves 8 April
   1943; Oakleaves with Swords, 17
   March 1945; German Cross in Gold,
   29 November 1941; SS Honour Ring;
   SS Honour Sword.

Having served in the campaign in France in 1940, Kumm's leadership ability was quickly recognised and he was given command positions during duty on the Russian Front as battalion and regimental commander. His dogged determination in the face of overwhelming odds was the force that inspired the SS-Panzergrenadier Regiment *Der Führer*. He was awarded the Knight's Cross of the Iron Cross for actions on the Russian Front, being personally invested by General Field Marshal Model.

While commanding the 4th SS-Panzergrenadier Regiment *Der Führer* he was awarded the Oakleaves for his leadership and bravery in the field, becoming the 221st recipient. Hitler was so impressed by him that he personally bestowed the award. Kumm went from staff officer to command the *Prinz Eugen* Division in the anti-partisan war against Tito in Yugoslavia. At the same time his troops were deployed in the front against the Soviet and Bulgarian forces. For these actions he was awarded the Swords, becoming the 138th recipient, which was bestowed by 'Sepp' Dietrich (q.v.). In the last few months of the war he was given the command of the *Leibstandarte* Division.

KUSKE, Ortwin

RANK: SS-Hauptsturmführer
BORN: 3 February 1921
DIED: 19 February 1972 (D)
PARTY NUMBER: —
SS NUMBER: —
AWARDS: 1939 Iron Cross Second Class,
   21 July 1941; 1939 Iron Cross First
   Class, 16 July 1944; Knight's Cross of
   the Iron Cross, 26 November 1944;
   Close Combat Clasp Bronze Class;
   Infantry Assault Badge; 1939 Wound
   Badge Silver Class.

Kuske fought in France in 1940 when he was attached to the 1st (Light) of the *Leibstandarte*. In November 1944 he was a company commander in the *Götz von Berlichingen* in the West. He became engaged in heavy fighting between Metz and Pont à Mousson in Lorraine. For three days and four nights the Americans attacked his position, until he was able to break out with two-thirds of his men and successfully return to German lines. He was awarded the Knight's Cross. He survived the war and became a mining technical officer in a large company. He died of leukaemia in 1972.

LAGES, Willi

RANK: SS-Sturmbannführer
BORN: 5 October 1901—
PARTY NUMBER: 3552661
SS NUMBER: 267729
AWARDS: War Merit Cross Second Class
with Swords; War Merit Cross First
Class with Swords; SS Honour Ring.

Lages was head of the Amsterdam branch of the Sipo and was
associated with Rauter (q.v.). Together they implemented, through
Schoengarth, Hitler's so-called Niedermachungsbefehl, the instruction to the police to execute publicly any *Todeskandidaten* (death
candidates) who were members of the Resistance.

LAMMERDING, Heinz

RANK: SS-Gruppenführer
und Generalleutnant der Waffen-SS
BORN: 27 August 1905
DIED: 13 January 1971 (D)
PARTY NUMBER: 722395
SS NUMBER: 247062
AWARDS: 1939 Iron Cross Second Class,
23 May 1940; 1939 Iron Cross First
Class, 22 June 1940; German Cross in
Gold, 25 April 1943; Knight's Cross,
11 April 1943; Demjansk Shield;
General Assault Badge, Badge of the SA
rally at Brunswick 1931, SS Honour
Ring; SS Honour Sword.

Left: Totenkopf *soldiers in the Demjansk Pocket,*
January 1942. The division lost over 6000 men
defending the pocket against the Soviet onslaught.

An engineer who served with the head office of the Training
Department of the Reichswehr, Lammerding joined the SS-
Verfügungstruppe as an engineering officer and then served during
the 1940 French campaign in the engineer battalion of the
Totenkopf Division.

Transferred to the Eastern Front, in the summer of 1941 he
was successful in breaking through the Stalin Line near Sebesh,
and was the first staff officer of the *Totenkopf* Division in the
Demjansk Pocket. In 1942 he commanded the Motorcycle
Regiment *Thule*, subsequently he commanded the armoured
Battle Group *Das Reich*. In March 1944 most of the division was
transferred for refit to Montauban in southern France. In June,
it was moved to the area around Chaumont and Viliedien. During
this transfer the French Resistance inflicted heavy casualties on
individual units, angering the Waffen-SS soldiers. After the Allied
landings on 6 June, the number of attacks intensified and SS-
Obersturmbannführer Kämpfe was captured and executed by the
Resistance on 9 June (his body was not found until after the war;
Kämpfe's companion, SS-Obersturmführer Gerlach, reported the

incident). In reprisal the men of Oradour-sur-Glane were shot, and the women and children locked in the church. The town was then put to the torch. The fire spread quickly to the church and all inside perished (the location has never been rebuilt; it stands in mute testimony to the ruthlessness of National Socialist ideology and Waffen-SS brutality).

Lammerding went on to become Himmler's chief of staff, Vistula Army Group, from January to March 1945. After the war Lammerding was tried in absentia in Bordeaux for the Oradour-sur-Glane massacre and sentenced to death. He never suffered this penalty or imprisonment; even though the French Government requested that the Bundesrepublik extradite him on several occasions, but the German Government steadfastly refused. It can thus be said that Lammerding, like so many in the SS as a whole, escaped lightly. He died of cancer in Bad Tölz in 1971 and was buried in Düsseldorf.

LAMMERS, Dr Hans

RANK: SS-Obergruppenführer
BORN: 27 May 1879
DIED: 4 January 1962 (D)
PARTY NUMBER: 1010255
SS NUMBER: 118404
AWARDS: Golden Party Badge; 1914 Iron Cross Second Class; 1914 Iron Cross First Class; Cross of Honour 1914-1918 Combatants; SS Honour Ring; SS Honour Sword.

Born at Lublinitz, Upper Silesia, Lammers was a brilliant lawyer who acted for the Nazi Party and distinguished himself by interpreting legal tangles for it. He was State Secretary from 1933 to 1945, becoming minister and head of the Chancellery. Hitler ordered his arrest for high treason on 23 April 1945, but the war ended before this order could be implemented.

Lammers was tried at Nuremberg in April 1949 for his part in drafting anti-Jewish decrees. In his defence he pleaded he was unaware of 'the Final Solution of the Jewish problem'. He was sentenced to 20 years' imprisonment for his part, but was released on 15 December 1951. He died in Düsseldorf 11 years later.

LANDWEHR, Paul

RANK: SS-Sturmbannführer und Major der Polizei
BORN: 21 November 1906
DIED: 28 April 1945 (K.I.A.)
PARTY NUMBER: —
SS NUMBER: —
AWARDS: 1939 Iron Cross Second Class; 1939 Iron Cross First Class; Knight's Cross of the Iron Cross, 17 March 1945; Infantry Assault Badge; Medal for the Winter Campaign in Russia 1941-1942; 1939 Wound Badge Black Class.

In March 1945 he was the commanding officer of the Second Battalion 14th Police Regiment, 40th Panzer Corps, on the Eastern Front in Germany. He was awarded the Knight's Cross of the Iron Cross. He was killed in action near Taubenford, Guben District, Eastern Germany, on 28 April 1945.

LAUTERBACHER, Hartmann

RANK: SS-Obergruppenführer, Gauleiter of South-Hanover-Brunswick 1940-45
BORN: 24 May 1909
DIED: 1989 (D)
PARTY NUMBER: 86837
SS NUMBER: 382406
AWARDS: SS Honour Ring; SS Honour Sword.

He joined a Nazi youth group in 1922 and his career was mainly with the Hitler Youth. Lauterbacher was Baldur von Schirach's chief of staff and personal representative from 1933 until 1940, when in August of that year, he was appointed Gauleiter of South-Hanover-Brünswick, replacing Bernhard Rust. He was the youngest of all the gauleiters and after the war he was interned. He escaped from a prison camp on 5 February 1948 and fled to Italy. The Italian authorities arrested him in 1950, returned him to Germany, where he apparently escaped again, this time to Argentina.

Junkerschule at Bad Tölz from 1935 to 1936. He was then transferred to the SS-Verfügungstruppe and served with the elite SS-Standarte *Germania*.

In 1942 Lehmann took the post of 1st Staff Officer of the *Leibstandarte* and proved to be an able strategist and tactician, establishing himself as one of the most accomplished officers; 'Sepp' Dietrich came to rely on him absolutely. Lehmann's talents shone when the Soviets' spearhead endangered the *Leibstandarte*'s headquarters. He carried out a successful counterattack with a force cobbled together from some staff officers, adjutants and orderlies. In recognition of his leadership he was awarded the Knight's Cross of the Iron Cross. When Werner Ostendorff (q.v.), the commander of the 2nd SS Panzer Division *Das Reich* was wounded in March 1945 in Hungary, Lehmann was given temporary command of the division from 9 March until 13 April. Fighting a string of defensive actions, the division retreated into Austria and continued its stubborn rearguard action south of Vienna. Elements of the *Das Reich* Division attempted to hold the Vitel-Danube canal bridges in the heart of Vienna on 13 April, but were forced out of the city on the 15th. Lehmann was awarded the Oakleaves, becoming the 849th recipient. He survived the war and died in Ettlingen in 1983.

LEHMANN, Rudolf
RANK: SS-Standartenführer
BORN: 30 January 1914
DIED: 17 September 1983 (D)
PARTY NUMBER: 3143188
SS NUMBER: 111883
AWARDS: 1939 Iron Cross Second Class,
14 November 1939, 1939 Iron Cross
First Class, 3 June 1940; German Cross
in Gold, 1 November 1943; Knight's
Cross of the Iron Cross, 23 February
1944; Oakleaves, 6 May 1945;
SS Honour Ring; SS Honour Sword.

Born in Heidleberg, Lehmann was a skilled staff officer and tactician. He joined the *Leibstandarte* in 1933 and attended the SS-

LEISTER, John
RANK: SS-Schütze
BORN: 19 June 1922
PARTY NUMBER: —
SS NUMBER: —

Born in London, Leister was the son of a north London baker who had served in World War I in the Middlesex Regiment, despite his German birth. In the interwar years he made frequent visits to his family in Germany, who were NSDAP members and took some delight in dressing their small English relation in party uniform. From 1935 to 1936 he lived with his great-aunt in Germany, attending school and learning to speak the native language fluently.

The outbreak of war in 1939 caused a conflict of loyalties and he decided to join the Peace Pledge Union Scheme, providing agricultural workers for the Channel Islands. The invasion of the Channel Islands in July 1940 put him in a difficult position. He became an interpreter for the Germans, while his friend Pleasants (q.v.) teamed up with Eddie Chapman, the notorious triple spy. Leister and Pleasants decided to escape to England, but were caught and sentenced to six months in prison. They were sent to France, and afterwards Leister was sent to a civilian internment camp where he attempted to escape again. He was apprehended and served a further six weeks in a Gestapo prison.

Finally, he and Pleasants were interned at Marlag-Milage, where they decided to join the British Freikorps. Leister also worked for the broadcasting service and subsequently joined the Kurt Eggers Regiment, and on a false pass, provided by his girlfriend Lena Jurgens, escaped to Italy in her company. They surrendered to the American authorities, who returned him to England, where he was tried at the Old Bailey, found guilty and sentenced to three years' penal servitude.

LEROY, Jacques
Rank: SS-Untersturmführer
Born: 10 September 1924
Died: 5 August 1996 (D).
Party number: —
SS number: —
Awards: 1939 Iron Cross Second Class, 11 November 1943; 1939 Iron Cross First Class, 8 July 1944; Knight's Cross of the Iron Cross, 20 April 1945; Close Combat Clasp Silver Class.

Leroy was born in Binche, Belgium, and volunteered for service in the Waffen-SS as a foreigner. He was the commanding NCO of the First Company SS-Panzergrenadier Regiment 69 in the 28th SS Freiwilligen-Panzergrenadier Division *Wallonien*, serving on the Eastern Front. He was awarded the Knight's Cross of the Iron Cross for his bravery in an action where he lost his eye and his arm. He was recovering in hospital when the award was made. He re-mustered with his unit, terribly wounded, to continue the fight, but the prestigious award was never actually bestowed upon him, nor did he receive the preliminary citation; worst of all, his name had not been entered on the role of winners. It was not until 20 May 1957 that his entitlement was proved by the division adjutant Roger Wastian, and it was confirmed on 8 December 1973 by Leroy's commander, Léon Degrelle (q.v.).

LIE, Jonas
Rank: SS-Oberführer
Born: 31 December 1899
Died: 1945 (D)
Party number: —
SS number: 401276
Award: 1939 Iron Cross Second Class; 1939 Iron Cross First Class; SS Honour Ring.

A Norwegian, Lie was a professional police officer and amateur author who used the pseudonym of Max Mauser. In 1934 he was chosen by the League of Nations to lead the peacekeeping force sent to the Saar to supervise the plebiscite held to determine the territory's future. By a strange turn of fate Lie met and struck up a friendship with Josef Terboven, the Gauleiter of Essen and later Reichskommissar of Norway. Later, Terboven was to make no secret of the fact that he would have preferred Lie, rather than Quisling, to have been the leader of the *Nasjonal Samling* (the Norwegian Nazi Party). Although a sympathiser, Lie never joined the party (in Germany membership of the SS also did not necessarily mean membership of the NSDAP), a state of affairs pertinent to many who enlisted in the Waffen-SS in Norway and other occupied countries. Lie, as with the majority of those responsible for recruiting, as well as the majority of the volunteers that joined the Waffen-SS to fight in Russia, was not by nature a sympathiser to the Nazi cause, but can be best described as a fervent anticommunist, who joined Hitler's 'crusade against communism' out of a fear of a communist takeover in his country. In the case of Norway it must be seen that the Russian war with Finland directly endangered it. Likewise Danish volunteers felt threatened, and hence the fervour for volunteering to fight in this campaign can be easily understood. Equally it must be noted that the British Government allowed serving British military personnel to stand down, appear in *mufti* and volunteer for service with the Finnish forces against the Soviet Union. This led to a number of Britons in fact serving in Russia with the Finns, supporting SS units. Of course these men were never brought to trial for serving in this manner and have only relatively recently been allowed to receive the Finnish Winter War Medal.

A patriot, in April 1940 Lie continued to fight against the Germans

A patriot, in April 1940 Lie ignored Quisling's 'demobilisation order' and continued to fight against the Germans until the end of the campaign; he was a patriotic Norwegian and therefore considered it his duty to uphold the integrity of his country against the invasion. His anti-communist views led him to having the position of responsibility in the police, plus the fact that due to his friendship with Terboven, which was formed in the 1930s, meant that when Terboven became commissioner for Norway he trusted Lie more than Quisling. Lie was altogether a more ruthless and unscrupulous character than Quisling. Enmity and jealousy soon sprang up between the two. Quisling had proposed a cabinet in which Lie was to be the minister of justice, but this was quashed. On 25 September 1941 Terboven dismissed the administrative council and replaced it by a Committee of Commissarial State Councillors, in which Lie was made responsible for the police.

SS recruiting propaganda in Norway was considered in rather nebulous National Socialist terms, but did claim that German intervention had foiled a British plot to occupy Norway. Quisling broadcast an appeal for volunteers for Regiment *Nordland* to participate in 'the war of freedom and independence against English despotism' on 13 January 1941. Recruitment was very slow to begin with; only around 300 volunteers came forward in the first year. Even after the commando raids on the Lofoten Islands, few Norwegians were concerned about this so-called threat to their homeland. Jonas Lie spoke of ancient claims to the Orkney and Shetland Isles and the Outer Hebrides. Few listened.

In the summer of 1942 Jonas Lie commanded the First Police Company, and in September it joined the rest of the legion outside Leningrad on the Eastern Front. The Norwegians did not take part in any major battles as such, but rather undertook patrols and reconnaissances. However, their attrition rate was high and their morale suffered as a result. Lie retained his position until its return to Norway on 6 April 1943.

In July 1942 the SS made a move calculated to weaken Quisling's grip on his own party. On the 21st Himmler let it be known that Norges SS had been transformed into the Germanske SS Norge and was now part of a new complex: non-Germanic Nordic Allgemeine-SS units, which were under the general leadership of the Germanic SS. This was directly responsible to Himmler and he confirmed Lie as leader of the new formation in Norway.

Lie survived the war and was arrested. The former chief of the Norwegian police and the police company died of a heart attack while awaiting trial in prison.

LINGE, Heinz

RANK: SS-Sturmbannführer
BORN: 22 March 1913
DIED: 9 March 1981 (D)
PARTY NUMBER: —
SS NUMBER: —

A bricklayer by profession, Linge joined the SS in 1933 and was subsequently posted to the SS-Begleitkommando which was charged with Hitler's protection. In July 1935, he undertook the task of Hitler's ordnance officer, and with the dismissal of Hitler's head valet, Karl Kruse (q.v.), in September 1939 Linge was appointed to the post. During his tenure Hitler became fond of him. After Hitler's suicide, it fell to Linge to help wrap the corpse in an army blanket and carry it into the Chancellery garden to be cremated alongside Eva Braun. He helped inter the charred remains in a shell hole. He was in the 'bunker breakout' but was subsequently captured and spent 10 years in Soviet captivity. After his release he became a successful businessman in Hamburg where he eventually died in 1981.

LIPPERT, Michael

RANK: SS-Standartenführer
BORN: 24 April 1897—
PARTY NUMBER: 246989
SS NUMBER: 2968
AWARDS: SS Honour Ring; SS Honour Sword.

Lippert was Eicke's (q.v.) adjutant and accompanied him and SS-Gruppenführer Heinrich Schmauser to Stadelheim Prison to murder Röhm in 1934.

He went on to become the first commander of Freiwilligen-Legion *Flandern* and was wounded during the fighting in the Volkhov Pocket and had to be evacuated. Lippert came in for a good deal of criticism for his alleged high-handed and disdainful attitude towards his Flemish charges, whom he was accused of treating as second-class soldiers.

LOEPER, Wilhelm

RANK: SS-Gruppenführer
BORN: 1883
DIED: 23 October 1935 (D)
PARTY NUMBER: 6980
SS NUMBER: 142592
AWARDS: 1914 Iron Cross Second Class; 1914 Iron Cross First Class; Military Merit Medal Second Class; Military Merit Medal First Class; Cross of Honour 1914-1918 Combatants; 1914 Wound Badge Silver Class; Blood Order No 47; Gau General Commemorative Badge 1923 or 1925.

Loeper served in World War I, after which he was demobilised. He returned to the colours in 1920, but was dismissed from the army in 1924 after his part in the 1923 Putsch.

On 1 April 1927, he was installed as Gauleiter of Anhalt province, north Saxony, which was renamed Magdeburg-Anhalt on 1 October 1928. He remained in this post until his death in 1935 after a long illness.

consisted of two mounted regiments, a mobile reconnaissance detachment and a small tank and anti-aircraft detachment.

Operation 'Barbarossa' in 1941 cut off large numbers of Soviet forces who concealed and regrouped themselves in the forests and marshes, and posed a considerable threat to the German frontline troops, as well as to the supply lines which grew increasingly elongated. The cavalry units were given the job of fighting these parties, a task for which they were eminently well qualified. Partisan attacks not only strained frontline troops, they drained urgently needed reinforcements. However, civilian resentment of the policies of Alfred Rosenberg's Ostministerium (administered by unfit, misguided and unsympathetic officials) in the occupied areas helped the partisans.

Cavalry units were rushed to these areas, and soon became known as 'fire brigades'. The German High Command further realised that it had made a fundamental mistake in converting all its cavalry into motorised units. When the fighting moved to the Russian Plains, the cavalry once more came into its own, and the Soviets continued to use cavalry to effect throughout the war.

LOMBARD, Gustav

RANK: SS-Brigadeführer
  und Generalmajor der Waffen-SS
BORN: 10 April 1895
DIED: 17 September 1992 (D)
PARTY NUMBER: 2649630
SS NUMBER: 185023
AWARDS: 1939 Iron Cross Second Class,
  15 December 1940; 1939 Iron Cross
  First Class, 3 September 1941; German
  Cross in Gold, 11 February 1943;
  Knight's Cross of the Iron Cross,
  10 March 1943; General Assault Badge;
  SS Honour Ring; SS Honour Sword.

Born in Klein-Spiegelberg, Brandenburg, Prussia, Lombard was a dedicated equestrian and hunter, which induced him to join the SS Totenkopf Cavalry Unit in Poland in 1940. The 1st and 2nd SS-Cavalry Regiments were eventually used to form the SS-Cavalry Brigade and later, the 8th SS Kavallerie Division *Florian Geyer* (named after a sixteenth-century Franconian knight), which

Lombard was awarded the Knight's Cross of the Iron Cross for his leadership and bravery. With Fegelein (q.v.), he played an important part in the development of cavalry within the Waffen-SS.

Accompanied by the remnants of his last command, the 31st Volunteer Grenadier Division, he went into Soviet captivity at the end of the war and was released on 10 October 1955. He died in Mühldorf, Bavaria, in 1992.

LORENZ ,Werner

RANK: SS-Obergruppenführer
BORN: 2 October 1891
DIED: 13 May 1974 (D)
PARTY NUMBER: 397994
SS NUMBER: 6636
AWARDS: SS Honour Ring; SS Honour Sword.

Born in Grünhof, Lorenz saw service in World War I as a pilot. He owned an estate in Danzig and became a zealous early party member, joining the SS in 1931. He headed the VOMI, the office charged with responsibility for the welfare of German nationals residing in other countries. From 1933 until the war's end he

was the driving force in Himmler's (q.v.) ambitions to absorb racial Germans into the Reich, thus being able to control and use the extra manpower this afforded in the occupied territories.

The stewardship he exercised over his office never resorted to brutality, but epitomised skill and dexterity. Lorenz was captured at Flensburg on 10 May 1945, brought to trial and sentenced on 10 March 1948 to 20 years' imprisonment, although he was released in 1955.

LORITZ, Hans

RANK: SS-Oberführer
BORN: 21 December 1895—
PARTY NUMBER: 298668
SS NUMBER: 4165
AWARDS: 1914 Iron Cross Second Class, Cross of Honour 1914-1918 Combatants, 1914 Wound Badge Silver Class, War Merit Cross Second Class with Swords, War Merit Cross First Class with Swords, SS Honour Ring, SS Honour Sword.

Loritz served in World War I and afterwards joined the SS, becoming one of its early members. He was one of Dachau's most sadistic commanders and was responsible, with the connivance of the politische Abteilung, for introducing one of the most appalling tortures known in Dachau, the Baum or Pfahl experience.

Twice a week, selected prisoners had their hands tied behind their backs, forced on to a stool and were then hung to hooks on a post by their wrists. The stool was kicked away and the victim remained suspended with his feet clear of the ground for up to two hours. The pain was excruciating. An added refinement was to make the body swing and flog it. The sudden drop caused broken joints, and even when there were no permanent effects, a victim could not use his arms for weeks afterwards. Unfortunately he escaped justice at the end of the war.

Right: Horsemen of the 8th SS Kavallerie Division Florian Geyer *on anti-partisan duties in Russia, 1942. The division had three cavalry regiments.*

MACHER, Heinz

RANK: SS-Sturmbannführer
BORN: 31 December 1919—
PARTY NUMBER: —
SS NUMBER: —
AWARDS: 1939 Iron Cross Second Class,
24 September 1941; 1939 Iron Cross
First Class, 15 March 1942; German
Cross in Gold, 7 August 1944; Knight's
Cross of the Iron Cross, 3 April 1943;
Oakleaves, 19 August 1944; Close
Combat Clasp Gold Class, 23 October
1944; Tank Destruction Strip Silver
Class; Medal for the Winter Campaign
in Russia 1941-1942; 1939 Wound
Badge Gold Class, July 1943.

Born in Chemnitz, Saxony, Macher served in the RAD before joining the Waffen-SS as a pioneer on 3 April 1939. He was posted to the Second Company of the SS-Pioneer Battalion at Dresden, and his unit was engaged in the Polish campaign. Macher's outstanding leadership qualities led to his selection for the SS-Junkerschule at Bad-Tölz from October 1939 to August 1940. On completion of the course, he was transferred to the SS-Junkerschule at Brünswick. In March 1941 he remustered with his old unit, now the pioneer battalion of the 2nd SS Panzer Division *Das Reich*.

Macher led his platoon on the Russian Front and was wounded during Operation 'Barbarossa'. He discharged himself from hospital and continued in various capacities. During the night of the 11/12 March 1943, Macher formed an assault group from his company and undertook a daring attack against Soviet positions on the outskirts of Kharkov. After infiltrating the Soviet lines the detachment took the Russian defenders completely by surprise. In fierce hand-to-hand fighting, Macher secured a substantial bridgehead within the Soviet positions, killing 90 or more of the Russian defenders and capturing 28, as well as substantial amounts of small arms, mortars and anti-tank weapons. Accomplished without loss of life, the bridgehead facilitated the German armoured units' drive deep into the Soviets' rear areas. Macher was awarded the Knight's Cross of the Iron Cross.

Macher's unit was transferred to France for a refit in March 1944, and after the Normandy landings it was positioned near St Lo. Here it suffered continual aerial bombardment and sustained ground attacks, repulsing 38 different assaults and engaging in equal numbers of counterattacks. Macher became the 554th recipient of the Oakleaves. He was critically wounded and evacuated through the rapidly closing Falaise Gap.

In January 1945 he was assigned as a staff officer at Army Group *Weichs*, then transferred to Pommerania and assigned to the Second Division under General Bleckwendt. Due to the severity of his wounds, he was transferred to WASAG, a company involved in the production of explosives, and was engaged in research on grenades and anti-tank mines. Macher was summoned to Himmler's (q.v.) headquarters on 30 March 1945 and was entrusted with the task of destroying Wewelsburg Castle, Himmler's SS shrine. Macher remained as part of Himmler's headquarters staff. The final and most bizarre escapade came when, in the company of SS-Obersturmbannführer Grothmann (q.v.), he accompanied Himmler in his attempt to escape disguised as an army sergeant. He and his comrades were captured.

MARTIN, Dr Benno

RANK: SS-Obergruppenführer
BORN: 12 February 1893
DIED: 2 July 1975 (D)
PARTY NUMBER: 2714474
SS NUMBER: 187117
AWARDS: 1914 Iron Cross Second Class;
1914 Iron Cross First Class; Cross of
Honour 1914-1918 Combatants; 1914
Wound Badge Silver Class; War Merit
Cross Second Class with Swords; War
Merit Cross First Class with Swords;
SS Honour Ring; SS Honour Sword.

Having studied law at Munich university, Martin passed his assessor's examination in 1922 and went on to join the Nuremberg police in 1923. He became a member of the NSDAP in the summer of 1933, and joined the SS the following year. From 1934 to 1942, he was police president of Nuremberg, taking over the duties of Higher SS and Police Leader for the 13th service command at Nuremberg. He also supervised all police forces in Bavaria. At the end of the war he was arrested by US forces, tried and sentenced to three years' imprisonment. In his defence it should be said that he saved Bamberg Cathedral from destruction, and for this act the Pope intervened several times on his behalf.

MARTINSEN, Knud Borge

RANK: Legions-Obersturmbannführer
BORN: unknown
DIED: 25 June 1949 (E.A.)
PARTY NUMBER: —
SS NUMBER: —
AWARDS: 1939 Iron Cross Second Class;
1939 Iron Cross First Class.

When the commander of the Freikorps *Danmark*, von Schalburg (q.v.), was wounded in the leg during an attack on 2 June 1942, and then killed by an artillery salvo, Martinsen, his second-in-command, took over and ordered a withdrawal. The assault company pulled back leaving the bodies of von Schalburg and

24 comrades buried beside the road near Biakovo. On 10 June 1942 Martinsen was replaced as commander by SS-Obersturmbannführer Hans-Albert von Lettow-Vorbeck, an appointment bitterly resented by the Danes, as they believed it broke the agreement that the Freikorps was essentially a Danish unit with Danish officers. What was more, Martinsen had proved himself to be more than a capable commander in the short time he had been in command. Lettow-Vorbeck only commanded the unit for nine days, however, when he was killed in action on 11 June 1942.

Martinsen took over once again and succeeded in extricating the Freikorps from a dangerous situation imposed by a surprise Soviet attack on Bolshoi Dubovitsky. Following this, Martinsen was promoted and confirmed as the Freikorps' commander. Having suffered 121 killed, the Freikorps was given home leave in September for four weeks. It returned to the front in October 1942 and was finally withdrawn in April 1943, being officially disbanded the following month.

On his return home, Martinsen set up, with German

connivance, a Danish branch of the Germanic SS. It was formed in April 1943 and Martinsen called it *Germansk* Korps, which he quickly renamed *Schalburg* Korps, in memory of the Freikorps' most popular commander. The corps opened its ranks to 'all young men of Nordic blood' without, theoretically, regard to their political affiliation. After the general strike in Denmark in June and July 1944, the corps was withdrawn from Copenhagen and moved outside the city to Ringstad and absorbed into the SS. In October 1944, ostensibly for criticising the Germans, Martinsen was relieved of his command.

After the war he was sentenced to death. The death penalty had been abolished in 1895 in Denmark, but was restored on 1 June 1945 for extreme cases of collaboration or crimes against humanity. Martinsen was executed on 25 June 1949.

MAURICE, Emil

RANK: SS-Oberführer
BORN: 19 January 1897
DIED: 6 February 1972 (D)
PARTY NUMBER: 39
SS NUMBER: 2
AWARDS: Golden Party Badge; Coburg Badge, 14 October 1932; Blood Order No 495; War Merit Cross Second Class without Swords; SS Honour Ring; SS Honour Sword.

A watchmaker by trade, Maurice was born in Westmoor. In 1919 he joined the German Workers' Party, the forerunner of the NSDAP, becoming Hitler's bodyguard and chauffeur. He took part in the

1923 Putsch and joined the fugitives on its failure, but was captured and imprisoned in Landsberg. He become an intimate of Hitler and acted as secretary, noting down *Mein Kampf* until Hess took over.

Following his release, he remained in Hitler's inner circle, continuing in his previ-

ous role. Tension broke out between them in 1927 because of Maurice's unwanted liaison with Hitler's niece, Geli Raubal. This ultimately ousted him from the inner circle. Nevertheless, in June 1934 Maurice was with Hitler when he raided Röhm and his associates, shooting the homosexual Edmund Heinz and the boy found in his bed. He is also credited with the murder of Father Stempfle.

By 1935 the tension between Hitler and Maurice had begun to subside, due in part to Maurice's application to marry; since he was in the SS, the couple both had to submit proof of Aryan purity. When Himmler announced that 'without question SS-Standartenführer Emil Maurice is, according to his ancestral table, not of Aryan descent', Hitler refused to expel him from either the party or the SS. Himmler was outraged, but promotion followed, with Maurice becoming SS-Brigadeführer. From 1940 to 1942 he served as an officer in the Luftwaffe. He also headed a Munich handicraft works guild. In 1948 a de-Nazification court sentenced him to four years in a labour camp. He died in Munich on 6 February 1972.

MEIERDREES, Erwin-Hubert

RANK: SS-Sturmbannführer
BORN: 11 December 1916
DIED: 4 January 1945 (K.I.A.)
PARTY NUMBER: 3601911
SS NUMBER: 265243
AWARDS: 1939 Iron Cross Second Class, 15 November 1939; 1939 Iron Cross First Class, 15 January 1942; Knight's Cross of the Iron Cross, 13 March 1942; Oakleaves, 5 October 1943; 1939 Wound Badge Gold Class; Demjansk Shield; SS Honour Ring; SS Honour Sword.

Meierdrees joined the *Totenkopf* Division and became the commanding officer of the 3rd SS-Assault Gun Battery. His first real military success came in the Demjansk area of Bjakow, where a Soviet strongpoint was holding up the German advance. With a small force of 120 men, Meierdrees took the position for the loss of only one dead and seven wounded. The Soviets mounted a

heavy counterattack in which he was severely wounded, but his command repulsed the attack and was able to secure the position. Awarded the Knight's Cross of the Iron Cross, Meierdrees was wounded a further five times in fierce fighting. His exemplary leadership and bravery, especially in close combat, earned him the Oakleaves, becoming the 310th recipient. He was killed in action in the area of Dunaalans, Hungary, on 4 January 1945 while commanding the First Battalion, 3rd SS-Panzer Regiment. After the war his body was exhumed and re-buried in Vienna, Austria, in 1947.

MEISSNER Otto
BORN: 1880
DIED: 27 May 1953 (D)

State Secretary and chief of the President's Chancellery from 1920 to 1933 under President Hindenburg, Meissner retained this position when Hitler assumed power and held it until 1945. In 1937 he was elevated to the higher position of Reichsminister.

Meissner was a functionary with little real power, but on the occasion of Heydrich's (q.v.) state funeral, Hitler told President Hacha and his Czech delegation that if he had any more trouble, he would deport the entire population. Thereupon, Meissner, who never had anything to do but arrange the seating at the dinner, took Dr Hacha for a walk in the garden and told him Hitler meant it. The result was a mass rally in Prague declaring the loyalty of the Czech nation. Hitler was deeply impressed. Meissner was arrested and tried at Nuremberg for war crimes on 11 April 1949 but was acquitted. He died in Munich in 1953.

MEYER, Kurt
RANK: SS-Brigadeführer und Generalmajor der Waffen-SS
BORN: 23 December 1910
DIED: 23 December 1960 (D)
PARTY NUMBER: 316714
SS NUMBER: 17559
AWARDS: 1939 Iron Cross Second Class, 20 September 1939; 1939 Iron Cross First Class, 8 June 1940; German Cross in Gold, 8 February 1942; Knight's Cross, 18 May 1941; Oakleaves, 23 May 1943; Oakleaves with Swords, 27 August 1944; Wound Badge Black Class; SS Honour Ring; SS Honour Sword; (Bulgaria: Military Order for Bravery).

One of the youngest generals in the Waffen-SS, Meyer was born in Jerxheim and originally served with the Mecklenburg Police, joining the *Leibstandarte* in Berlin in 1934. He saw service during the campaigns in Poland and France.

The LSSAH marched through Yugoslavia on its way to Greece in early 1941, where his impressive leadership was largely responsible for the defeat of Greek resistance near Lake Castoria. Always at the front of his reconnaissance unit and later his division, Meyer's daring actions earned him the nicknames 'Panzermeyer' and 'Schnell Meyer' during the early days of the war. He won the Knight's Cross of the Iron Cross, continually demonstrating the type of courage and leadership that is commensurate with getting the mission done.

Meyer was in charge of the Reconnaissance Detachment during the Russian campaign, and led his men to Uman, Cherson, Perikop, Taganrog and Rostov on the Don river. In recognition of his achievements, he became the 195th recipient of the Oakleaves.

In 1943 'Panzermeyer', as he was now known, left the *Leibstandarte*, taking command of his own regiment in the 12th SS-Panzer Division Hitlerjugend. When the commander, SS-Brigadeführer Fritz Witt (q.v.), was killed in action on 16 June 1944 by Allied naval gunfire, Meyer assumed command of the division, and led it aggressively in an unsuccessful effort to counter the advancing Allied invasion. His leadership and bravery in France, however, earned him the Oakleaves and Swords, of which he was the 91st recipient.

By now a major-general in the Waffen-SS, he was severely wounded on 6 September and captured at Amiens on 17 November 1944, falling into the hands of Belgian partisans. He would have preferred to have been killed on the spot, but the Americans intervened, dressing him in uniform of an army oberst and turning him over to the British. After he had made a limited recovery he was transferred to England.

After the war he was brought before a Canadian military court at Aurich, tried for war crimes (the murder of Canadian prisoners in Normandy by troops under his command) and convicted with a sentence of execution by firing squad. However, this sentence was commuted to life imprisonment and he was taken to Canada. Several years later he was transferred to West Germany, and finally released on 6 September 1954 after a number of appeals. As a result of his war wounds and his tireless personal engagements on behalf of his former comrades, his health deteriorated. While celebrating his 50th birthday he suffered a fatal heart attack, from which he died on 23 December 1960 in Hagen, Westphalia.

MEYER, Otto
RANK: SS-Obersturmbannführer
BORN: 23 December 1912
DIED: 28 August 1944 (K.I.A.)
PARTY NUMBER: —
SS NUMBER: —
AWARDS: 1939 Iron Cross Second Class, 29 May 1940; 1939 Iron Cross First Class, 8 August 1940; German Cross in Gold, 14 January 1942; Knight's Cross of the Iron Cross, 4 June 1944; Oakleaves, 30 September 1944.

Otto Meyer was born in Moldenit, Schleswig. He saw service in the French campaign of 1940 and went east with Operation 'Barbarossa'.

Meyer was the commanding officer of the 9th SS-Panzer Regiment, 9th SS Panzer Division *Hohenstaufen*, II SS Panzer Corps, in 1944. This was a grave period for the German forces in the East, and in March the situation was nearing disaster with the German First Armoured Army encircled by the Soviets at Tarnopol. By the middle of the month, the Russians were at the Polish border and Hitler ordered four of his panzer divisions to the Eastern Front: the Waffen-SS divisions *Hohenstaufen* and *Frundsberg* made up II SS Panzer Corps, plus the Army's Panzer Lehr Division and the 349th Division. *Hohenstaufen* moved eastwards to Poland, then from Lvov, farther east to Tarnopol. The Germans launched a counterattack, but were hindered by the mud of the spring thaw; the tanks were bogged down and the unit sustained serious losses.

On 5 April the 4th Armoured Army, which included *Hohenstaufen*, attacked the Russians in force. In a violent offensive, *Hohenstaufen* penetrated the front held by the First Soviet Tank Army. On the 9th, the division's forward tanks met up with the beleaguered German First Panzer Army, which was finally freed. Otto Meyer distinguished himself in this action and he was rewarded with the Knight's Cross of the Iron Cross.

With the Allied landings in Normandy on 6 June 1944, the division was withdrawn to France where Meyer and his men fought near Caen, Avranches and Vire; he also stopped the British tank attack at Caumont. His tank regiment was one of the most successful on the Western Front, destroying more than 300 Allied tanks in a fierce campaign. Meyer was killed in action near Dualair in France and was posthumously awarded the Oakleaves, becoming the 601st recipient.

MODER, Paul

RANK: SS-Gruppenführer
BORN: 1 October 1896
DIED: 8 February 1942 (K.I.A.)
PARTY NUMBER: 9425
SS NUMBER: 11716

Moder was SS and police commander in Warsaw from October 1939 to June 1940. He then served as a staff officer with SS-Oberabschnitt Ost until 19 July 1941. Awaiting Himmler's (q.v.) decision on a new police assignment for him in the East, he joined the *Totenkopf* Division. With a combat rank of SS-Sturmbannführer, Moder was attached to the motorcycle battalion in Russia. At his own request he was given an extension of his stay, and in the autumn of 1941 became involved in the extremely bitter fighting south of Lake Ilmen. At the height of the Soviet winter counteroffensive in the Demjansk sector, he was killed in action on 8 February 1942.

MOHNKE, Wilhelm

RANK: SS-Oberführer
BORN: 15 March 1911—
PARTY NUMBER: 649684
SS NUMBER: 15541
AWARDS: 1939 Iron Cross, 21 September 1939; 1939 Iron Cross First Class, 8 November 1939; German Cross in Gold, 26 December 1941; Knight's Cross of the Iron Cross, 11 July 1944; SS Honour Ring; SS Honour Sword.

Born in Lübeck, Mohnke was a fervent Nazi, an original member of the *Leibstandarte* who commanded Hitler's bodyguard during the 1930s.

Mohnke fought in France in 1940 and is notorious for shooting prisoners of war. On 28 May 1940 his commanding officer, 'Sepp' Dietrich, (q.v) ordered him to attack and secure the village of Wormhoudt, which lay between Kassel and Dunkirk. It was held by men of the British 48th Division with troops from the Second Royal Warwicks and machine gunners of the 4th Cheshire Regiment. Resistance was determined, and when eventually the *Leibstandarte* secured the village they had to repulse fierce counterattacks. The *Leibstandarte* lost 23 men killed and many more were wounded, including SS-Sturmbannführer Schutzeck, the second battalion commander.

Many prisoners were taken and some appear to have been reasonably treated. One group of between 80 and 90 Royal Warwicks, Cheshires and a few artillery men were seen late in the afternoon by the new commander of the second battalion, Mohnke. He was in an angry mood. Completely losing his temper, he accused the NCO in charge of the escort of disobeying orders by taking prisoners instead of shooting them. Mohnke ordered them to be escorted by a detail from the No 7 Company to a nearby barn and killed. He ordered a detachment of No 8 Company to carry out the execution. First, a salvo of grenades was thrown into the small, crowded barn. This was followed by small-arms fire. The survivors were ordered out in groups of five, and the first two were immediately executed, although one badly wounded private feigned death and later managed to crawl into the barn and lie among the dead.

Only 15 men survived the massacre (although one was to die shortly afterwards), and when four of the survivors were repatriated in 1943, they reported the atrocity to the British authorities.

In 1941 Mohnke served with the *Leibstandarte* in the Balkans and was badly wounded in the foot by a Yugoslav air strike on the opening day of the campaign. Later, he rejoined the *Leibstandarte* in Russia, but in mid-1943 was transferred to the newly formed 12th SS Panzer Division *Hitlerjugend* and was given command of the 26th SS-Panzergrenadier Regiment. In June 1944, Mohnke's regiment was on the Normandy invasion front, where it was locked in battle with elements of the Canadian 3rd Infantry Division. Three Canadian soldiers, riflemen A. R. Owens of the Royal Winnipeg Rifles, Sapper Jionel and G. A. Benner of the Royal Canadian Engineers, were captured and escorted to the HQ of the 26th SS-Panzergrenadier Regiment. Mohnke interrogated them for 20 minutes. After its conclusion two Feldgendarmerie marched the prisoners to a nearby bomb crater and shot them, while Mohnke watched impassively. Mohnke was also implicated in four other separate similar incidents, involving another nine Canadian prisoners.

Mohnke assumed command of the *Leibstandarte* after its commander, Theodor Wisch (q.v), had been badly wounded. He led it in the Ardennes counteroffensive of December 1944 and he was implicated in the Malmédy Massacre as the commanding officer who transmitted orders to 'take no prisoners'. After the failure in the Ardennes, 6th SS Panzer Army was withdrawn for refitting and sent to Hungary. Mohnke was transferred to Berlin as Commandant of the Reich Chancellery. He was in the Führer bunker when Hitler committed suicide and an eyewitness reported that he wept openly. It was Mohnke who set fire to the bunker on the following day, 1 May, and he joined one of the escape groups that night. He was captured by the Russians while hiding in a cellar in the Schönhauser Allee. In October 1955 he was one of the first Germans to be released from Soviet captivity. Mohnke now lives quietly on the outskirts of Hamburg.

MOOYMAN, Gerardus

RANK: SS-Untersturmführer
BORN: 23 September 1923
DIED: 21 June 1987 (D)
PARTY NUMBER: —
SS NUMBER: —
AWARDS: 1939 Iron Cross Second Class, 4 February 1943; 1939 Iron Cross First Class, 10 February 1943; Knight's Cross of the Iron Cross, 20 February 1943; Medal for the Winter Campaign in Russia 1941-1942.

Mooyman was born in Apeldoorn in Holland and was one of the first 'Germanic' volunteers in the Waffen-SS, joining the SS-Volunteer Legion *Nederland* as a gunner in the 14th anti-tank company. During the fierce fighting on the northeastern front in February 1943, he destroyed more than 15 Russian tanks south of Lake Ladoga with his anti-tank gun.

He became the first Germanic volunteer to be awarded the Knight's Cross

He became the first Germanic volunteer to be awarded the Knight's Cross, on 20 February 1943, and General Major Fritz von Scholz (q.v) decorated him personally on 17 March 1943. Subsequently, he was paraded for propaganda purposes, first in Berlin, where he met Dutch journalists on 23 March, and notably by being welcomed in April in Holland by SS-Gruppenführer Reuter and Seyss-Inquart (q.v). He made further photo calls in Belgium.

After the war he was sentenced to six years' imprisonment for his involvement in the Waffen-SS, but was released after only two years. He was involved in a road accident and died from his injuries in 1987.

MORGEN, Konrad

RANK: SS-Obersturmbannführer
BORN: 1909
PARTY NUMBER: —
SS NUMBER: —

An assistant SS judge, Morgen's function was to investigate irregularities in the administration of the concentration camps. His brief, astonishingly, was to ensure that no brutality took place. Considering the transportations to Auschwitz and Treblinka, the gassing and cremations, it depicts an extraordinary ambivalence in SS attitudes towards its purpose as exterminator.

Morgen was also instructed to investigate theft by guards or SS officers. In both functions he acted scrupulously. In camp after camp he obtained sentences against SS personnel for brutality. In 1943 he discovered the camp commandant of Buchenwald, Karl Koch (q.v), had concealed murders, falsified documents and embezzled over 100,000 Marks. Morgen presented his report to SS headquarters, where it was directed to Kaltenbrunner (q.v) who passed it to the legal department, both authorities preferring not to handle it. Himmler (q.v) acted on it, and Koch was found guilty and executed. Belzec, Majdanek, Sobibor and Treblinka extermination camps built by Wirth (q.v) were subsequently inspected and Morgen found not less than 800 cases of corruption and murder. After the war he was a Nuremberg witness and then he disappeared into obscurity.

MRUGOWSKY, Prof Dr Joachim
RANK: SS-Oberführer
BORN: 15 August 1905
DIED: 2 June 1948 (E.A.)
PARTY NUMBER: 210049
SS NUMBER: 25811
AWARDS: 1939 Iron Cross Second Class; War Merit Cross Second Class with Swords; War Merit Cross First Class with Swords; SS Honour Ring; SS Honour Sword.

A professor of bacteriology, Mrugowsky joined the SS in 1931 and became head of the SS health department Hygiene Institute in Berlin in 1939, a post he held until the end of the war. He believed in the doctor's function as 'the priest of the holy flame of life' and wrote of the 'art of healing' as the doctor's 'divine mission'.

In March 1942, Himmler (q.v) was greatly impressed with Zyklon B because it offered no possibility of a mechanical breakdown and in August commissioned Mrugowsky to send a demonstrator to Wirth, (q.v) the commander in Poland. From then on the distribution of Zyklon B within the SS became centrally regulated by the SS Hygiene Institute in Berlin. Mrugowsky also ordered experimentation with phenol in Buchenwald after it had been noted that tiny percentages of carbolic acid preservative in serum had contributed to the accidental death of several German soldiers. He also observed the effect of poison bullets on inmates.

Tried in the doctors' trials, Mrugowsky was found guilty of extensive involvement in fatal medical experiments. He was hanged at Landsberg Prison on 2 June 1948.

MÜHLENKAMP, Johannes Rudolf
RANK: SS-Standartenführer
BORN: 9 October 1910
DIED: 23 September 1986 (D)
PARTY NUMBER: 2800042
SS NUMBER: 86065
AWARDS: 1939 Iron Cross Second Class, 3 October 1939; 1939 Iron Cross First Class, 11 November 1939; German Cross in Gold, 2 January 1942; Knight's Cross of the Iron Cross, 3 September 1942; Oakleaves, 21 September 1944; 1939 Wound Badge Silver Class; Silver Tank Battle Badge; SS Honour Ring; SS Honour Sword.

Mühlenkamp commanded the first tank detachment of the Waffen-SS. He joined the SS-Verfügungstruppe in 1934 and attended the officers' training school. Subsequently attached to the SS-Standarte *Germania*, he commanded the 15th (Motorcycle) Company, which he led in the Polish campaign. He served as an adjutant to

Paul Hausser (q.v) and was subsequently given command of the reconnaissance detachment of the SS-Verfügungsdivision, seeing action in Yugoslavia, followed by a few months in Russia.

Mühlenkamp attended courses with army panzer troops to gain experience for the formation of the first tank detachment of the Waffen-SS. This new unit was finally assigned to the *Wiking* Division and played a large part in the division's successes in Russia. He continued to lead it with outstanding success after it had reached regimental strength and was awarded the Knight's Cross of the Iron Cross. He took over command of the division on 8 August 1944 until 9 October 1944, after Gille (q.v) had formed an SS panzer corps, and was awarded the Oakleaves, becoming the 596th recipient. Mühlenkamp's last command was inspector general of Waffen-SS panzer troops. He died in Goslar in late 1986.

MÜLLER, Heinrich
RANK: SS-Gruppenführer
    und Generalleutnant der Polizei
BORN: 28 April 1900
DIED: May 1945 (M.I.A.)
PARTY NUMBER: 4583199
SS NUMBER: 107043
AWARDS: 1914 Iron Cross Second Class;
    1914 Iron Cross First Class; Cross of
    Honour 1914-1918 Combatants;
    1939 Iron Cross Second Class Bar,
    29 October 1940; 1939 Iron Cross First
    Class Bar, 29 October 1940; War Merit
    Cross Second Class with Swords; War
    Merit Cross First Class with Swords;
    Knight's Cross to the War Merit Cross
    with Swords, 5 October 1944;
    SS Honour Ring; SS Honour Sword.

Born in Munich, Müller served as an NCO and pilot in the Fliegerabteilung 287A on the Western Front in World War I. From 1919 to 1934, he served in the Bavarian Police as an official of the Munich political police, employed as an expert on politics and the surveillance of communists. In 1931, when Hitler's niece,

Geli Raubal, was shot, Bormann (q.v), using the 'Adolf Hitler Fund', allegedly paid Müller, the investigating police inspector, to ensure that no whiff of scandal tainted Hitler. Müller proved himself reliable, and Bormann recruited him to the party. Heydrich (q.v) selected him to take over the Gestapo from Diels (q.v), who was Göring's man.

As head of the SS-RSHA Amt IV, the bureaucratic office that was Gestapo headquarters, 'Gestapo' Müller directed the department run by Eichmann (q.v), and his position remained unchanged for the remainder of the war. The promotions and changes that followed Heydrich's assassination in 1942 did not affect him and he continued to serve under Kaltenbrunner (q.v). He headed the investigation committee that sought out the 20th July conspirators and was awarded the Knight's Cross of the War Merit Cross with Swords for its success. He shunned publicity and is believed to have planned an escape well in advance of the inevitable defeat. He was last seen in Berlin in the closing weeks of the war, but then vanished. The mystery of his disappearance remains, but it has been reported in a recent publication that he was recruited into the CIA and thus made his way to America.

NAUJOCKS, Alfred

RANK: SS-Sturmbannführer
BORN: 20 September 1911
DIED: 4 April 1960 (D)
PARTY NUMBER: 26240
SS NUMBER: 624279

An engineering student at Kiel University, Naujocks spent more time brawling than studying. He joined the SS in 1931, and became an official of the Amt VI of the SS security service in 1934 and was one of the most audacious commanders of the SD. He was not an intelligent leader and lacked the mental capacity for creating intricate plans such as those conceived by Heydrich (q.v). However, he was expert at carrying out an operation once it was explained clearly to him.

A trusted associate of Heydrich, Naujocks was involved in a number of shady but important operations. He helped Heydrich with the Tukhachedsky affair and staged some bombings in Slovakia, which were blamed on Slovak nationalists. Heydrich chose him to lead the simulated attack on the Gleiwitz radio stations in Poland on 10 August 1939, which provided Germany with justification for invasion. He was also involved in the Venlo incident, abducting two British intelligence officers, Captain S. Payne-Best and Major R. H. Stephens, in the Netherlands in order to accuse them of involvement in the 1939 Munich bomb plot. The Venlo incident provided the excuse for invading the Low Countries.

Alfred Naujocks was described as an 'intellectual gangster'

Naujocks worked on Operation 'Bernhard', the operation of faking British bank notes by inmates of the Sachsenhausen concentration camp. The escapade gives a prime example of the bizarre nature of the Third Reich's leaders. The Nazi authorities were so pleased with the results that 12 prisoners, three of whom were Jews, were awarded the War Merit Medal, and six of the SS guards the War Merit Cross Second Class without Swords. One wonders what the Jewish medal winners thought of their awards.

Dismissed by the SD for disobedience, Naujocks joined the Waffen SS in 1943 and was responsible for the murder of members of the Danish Resistance. In November 1944 he deserted to the Americans and at the war's end he escaped from a US internment camp, suspected of organising the ODESSA operation that provided ex-SS members with an escape route. He died in 1960 in Germany. Naujocks has been described as being an 'intellectual gangster'. He was certainly one of Heydrich's most ruthless assassination squad leaders. During the attack on the Gleiwitz radio station, for example, he had no qualms about shooting a dozen concentration camp inmates in Polish uniforms and leaving their bodies scattered around the site. He was very fortunate to have escaped a death sentence in 1945.

NEBE, Artur

RANK: SS-Gruppenführer
BORN: 13 November 1894
DIED: 3 March 1945 (unverified)
PARTY NUMBER: 280152
SS NUMBER: 574307
AWARDS: 1914 Iron Cross Second Class;
   1914 Iron Cross First Class; Cross
   of Honour 1914-1918 Combatants;
   1939 Iron Cross Second Class Bar; War
   Merit Cross Second Class with Swords;
   Police Long Service Cross, 18 Years;
   Army Long Service Medal, NSDAP
   Long Service Cross, 10 Years;
   Commemorative Medal of 13 March
   1938; Commemorative Medal of
   1 October 1938; Prague Castle Bar.

The director of Kripo led something of a double life; he was a survivor who obeyed his instincts. In February 1934 he and Gisevius were summoned by 'Sepp' Dietrich (q.v) to Lichterfelde barracks and asked to compile a report for Himmler (q.v) and Heydrich (q.v) stating all known excesses committed by the Gestapo and SA. In typical character during 1933-34, Nebe sided with Himmler against Göring over Gestapo control, and later became a very questionable member of the Resistance Circle before the 20 July Bomb Plot. Principally, he was an old-style police officer who, since 1934, had seen his criminal police department infiltrated by amateur Gestapo officers and finally absorbed by Heydrich in 1939.

Nebe was a mere shadow of himself and on the verge of a nervous breakdown

Nebe's retention of office was due to the five months he spent in Russia heading Einsatzgruppe B, which worked with Army Group Centre in the Soviet Union in the area between the Baltic states and the Ukraine. Nebe's headquarters were at Minsk and later Smolensk where he was in touch with Hans Oster, an old friend and an opponent of Hitler's war aims. Nebe supposedly fought against Heydrich's orders, disclosing them to the Oster circle, who had used him as an information post for four years. This may explain why Heydrich's reports credit Nebe with a quite modest score of 46,000 liquidations compared to Stahlecker's (q.v) 221,000.

The winter of 1941-42 had taken a toll on the Einsatzgruppen leaders, who were feeling the effects of the murders. Nebe was a mere shadow of himself and on the verge of a nervous breakdown. One of his associates had described him as being 'a mere shadow of his former self, nerves on edge and depressed'. Nebe's driver, a man called Köhn, had shot himself in horror at the actions being taken against the Jews, which must have depressed and shaken Nebe even further.

Himmler travelled to Minsk to encourage his executioners, asking to witness a liquidation, and obligingly supplying 100 partisans from the city jail, all but two being men. According to one account, Himmler ordered Nebe to seduce the two women before shooting them, thinking it a useful way of obtaining information regarding partisan activities. Himmler became hysterical and nearly collapsed on witnessing the shootings (he was splattered with victims' brains) and ordered Nebe to develop a method of killing less distressing to the executioners! Nebe readily agreed, for the psychological effect on those who had to carry out the executions was very great.

Nebe began experimenting with killing people, using exhaust gases from his car, an eight-cylinder Horch. A keen amateur film maker, he enthusiastically filmed his work. After the war footage showing a gas chamber, worked by the exhaust of a lorry, was found in his Berlin flat.

On the dismissal of Diels (q.v), Himmler rearranged the police organisations. Nebe controlled the Kripo, the frontier police and counter-espionage police. His brinkmanship foundered with the 1944 Bomb Plot. He supported the plotters and with the failure of the early stages of the revolt, Nebe played the tireless policeman rooting out the guilty. The arrest of his colleague Helldorf brought the Gestapo too close for comfort. Nebe had not even been suspected at the time of his colleague's arrest and he might not have been pulled in at all had he not chosen to hide.

'Nebe had maintained close relations with people involved in the Putsch'

On 23 August 1944, SS-Standartenführer Werner of the RSHA issued a description and offered a reward of 50,000 Reichsmarks for Nebe. Himmler expelled Nebe from the SS on 30 November, adding, 'It has been proved by documents found and investigations carried out by the state police, that for years Nebe had maintained close relations with people directly involved in the Putsch of 20 July. His betrayal had been to support the Putschists, breaking his allegiance to the Führer.' The latter was certainly true, for as early as 1941, when he was involved in Einsatzgruppe activities, he had secretly urged the murder of Hitler as the only way of ending the Nazi regime. However, he was appalled by the poor security measures taken by his fellow conspirators. He himself was always careful to cover his tracks and avoid any danger.

Nebe was arrested on 16 January 1945, evidently betrayed by a girlfriend, and sentenced by the People's Court to death. There is no official mention of a Volksgericht trial, however, and Nebe is not on Pechel's list of Plötzensee executions. The author Gregory Douglas suggests in his book that Müller became a CIA agent. Could Nebe have followed the same route?

NEUMANN, Eggert
RANK: SS-Sturmbannführer
BORN: 30 December 1912
DIED: 28 May 1970 (D)
PARTY NUMBER: 1162622
SS NUMBER: 45654
AWARDS: 1939 Iron Cross Second Class; 1939 Iron Cross First Class; Knight's Cross of the Iron Cross; SS Honour Ring.

Neumann was the commander of SS Gebirge Aufklärungsabteilung 7 of the 7th SS Freiwilligen-Gebirgs Division *Prinz Eugen*, where he distinguished himself through his personal courage and initiative. For this he was awarded the Knight's Cross of the Iron Cross. employed in actions against Tito's partisans in Yugoslavia, in October 1944, the division was transferred to Belgrade to cover the flank of the German retreat through Yugoslavia after the Romanian and Bulgarian defections to the Allies. Here, the division suffered appalling losses at the hands of the Soviet forces. Reconstructed and redeployed against the partisans, the division was held responsible for some of the worst atrocities carried out in the war, although the partisan fighting was particularly brutal. In one incident, an NCO had placed some young recruits in a house and paid the lady of the house for their keep. After half an hour he returned to find the young soldiers being emasculated by a group of women. He felt he had little option but to throw two grenades into the house, to save his recruits further agony and to punish the women.

When the division surrendered to Soviet forces it numbered only a few hundred

When the division surrendered to the Soviet forces in May 1945 it numbered only a few hundred troops, who were brutally treated by their captors. The division, which had contained Serbs, Romanians and Hungarians, had always been viewed as a unit for anti-partisan duties. As such, it had never been allocated first-rate weapons and equipment to fight with. Neumann died in Hamburg in 1970.

OBERG, Carl-Albrecht
RANK: SS-Obergruppenführer
BORN: 27 January 1897
DIED: 3 June 1965
PARTY NUMBER: 575205
SS NUMBER: 36075
AWARDS: 1914 Iron Cross Second Class;
  1914 Iron Cross First Class; Cross
  of Honour 1914-1918 Combatants;
  War Merit Cross Second Class with
  Swords; War Merit Cross First Class
  with Swords; SS Honour Ring; SS
  Honour Sword.

Oberg, along with millions of others, had been thrown on the streets in the Depression, where he had been an executive with a firm of banana importers. His motive in joining the SS had been partly monetary: it had meant an end to financial problems. Oberg trailed Heydrich (q.v.) to Munich within months of the Nazis coming to power, feeling that he held the key to his future. His rate of promotion in the intervening nine years was impressive: on 1 July 1933 he was a mere SS-Untersturmführer, but by September 1941 he was SD and Polizeiführer at Radom in Poland, where he had been most assiduous in his pursuit of Jews.

Escorted by Heydrich, Oberg departed for Paris on 7 May 1942 to reorganise the regional branches of the SS and Gestapo in France in an attempt to quash the French Resistance. The SD took over surveillance of the French police, and the head office of the German police service in Paris was modelled on RSHA in Berlin, with regional offices established throughout occupied France. The actual Gestapo was controlled by Sonderkommando

---

Left: A gilded SS eagle bearing the Waffen-SS's motto,
Meine Ehre Heisst Treue *(Loyalty is My Honour). The*
motto was also inscribed on SS daggers.

IV, later IV B4, engaged in the anti-Jewish campaign and under the control of Theo Dannecker.

Many members of the staff of Heinrich von Stülpnagel, the military governor of France, were part of the 1944 Bomb Plot conspiracy, and Oberg and Helmuth Knochen (q.v), the Paris commander of the security police, were arrested with the entire staff of the Gestapo and the SD, although they only spent three hours in captivity. At 0130 hours in the morning, on the threat of armed intervention, Stülpnagel released his captives and the affair ended with an all-night drinking party in the Hotel Raphael, where ambassador Abtez made Stülpnagel and Oberg shake hands.

Oberg was sentenced by a British court for the execution of captured airmen

On Oberg's suggestion, the troops who had conducted the arrests and who had got the sand ready for the executions in the Ecole Militaire, were thanked at morning parade for carrying out a practical exercise with the higher SS police leader. At the end of the war Oberg went into hiding. As Albrecht Heintze he had a fleeting period of anonymity in Kirchberg, a small Tyrolean village near Kitzbühel. However, his real identity was soon established and in August he was handed over to the French authorities at Wildbad. Oberg was sentenced by a British court in 1946 for the illegal execution of captured airmen in his capacity as SS police commander in France. He was further sentenced to death in Paris in October 1954 and was imprisoned in Cherche-Midi Prison, where he remained until December 1959 when his sentence was commuted to 20 years' forced labour.

OHLENDORF, Otto

RANK: SS-Gruppenführer
BORN: 4 February 1907
DIED: 8 June 1951 (E.A.)
PARTY NUMBER: 6531
SS NUMBER: 880
AWARDS: Golden Party Badge; War Merit Cross Second Class with Swords; War Merit Cross First Class with Swords; SS Honour Ring; SS Honour Sword.

A Hanoverian farmer, who was both a lawyer and an economist, Ohlendorf was an early member of the NSDAP, although he soon discovered that he did not agree with all of its policies.

While a member of the Institute of World Economics in Kiel, he came to the conclusion that the NSDAP had collective socialist tendencies and spoke out against this flaw. The Gestapo arrested him for his continued lecturing and after the Gestapo's investigators had concluded their work, he had no wish to speak out further against party policies. Ohlendorf thought his party career was ended, but a chance introduction to Professor Reinhard Höhn in Berlin, who headed an SD section, led to his appointment as an economic adviser.

Catapulted to the centre of the Nazi Party movement, Ohlendorf assembled a staff of economists from all over Germany and analysed the economic affairs of the Third Reich. He expanded his activities to include reporting on culture, science, education, law, administration, and even the hallowed ground of the party and the state. Initially these reports found little favour with Hitler and Himmler (q.v), who tended to disregard them, but Himmler began to call him 'Nazism's Knight of the Holy Grail'. However, when Ohlendorf overstepped the mark, Himmler explained to him in no uncertain terms that his reports were illegal and unwanted and he was to concentrate on less critical economic accounts in the future. Ohlendorf tended his resignation; Himmler ignored it. Ohlendorf became chief of the inland (internal) SD and acquired a reputation as an administrator who was intelligent and humane.

The Führer's plan for the invasion of Poland was simple: Himmler was to form Einsatzgruppen which were to follow the German troops and liquidate the upper classes. A month after the invasion Heydrich was able to announce: 'Of the Polish upper classes in the occupied territories only a maximum of three per cent is still present.' With the invasion of Russia and the decision to liquidate the Jews, the SS and OKW came to an agreement in April 1941 stating that 'the Einsatzgruppen are authorised, within the framework of their task and on their own responsibility, to take executive measures affecting the civilian population.'

By the winter of 1941-42 his command had murdered 92,000 Jews

Commander of Einsatzgruppe D in the Ukraine, Ohlendorf immediately became an expert on extermination, keeping exact scores of his achievements. By the winter of 1941-42 his command had murdered 92,000 Jews and was still going strong. The other groups were feeling the psychological strain and replacements were made. Ohlendorf, however, became more fanatical.

On 30 April 1945 he travelled to Flensberg, where Himmler had established his HQ, and advised him to surrender to the Allies. Himmler refused. Ohlendorf accompanied Himmler in his escape from Flensberg, until they were apprehended by the British. Ohlendorf learnt of Himmler's suicide, but suicide was furthest from his own thoughts. He was convinced he could justify all his actions and looked forward to the opportunity to do so. He was tried for war crimes and on 10 April 1948 was found guilty and sentenced to death. After all appeals had been heard, he was hanged at Landsberg Prison on 8 June 1951.

OSTENDORFF, Werner

RANK: SS-Gruppenführer
und Generalleutnant der Waffen-SS
BORN: 15 August 1903
DIED: 5 May 1945 (K.I.A.)
PARTY NUMBER: 4691488
SS NUMBER: 257146
AWARDS: 1939 Iron Cross Second Class,
19 May 1940; 1939 Iron Cross First
Class, 23 June 1940; German Cross
in Gold, 5 June 1942; Knight's Cross,
13 September 1941; Oakleaves,
6 May 1945; SS Honour Ring;
SS Honour Sword.

Born in Königsberg in East Prussia, Ostendorff served in the First Infantry Regiment of the Reichswehr stationed at Königsberg. He also became a member of the German flying club, the DLV, which taught young Germans flying skills and became the basis of the Luftwaffe. In 1935 he joined the SS-Verfügungstruppe, being posted to the SS-Junkerschule at Bad Tölz as a tactical instructor.

In September 1939, during the Polish campaign, Ostendorff served as a staff officer with Panzer Group *Kempf* a combined army and SS-Verfügungstruppe force. He became the first staff officer of the SS-Verfügungsdivision in France and first general staff officer to Paul Hausser (q.v.) during the campaign in Yugoslavia and later in the Soviet Union (the SS-Verfügungsdivision was reorganised at the end of 1940 and renamed *Das Reich*). The 2nd SS Division *Das Reich*, which had been attached to Army Group Centre, was particularly effective in conflict and in August 1941 achieved distinction in the battle of Yalnya, east of Smolensk. Ostendorff was awarded the Knight's Cross of the Iron Cross for his outstanding bravery.

During the winter campaign of 1941-42, *Das Reich* took part in the fatally delayed assault on Moscow, an action which depleted the division to 60 per cent of its combat strength by the middle of November 1941. Ostendorff commanded the decimated *Das Reich* which spearheaded the attack on Moscow, penetrating the Moscow defences south of Borodino and coming within a few miles of the Russian capital. In early 1943, during the Battle of Kharkov, he was made first staff officer of I SS Panzer Corps.

In January 1944 he took command of the Panzergrenadier Division *Götz von Berlichingen* and led it in the early stages of the fighting in Normandy. He was badly wounded near Carentan and was relieved of his command on 15 June 1944. The division was badly mauled trying to retake the town.

Ostendorff was posthumously awarded the Oakleaves for his bravery

He became chief of staff of Army Group *Oberheim* on his recovery and then took command on 4 February 1945 of the 2nd SS Panzer Division *Das Reich* in Hungary. The division was now a shadow of its former self, having little equipment, fuel and ammunition. He was wounded near Stuhlweissenburg and died in a military hospital in Bad Aussee in Austria. He was posthumously awarded the Oakleaves for his bravery and leadership in the Hungarian campaign.

PEICHL, Adolf

RANK: SS-Untersturmführer
BORN: 8 December 1917
DIED: 4 June 1969 (D)
PARTY NUMBER: —
SS NUMBER: —
AWARDS: 1939 Iron Cross Second Class,
23 August 1941; 1939 Iron Cross First
Class, 28 October 1941; German Cross
in Gold, 16 September 1943; Knight's
Cross of the Iron Cross, 16 October
1944; Medal for the Winter Campaign
in Russia 1941-1942; two Gold Tank
Destruction Strips; one Silver Tank
Destruction Strip; Infantry Assault
Badge; Close Combat Clasp in Gold,
26 October 1943; 1939 Wound Badge
Gold Class.

An Austrian, Peichl fought on the Eastern Front and gained a reputation for his ability as a 'lone fighter'. He distinguished himself through the destruction of several enemy tanks: by 1943 he had eliminated six and his final score was eleven.

Transferred to France, where in June 1944 the *Das Reich* Division was one of four Waffen-SS divisions in France, Peichl was sent north to the Normandy area shortly after the Allied armies had launched their invasion of Europe. Peichl was platoon leader in the 12th (Armoured) Company, 4th SS-Panzergrenadier Regiment *Der Führer, Das Reich*, and engaged in the fierce fighting in the hedgerows of Normandy.

An exceptionally tough and brave man, Peichl won the Knight's Cross of the Iron Cross, as well as the Close Combat Clasp in Gold, which was regarded by Hitler as the highest infantry decoration short of the Knight's Cross. Hitler reserved the right to bestow the award personally and only 403 were presented during the entire war. The criteria were that the recipient had been wounded in 50 days of hand-to-hand or close combat. Despite his fondness for fighting the enemy at close quarters, Peichl survived the war and died in Vienna in 1969.

PEIPER, Joachim

RANK: SS-Standartenführer
BORN: 30 January 1915
DIED: 14 July 1976 (M)
PARTY NUMBER:
SS NUMBER: 132496
AWARDS: 1939 Iron Cross Second Class,
31 May 1940; 1939 Iron Cross First
Class, 1 July 1940; Knight's Cross of the
Iron Cross, 9 March 1943; Oakleaves,
27 January 1944; Swords, 11 January
1945; Close Combat Clasp Silver Class,
SS Honour Ring; SS Honour Sword.

Peiper was born in Berlin-Wilmersdorf, the son of an army officer. He volunteered for duty with the *Leibstandarte* in October 1934 and attended the SS-Officers' school at Brünswick. He served as Himmler's (q.v.) adjutant from 1938 to 1939, and when war broke out served with the motorised regiment *Leibstandarte* in the Western campaign. He was transferred to the Eastern Front, and while serving as commanding officer of the 3rd Battalion, SS-Panzergrenadier Regiment 2, LSSAH, was awarded the Knight's Cross of the Iron Cross for his bravery in action near Kharkov.

In autumn 1943 Peiper took command of the panzer regiment of the *Leibstandarte*, and as commanding officer of the 1st Regiment was awarded the Oakleaves, becoming the 277th recipient. His command was transferred to the Western Front and during the defensive withdrawal following the Allied invasion in 1944 he was awarded the Swords, becoming the 119th recipient.

During the Ardennes Offensive men of Peiper's unit took a number of American prisoners at a small crossroads in Malmédy, Belgium. The events that surrounded the incident are confused, but 74 Americans were murdered, and after the war the senior commanders were tried at Dachau for war crimes as a result of this massacre. On 16 July 1946, 43 death sentences were handed down to the 74 defendants on trial. Thanks to the energetic efforts of the American prosecution council, Major Everett, none of the controversial sentences were ever carried out. Peiper was one of those condemned, and his sentence was commuted to life imprisonment in 1951.

He was released from Landsberg Prison on 22 December 1956. He changed his name and settled in France, but on 13 July 1976 he was brutally murdered, probably by former French Resistance members.

PFEFFER-WILDENBRUCH, Karl
RANK: SS-Obergruppenführer und General der Polizei
BORN: 12 August 1888
DIED: 29 January 1971 (D)
PARTY NUMBER: —
SS NUMBER: —
AWARDS: 1914 Iron Cross Second Class; Cross of Honour 1914-1918 Combatants; 1939 Iron Cross Second Class Bar; 1939 Iron Cross First Class Bar; Knight's Cross of the Iron Cross, 11 January 1945; Oakleaves, 1 February 1945.

Born in Kalkberge-Rüderodorf, near Berlin, Pfeffer-Wildenbruch's military service began in 1906 as an officer candidate with the 2nd (Prussian) Field Artillery Regiment, and, like many Waffen-SS members, he enjoyed a distinguished career in World War I.

He joined the security police in 1919 in Münster, and also served in Osnabrück and Magdeburg. He was posted to Chile as a police instructor 1928-30. On his return he became Inspector-General of National Police at Kassel and Frankfurt, and Inspector-General of all police schools.

Pfeffer-Wildenbruch saw service in the Polish campaign and helped in forming the SS police division, the 4th SS Panzergrenadier Division *SS-Polizei,* in the autumn of 1939. He became commanding officer on 10 October 1939, relinquishing the post on 10 November 1940. The division received its training at Truppen-Übungsplatz Wandern, and during the invasion of France was held in reserve at Reutlingen and Tübingen, seeing its first action on 9 June. On 10 June the division was taken out of the line and placed in reserve. Due to its inexperience it suffered fairly high casualties. In addition, its equipment was poor compared to the other Waffen-SS divisions and those of the army. It performed poorly later in Russia.

Pfeffer-Wildenbruch became commanding general of IX SS Mountain Army Corps in 1944. He was awarded the Knight's Cross of the Iron Cross for actions on the southeastern front in Hungary, especially in and around Budapest. A mere 21 days later he won the Oakleaves, becoming the 723rd recipient. He was taken prisoner by the Russians at the end of the war and repatriated on 9 October 1955. He died in Bielefeld in 1971.

PISTER, Hermann
RANK: SS-Standartenführer
BORN: 21 February 1885
DIED: 11 April 1947 (E.A.)
PARTY NUMBER: 918391
SS NUMBER: 29892
AWARDS: 1914 Iron Cross Second Class;
Cross of Honour 1914-1918
Combatants; War Merit Cross Second
Class with Swords; War Merit Cross
First Class with Swords; SS Honour
Ring; SS Honour Sword.

Pister was in command of concentration camps in the south and commandant of Buchenwald, which supplied prisoners on 12-hour shifts to local armaments factories. In the closing weeks of the war Hitler told Pister that Dachau, Mauthausen and Theresienstadt were to be blown up, together with their inhabitants if they could not be evacuated before the arrival of the Allies. But in fact there was little will left to carry out the order. One view was that Pister only carried out the terrible evacuations from Buchenwald under direct pressure from Erbprinz Waldeck-Pirmont (q.v.), who had persistently sheltered the worst Buchenwald criminals. Liberated by the US 80th Division in April 1945, Pister was tried at Dachau on 11 April 1947 and sentenced to death. The sentence was carried out without any delay.

PLEASANTS, Eric
RANK: SS-Schüte
BORN: 1911
PARTY NUMBER: —
SS NUMBER: —

Pleasants was born in Norfolk, the son of a gamekeeper. As a youngster he became interested in body building, physical fitness and sport, taking up amateur boxing and wrestling. He attended Loughborough College under the patronage of the Bowes-Lyon family. He there obtained a diploma in physical education and physiotherapy.

The Norwich branch of the BUF (British Union of Fascists) asked him to become a member of their protection squad in the mid-1930s. He held pacifist views, and when war broke out was offered the opportunity, through the Peace Pledge Union, to work as an agricultural labourer in Jersey. He arrived in May 1940, one month before the Germans invaded.

On his way out of Berlin he had to kill two Russians with his bare hands

Pleasants stole a motor boat and attempted to escape to Britain with Leister (q.v.) and Keith Barnes. They were caught, and Pleasants and Leister were given six months' imprisonment which they served in Dijon. Being of military age they were then sent to Kreuzberg, a civilian internment camp. They claimed to be merchant seamen and demanded transfer to a POW camp, thinking the rations were better.

Pleasants decided to volunteer for the British Freikorps, becoming the Korps' physical training instructor. His time in the Korps was uneventful. He married a German girl, Annelise, and

together they escaped from Berlin in 1945, taking first to the underground and then through the sewers with the hope of reaching her parents' home near Dresden. On the way, despite his pacifist leanings, he had to kill two Russian soldiers with his bare hands. Despite the countryside being filled with Red Army patrols, they got to Dresden. Reaching her parents' home, they hid for some months, and Pleasants even earned a modest living doing a strong man act to entertain the occupying Russian soldiers until they were both arrested in early 1946 on suspicion of spying. He received a quick trial and was sent to the 'Inter' camp in the Russian Arctic. He was released seven years later and was the subject of a German newsreel. As for Annelise, she was never heard of again.

POHL, Oswald

RANK: SS-Obergruppenführer
   und General der Waffen-SS und Polizei
BORN: 30 June 1892
DIED: 8 June 1951 (E.A).
PARTY NUMBER: 30842
SS NUMBER: 147614
AWARDS: 1914 Iron Cross Second Class; 1914 Iron Cross First Class; Cross of Honour 1914-1918 Combatants; 1914 Wound Badge Silver Class; War Merit Cross Second Class with Swords; War Merit Cross First Class with Swords; Knight's Cross of the War Merit Cross with Swords, 10 October 1944 (16 November 1944); German Cross in Silver; Gold Sports Badge; SS Honour Ring; SS Honour Sword.

In 1912 Pohl joined the navy to follow an administrative career. His training ended in April 1918 with his promotion to naval paymaster. After World War I he completed a law degree at Kiel University. Until taking charge of the Reichs-marine in 1920, he was with the Loewenfeld Freikorps in Oberschlesien and in the Ruhr, and in the summer of 1923 he joined the Uwe Jens Lornsen Volksbund, a disguised NSDAP organisation. In 1929 became a full member of the NSDAP, running for election to Kiel council. From 1929 to 1931 Pohl was the Ortsgruppenleiter and SA-Führer in Swinemünde, returning to Kiel in 1932, where he founded the town parliament and the Marine-SA.

In May 1933 Pohl met Himmler (q.v.), and after some initial hesitation took up his offer to construct an SS administration office. His rise was meteoric. From 1 February 1934 he belonged to the SS with the rank of Standartenführer. After the extension of his powers to include the SS-Verfügungstruppen and SS-Totenkopfverbände (KL-Wacheinheiten), Pohl was raised to the post of Verwaltungschef and Reichskassenverwalter of the SS (SS Chief of Administration and Reich Treasurer) on 1 June 1935, and on 20 April 1939 he was made head of an independent Hauptamt. In June he accepted the appointment of Ministerialdirektor und Leiter vom Hauptamt Haushalt und Bauten im Reichsministerium des Innern – permanent secretary and leader of the main *Amt* economy and construction.

Pohl was an administrative schemer who developed a number of economic projects for the SS, the full details of which are still not known over 50 years later. By 1945 the SS was the owner of over 40 enterprises with around 150 firms and factories. They included very different areas of business, among them food and drink (*Apollinaris*), textiles, agriculture and forestry, distribution, stone and soil.

The WVHA also controlled the administration of all concentration camps. Because of this, Pohl was indicted by the American Military Tribunal IV in Nuremberg, condemned to death and hanged on 8 June 1951 in Landsberg.

PÖTSCHKE, Werner
RANK: SS-Sturmbannführer
BORN: 6 March 1914
DIED: 24 March 1945 (K.I.A.)
PARTY NUMBER: —
SS NUMBER: —
AWARDS: 1939 Iron Cross Second Class,
    27 September 1939; 1939 Iron Cross
    First Class, 2 June 1940; German Cross
    in Gold, 5 November 1942; Knight's
    Cross of the Iron Cross, 4 June 1944;
    Oakleaves, 12 March 1945.

Pötschke was born in Brussels and fought in the Polish campaign in 1939 and in France the following year. With Operation 'Barbarossa' his unit was transferred to Russia in 1941.

In 1944 he became commanding officer of 1st Company, 1st Panzer Regiment, 1st SS Panzer Division LSSAH, and was awarded the Knight's Cross of the Iron Cross for his work during the encirclement of Kamenets-Podolsk. The *Leibstandarte*, which was

now a shadow of its former self, was stationed in Bonn where it prepared for its next action, meeting the coming Allied attack.

On 12 January 1945, the Russians initiated their long-expected winter offensive in the East. When wide gaps were ripped open in the German lines in early March, the whole of 'Sepp' Dietrich's panzer army was transferred to Hungary in an attempt to relieve the garrison in the embattled city of Budapest. The SS panzer units, which were thrown into the ensuing battle without artillery preparation or air cover, were disabled immediately. Pötschke was detachment commander of the *Leibstandarte*'s panzer regiment, and was awarded the Oakleaves for his leadership and bravery at Gran Bridgehead, becoming the 783rd recipient. He was severely wounded near Veszprem and died as a result.

PREISSLER, Fritz
RANK: SS-Hauptsturmführer
BORN: 2 December 1899—
AWARDS: War Merit Cross Second Class
    with Swords; War Merit Cross First
    Class with Swords; Knight's Cross of
    the War Merit Cross First Class with
    Swords, 18 November 1944.

Preissler was born in Chemnitz in Saxony and became the commanding officer of the maintenance and repair detachment of the *SS-Polizei* Division. His division performed a vital task in the desperate fighting in the autumn of 1944 in the East, and Preissler won Knight's Cross of the War Merit Cross. The citation explains that it was 'for the successful execution of the retreat of the complete panzer division in the north battle areas, although temporarily half of the vehicles could not move under their own power. In the new combat area the panzers were once again repaired in unbroken work under the expert leadership of SS-Hauptsturmführer Preissler.'

The *SS-Polizei* Division had improved in quality by 1944, having put in a poor performance during the early part of the Russian campaign. The maintenance of vehicles was a constant problem for the German Army in the East. On 1 March 1942, for example, the Wehrmacht had 4462 tanks in the East, of which only 2468 were serviceable.

PRIESS, Hermann

RANK: SS-Gruppenführer
BORN: 24 May 1901
DIED: 2 February 1985 (D)
PARTY NUMBER: 1472296
SS NUMBER: 113258
AWARDS: 1939 Iron Cross Second Class,
   22 September 1939; 1939 Iron Cross
   First Class ,15 October 1939; German
   Cross in Gold, 6 January 1942; Knight's
   Cross of the Iron Cross, 28 April 1943;
   Oakleaves, 9 September 1943;
   Oakleaves with Swords, 29 April 1944;
   SS Honour Ring; SS Honour Sword.

Preiss joined the 18th Volunteer-Dragoon Regiment on 12 January 1919 and was engaged in the fighting on Germany's eastern border, subsequently serving in the Reichswehr. He joined the SS-Verfügungstruppe in 1934 and went on to serve in the SS-Standarte *Germania* in 1939. As a qualified artillery man, he developed artillery use within the Waffen-SS and the unit became part of the *Totenkopf* Division. He commanded this regiment in 1941 when it proved its worth as an infantry unit. He was awarded the Knight's Cross of the Iron Cross for actions on the Russian Front while leading Artillery Regiment 3 of the *Totenkopf* Division.

On Eicke's (q.v.) death Priess took command of the *Totenkopf* Division. He was largely responsible for the achievements of the division during the bitter fighting of 1943-44, and was awarded the Oakleaves, becoming the 297th recipient. Six months later he became the 65th recipient of the Swords.

In late 1944 Priess assumed command of I SS Panzer Corps

and led it during the Battle of the Bulge, and later in Hungary and Austria. After the war he was tried at Dachau in the Malmédy trial. He was found guilty and sentenced on 16 July 1946 to 20 years' imprisonment, but was released from Landsberg prison in 1954. He died in Ahrensburg in 1985.

PRÜTZMANN, Hans

RANK: SS-Obergruppenführer und General
   der Waffen-SS und der Polizei
BORN: 31 August 1901
DIED: 21 May 1945 (S)
PARTY NUMBER: 142290
SS NUMBER: 3002
AWARDS: Golden Party Badge; German
   Cross in Gold; 1939 Iron Cross Second
   Class; 1939 Iron Cross First Class;
   War Merit Cross Second Class with
   Swords; War Merit Cross First Class
   with Swords; SS Honour Ring;
   SS Honour Sword.

Prützmann was the higher SS police chief in the Ukraine from 1942 until 1944 when he was made head of the 'Werewolf' organisation, a body invented by Himmler (q.v.) for last-ditch resistance. The Werewolf organisation was the very embodiment of Himmler's muddled thinking after the 20 July Bomb Plot, when he was catapulted into military prominence out of his depth. If Himmler believed that within a few months the Western Allies would ask him to restore order in Europe and would require his SS to combat the menace of communism, what purpose could Himmler or the SS achieve by sabotaging the Western Allies which was the purpose of the organisation, in an attempt to slow or halt the advance on the Western and Eastern Fronts? They had few achievements in this area, but claimed some small successes behind the Allied lines, such as the American appointed mayor of Aachen and in April an American divisional commander being shot in March 1945.

Dönitz learned from General Kinzel that the personnel of a Luftwaffe squadron were following Himmler's orders and forming themselves into a 'Werewolf' unit. Dönitz sent for Prützmann, who had, for the last six months, been in charge of these daydreams, and warned him that he had forbidden 'Werewolf' activities for the end of resistance by regular troops had rendered it obsolete. The only achievement of the 'Werewolves' was to make Allied soldiers more suspicious of the German population as a whole, which ultimately harmed only the Germans. Prützmann committed suicide at Lüneburg.

PRZEDWOJEWSKI, Felix

RANK: SS-Unterscharführer
BORN: 7 December 1920
DIED: 15 August 1986 (D)
PARTY NUMBER: —
SS NUMBER: —
AWARDS: 1939 Iron Cross Second Class,
    6 August 1943; 1939 Iron Cross First
    Class, 14 November 1943; Knight's
    Cross of the Iron Cross, 16 December
    1943.

Felix Przedwojewski was a commander in the Second Anti-Tank Gun Company, *Totenkopf* Division, in 1943 when the division found itself in many critical situations on the Eastern Front. During a very dangerous point in the fighting he took the initiative and destroyed more than 10 Soviet tanks in one single action, winning the Knight's Cross of the Iron Cross. He survived the war and died in Karlsruhe in 1986.

QUIST, Arthur

RANK: SS-Sturmbannführer
PARTY NUMBER: —
SS NUMBER: —
AWARDS: 1939 Iron Cross Second Class;
    1939 Iron Cross First Class.

Quist commanded the Norwegian Freiwillige Legion from 1942. Quisling's exhortations to his Norwegian brethren to join the fight against 'English despotism' fell on deaf ears, although Hitler's 'crusade against Bolshevism' was a more effective propaganda weapon. Stalin's unprovoked attack on Finland had already angered Norwegians, causing some to volunteer for a legion of Scandinavians to fight the 'Red Menace'. On 29 June 1941, the formation of a Norwegian Legion was announced, with Quisling declaring on 4 July that it would comprise two battalions. They were named after the two Oslo district regiments of the Rikshird Viken Viking, and commanded by career officers of the Norwegian Army, Major Jorgen Bakke and Major Kjellsturp. The legion was

officially christened Freiwillige Legion *Norwegen* on 1 August and came under the command of Arthur Quist on 1 February 1942. He held this position until 5 May 1943 when the legion was brought home from Russia and disbanded. After the war he was captured, subsequently found guilty of treason and given 10 years' imprisonment.

Right: A Norwegian SS volunteer grabs a bite to eat while on campaign in Russia. The first Norwegian SS unit was commanded by Arthur Quist.

RAINER, Dr Friedrich

RANK: SS-Obergruppenführer,
    Gauleiter of Salzburg 1938-41,
    Gauleiter of Corinithia 1941-45
BORN: 28 July 1903
DIED: 18 August 1947 (E.A.)
PARTY NUMBER: 301860
SS NUMBER: 292774
AWARDS: Golden Party Badge; War Merit
    Cross Second Class without Swords;
    War Merit Cross First Class without
    Swords; SS Honour Ring; SS Honour
    Sword.

Born in Corinthia, Rainer held a series of positions in the Austrian Nazi Party. With the absorption of Austria into the Reich in 1938 he was appointed Gauleiter of Salzburg, and was transferred to Corinthia in 1941. In 1945 he was captured by American forces. Yugoslavia extradited and executed him in 1947.

RASCHER, Sigmund

RANK: SS-Sturmbannführer
BORN: 1909
DIED: May 1945 (E.R).
PARTY NUMBER: —
SS NUMBER: —

A particularly unpleasant character, Sigmund Rascher was urged to join the Allgemeine-SS when he demonstrated considerable Nazi spirit by denouncing his own father. He married a woman 15 years his senior, and as mother worship formed an essential part of Heinrich Himmler's (q.v.) folklore, he became very interested in the young man.

Rascher was engaged on a boring medical course with the Luftwaffe in Munich in May 1941 when he wrote to Himmler, asking if he could have human guinea pigs for high-altitude experiments using a pressure chamber which involved the death of the victims. Himmler agreed, and Rascher undertook the experiment at Dachau. Luftwaffe Colonel-General Milch had some misgivings a year later, and wrote to Karl Wolff (q.v.), requesting that the apparatus be returned to the Luftwaffe and suggesting that Rascher should undertake freezing experiments.

Himmler visited him at Dachau in November 1941, and Rascher discussed the use of animal heat in reviving frozen airmen. Himmler found this fascinating, although Rascher's report showed that the experiment had been useless. Himmler ordered Pohl (q.v.) to have four prostitutes sent to Dachau for further experiments in reviving the frozen bodies, although he later protested that Pohl should not have selected girls of German blood.

Himmler had Rascher transferred to the Waffen-SS and permanently situated at Dachau, where he worked until May 1945, when Karl von Eberstein (q.v.) came to arrest him, not for his experiments, but because his wife had kidnapped children from orphanages. The camp commandant and the chief medical officer seized their chance, emitting a flood of complaints against Rascher, whom they described as a 'dangerous, incredible person' who had Himmler's patronage in performing 'unspeakable horrors'. Himmler would not countenance a trial of the Raschers, but they were confined in the political bunkers of Dachau and Ravensbrück, the fate of people who knew too much. It is believed they both perished at the beginning of May 1945.

RATTENHUBER, Hans

RANK: SS-Brigadeführer
BORN: 30 April 1897—
PARTY NUMBER: 3212449
SS NUMBER: 52877
AWARDS: Golden Party Badge; 1914 Iron Cross Second Class; 1914 Iron Cross First Class; Cross of Honour 1914-1918 Combatants; SS Honour Ring; SS Honour Sword.

Head of the Reich security service and Hitler's personal safety, Rattenhuber held this position from the beginning of the war until Hitler's suicide. During this time he was also Hitler's personal security officer. After Hitler's death it should have been Rattenhuber who bargained for the lives of those left in the bunker, but it fell on the shoulders of Hans Krebs, the last Chief of Staff of the German Army, who hoped to bargain the lives of Hitler's court against the surrender of Berlin.

In the general panic, the fate of the men fighting in Berlin was disregarded

Russian General Vassili Chuikov demanded nothing less than the unconditional surrender of all those in the bunker. When Krebs returned with the terms, Göbbels, Burgdorf and Krebs chose suicide; Bormann (q.v.), Hewel (q.v.) and Rattenhuber, together with a group of minor officials and officers, chose escape. In the general panic, the fate of the men fighting in Berlin was totally disregarded. Most of the Waffen-SS troops fighting in the city in the defence of Hitler were actually non-Germans. They comprised men of the *Nordland* and *Charlemagne* Divisions, a battalion of Latvians from the 15th Waffen-Grenadier Division der SS and 600 men of Himmler's Escort Battalion, who fought much better than their commander.

The arrangements for a ceasefire were undertaken by a mere civilian, Hans Fritsche, the head of the broadcasting service. Rattenhuber was captured by the Russians while escaping from the Reich Chancellery on 2 May 1945. After serving a prison term he was repatriated to Germany on 10 October 1955.

RAUTER, Hanns Albert

RANK: SS-Obergruppenführer
BORN: 4 February 1895
DIED: 25 March 1949 (E.A.)
PARTY NUMBER: —
SS NUMBER: 262958
AWARDS: Cross of Honour 1914-1918 Combatants; 1914 Wound Badge Black Class; 1939 Iron Cross Second Class; 1939 Iron Cross First Class; War Merit Cross Second Class with Swords; War Merit Cross First Class with Swords; SS Honour Ring; SS Honour Sword.

Born in Klagenfurt in Austria, Rauter joined the Styrian Home Guard, a pan-German, fanatically anti-Semitic, paramilitary organisation during the 1920s. This group formed links with the newly emergent NSDAP, and Hanns Rauter, a crude street fighter, was drawn to the potential of a powerful police formation within the Third Reich.

With the outbreak of war, Rauter became Higher SS and Police Chief of the Netherlands, a position he held until the end of the war. In addition to detecting and repressing political crimes, he

undertook wider activities, particularly informing a network of Dutch informers, called 'V men,' who had the job of infiltrating the underground organisations. Rauter ruthlessly suppressed the Jews and undertook their deportation to the concentration camps. Hitler's Niedermachungsbefehl, the instructions to the police to publicly execute any Todeskandidaten (death candidates) who were Resistance members, was also strictly enforced.

By the end of the first few months of 1945, the Dutch hoped that they had endured the worst of the terror. However, a single incident brought about a blood bath on an unprecedented scale. Members of the Resistance shot and badly wounded Rauter on the night of 6/7 March, an unintentional attack, as they really only wanted to hijack an army vehicle to seize food destined for the Wehrmacht. Retribution was swift and decisive: the definition of Todeskandidaten was expanded to include not only Resistance members, but also looters and curfew breakers.

After the war, Rauter was tried by the Dutch for war crimes. In his defence he declared that he had begged Seyss-Inquart (q.v.) and Schoengarth to refrain from the reprisals. His protestations were not believed and he was found guilty and sentenced to death. He mounted the gallows on 25 March 1945.

REBANE, Alfons
RANK: Standartenführer der Waffen-SS
BORN: 24 June 1908
DIED: 3 March 1976 (D).
PARTY NUMBER: —
SS NUMBER: —
AWARDS: 1939 Iron Cross Second Class; 1939 Iron Cross First Class; Knight's Cross of the Iron Cross, 23 February 1944, Oakleaves, 9 May 1945; Close Combat Clasp Bronze Class, Infantry Assault Badge in Silver.

Born in Walk, Estonia, Rebane volunteered for service in an Estonian legion to fight alongside the Germans in the common struggle against Bolshevism. This was launched on 28 August 1942, the first anniversary of the liberation of the Estonian capital Tallin, by Generalkommissar Litzman. The 1st battalion of the

new regiment was despatched in March 1943 for active service with the 5th SS Panzer Division *Wiking*. It was popularly called the Estonian Volunteer Battalion *Narwa* while it served with the division. At the beginning of 1944 Himmler (q.v.) decided to increase the Estonian contribution to the Waffen-SS by absorbing the existing German Army's Estonian battalions and the Estonian police formations and combining these with the brigades, creating an Estonian division. The brigade's two existing regiments, SS-Freiwilligen Grenadier Regiments 45 and 46, were supplemented by a new regiment, 47. This was formed by the amalgamation of two Estonian battalions, 658 and 659, serving with the German Army.

Major Alfons Rebane, a distinguished Estonian officer, commanded 658 Battalion and was the country's first recipient of the Knight's Cross of the Iron Cross. To celebrate, he was a guest of honour at a grand reception held in Kadriorg Palace in Tallin. On 19 March 1945, the commanding officer, Augsberger, was killed in action and Rebane was promoted to deputy divisional commander. His superb leadership and bravery earned him the Oakleaves; he became the 875th recipient; a rare distinction for a foreigner. He survived the war and died in Augsburg, Bavaria in 1976.

REDER, Walter
RANK: SS-Sturmbannführer
BORN: 4 February 1915
DIED: 26 April 1991 (D)
PARTY NUMBER: 5020869
SS NUMBER: 58074
AWARDS: 1939 Iron Cross Second Class, 31 May 1940; 1939 Iron Cross First Class, 28 July 1941; German Cross in Gold, 17 October 1942; Knight's Cross of the Iron Cross, 3 April 1943; SS Honour Ring; SS Honour Sword.

Born in Freiwald, Austria, Reder fought in the French campaign of 1940 and then in Russia. He became commanding officer of a battalion in the SS-Panzer-grenadier Regiment *Totenkopf*, and for his bravery was awarded the Knight's Cross of the Iron Cross.

In the summer of 1944 he commanded the reconnaissance detachment of the 16th SS Panzergrenadier Division *Reichsführer-SS* in Italy. The unit was engaged in combat on the Arno Front in August 1944 against the Allies, who were advancing from the south and also against partisan units such as the 'Stella Rossa'. The *Reichsführer-SS* massacred 2700 Italian civilians soon afterwards, as reprisal for the activities of a partisan brigade in the Apennines.

Max Simon (q.v.), the divisional commander, was condemned to death by a British court in Padua, but the sentence was commuted and he was freed in 1954. For his connection with this massacre, Reder was sentenced to life imprisonment by a Milan court in October 1951. On 24 January 1985 he was released from the fortress prison at Gaeta, Italy. He died of an incurable illness in Vienna in 1991.

REINECKE, Dr Günther

RANK: SS-Oberführer
BORN: 18 April 1908—
PARTY NUMBER: 3257841
SS NUMBER: 77151
AWARDS: War Merit Cross Second Class with Swords; War Merit Cross First Class with Swords; SS Honour Ring; SS Honour Sword.

Head of the department of the SS courts and chief judge of the highest court of the SS and police, at Nuremberg where he could not make up his mind whether the 24,000 men of Oswald Pohl's (q.v.) WVHA office were concentration camp guards or personnel of Himmler's many business enterprises.

REINEFARTH, Heinz

RANK: SS-Gruppenführer und Generalleutnant der Polizei
BORN: 26 December 1903
DIED: 7 May 1979 (D)
PARTY NUMBER: 1268933
SS NUMBER: 56634
AWARDS: War Merit Cross Second Class with Swords; 1939 Iron Cross Second Class, 25 September 1939; 1939 Iron Cross First Class, 28 May 1940; Knight's Cross of the Iron Cross, 25 June 1940; Oakleaves, 30 September 1944; Close Combat Clasp; SS Honour Ring; SS Honour Sword.

Reinefarth was born in Gresen Posen district, West Prussia. While serving in the French campaign as a Feldwebel with the 337th Infantry Regiment of 208th Infantry Division, 18th Army, Army Group B, he was awarded the Knight's Cross of the Iron Cross. On 1 August 1944 the Second Warsaw Revolt broke out, and for his bravery in leading four battalions of German regular police against hard-pressed and exhausted Poles, he was awarded the Oakleaves, becoming the 608th recipient.

A few days before the opening of the Ardennes Offensive, Himmler (q.v.) took up his duties as commander of the Upper Rhine Army Group. He also formed the XIV and XVIII SS Army Group under the command of the heroes of Warsaw, Reinefarth and von dem Bach-Zelewski (q.v.). This army was formed in a matter of six weeks; while a triumph of improvisation, it was unfortunate that it served in a sector where the Allies never attacked. Reinefarth finally commanded the encircled East Prussian fortress of Küstrin until it fell on 2 March 1945.

Reinefarth survived the war and surrendered to the Americans in Austria on 25 May 1945 in the company Arthur Greiser (q.v.). He died in Westerland, Island of Sylt in 1979.

REITZENSTEIN, Hans-Albin von

RANK: SS-Obersturmbannführer
BORN: 4 March 1911
DIED: 30 November 1943 (S)
PARTY NUMBER: —
SS NUMBER: —
AWARDS: 1939 Iron Cross Second Class, 24
    September 1939; 1939 Iron Cross First
    Class, 2 October 1939; Knight's Cross
    of the Iron Cross, 13 November 1943.

Born in Berlin, Reitzenstein joined the SS in 1933 and was posted to the *Leibstandarte SS Adolf Hitler*. He saw service in the Polish campaign. In November 1943 he was the commanding officer of the 2nd SS-Panzer Regiment, *Das Reich* Division, 4th Panzer Army, Army Group South. The division reported the destruction of its 2000th enemy armoured vehicle on 6 November 1943, and under Reitzenstein's leadership the tank regiment had made a considerable contribution to this success. He was considered a brave and exemplary officer, and was awarded the Knight's Cross of the Iron Cross. Shortly after the award he chose to commit suicide on the Russian Front.

RENTROP, Fritz

RANK: SS-Sturmbannführer
BORN: 19 November 1917
DIED: 2 February 1945 (M.I.A.)
PARTY NUMBER: —
SS NUMBER: —
AWARDS: 1939 Iron Cross Second Class,
    18 June 1940; 1939 Iron Cross First
    Class, 27 November 1940; Knight's Cross
    of the Iron Cross, 13 October 1941.

Rentrop was born in Münster, Westphalia. Having fought in France in 1940, he went to the Eastern Front with Operation 'Barbarossa'. While fighting in the 2nd Battery, SS-Anti-Aircraft Detachment, Das Reich Division, Army Group Centre, in 1941, he was awarded the Knight's Cross of the Iron Cross. In 1945 Rentrop served as first staff officer of IV SS Panzer Corps, fighting on the Southeastern

Front in Hungary. There he was severely wounded and on 2 February fell into Soviet captivity. He was listed as missing in action and his fate remains a mystery.

RIBBENTROP, Joachim von

RANK: SS-Obergruppenführer,
    Foreign Minister
BORN: 30 April 1893
DIED: 16 October 1946 (E.A.)
PARTY NUMBER: 1199927
SS NUMBER: 63083
AWARDS: Golden Party Badge; Meritorious
    Order of the German Eagle; Grand
    Cross in Gold; 1939 Decoration of the
    Red Cross; Grand Cross Special Grade
    1934; SS Honour Ring; SS Honour
    Sword; Japan – Order of the Rising Sun
    with Pavlovnia-Flowers Grand Cross
    Badge and Breast Star.

Handsome, humourless and arrogant, von Ribbentrop was the son of an artillery officer, born in Wesel and raised in Kassel. His mother died when he was 15 and two years later he left for Canada, where he remained for four years until 1914, when he joined the Torgauer Husarenregeiment Nr. 12 as an officer. He served with bravery and was transferred to the intelligence service where he was tutored by von Papen.

He greeted the King of England at a court reception with 'Heil Hitler!'

He became a vintner after the war and in 1920 married Annalies Henkel of the wine and champagne family. He travelled extensively as a salesman for the firm, and this elevated position and wealth made him eager to join society; he added von to his name by grace of an aunt who adopted him.

Von Ribbentrop joined the NSDAP in 1932, and was immediately useful. Von Papen and Hitler used his house in Berlin-Dahlem on 22 January 1933 to plot their secret plan to make Hitler Chancellor-designate. Under Hess's secretariat, the Ribbentrop Bureau was established in 1933 in the Wilhelm Strasse, (provocatively just across the street from the Foreign Office). Staffed by careerists and journalists of dubious qualifications, it operated in direct opposition to the foreign ministry, with the objective of proving Nazi methods more effective than the foreign ministry's traditional policies. Having served in 1934 as special commissioner for disarmament, von Ribbentrop's career took off when he was able to conclude the Anglo-German naval treaty in May 1935, unaided by foreign ministry officials. The following year he cajoled Japan into joining an anti-Comintern pact, which Mussolini signed in 1937 (this was designed to combat the worldwide spread of communism; it talked of the blood of Japan containing Nordic virtues).

In 1936 Hitler appointed him ambassador to Great Britain. Von Ribbentrop's ambition was to replace von Neurath as Foreign Minister and he accepted the appointment with reluctance, fully believing that von Neurath was trying to sideline him. His reluctance was illustrated by the fact that he didn't take up the post for three months. Once ensconced, he shuttled between the two capitals. Diplomat he was not, for he greeted the King of England at a court reception at St Jame's in 1937, with 'Heil Hitler!' As a result British society rejected him, deeply offending his sensibilities, and causing a deeply held hatred of everything British, a situation that certainly contributed to the reports he sent Hitler, and thus Hitler's beliefs of British intentions in the pre-war years.

In February 1938 Hitler dismissed von Neurath and appointed von Ribbentrop as Foreign Minister. Himmler (q.v.) considered it a major victory for SS prestige, with the SS uniform to be seen in that bastion of conservatism, the Foreign Office. In August 1939 von Ribbentrop negotiated the agreement between Russia and Germany by which the two countries agreed to divide Poland. With the coming of the war in September 1939, von Ribbentrop's career as a diplomat effectively ceased. He was arrested on 14 June 1945 in Hamburg by Sergeant R. C. Holloway, accompanied by two British and one Belgian soldier. He was tried at Nuremberg, found guilty and hanged.

RICHTER, Wilfried
RANK: SS-Hauptsturmführer
BORN: 9 May 1916
DIED: 18 April 1981 (D)
PARTY NUMBER: —
SS NUMBER: —
AWARDS: 1939 Iron Cross Second Class,
    14 September 1941; 1939 Iron Cross
    First Class, 22 October 1941; Knight's
    Cross of the Iron Cross, 21 April 1942;
    Demjansk Shield.

In 1937 Wilfred Richter joined the SS and was attached to the 15th Company, SS-Standarte *Deutschland*. He went to the SS-Junkerschule and afterwards became a member of Eicke's (q.v.) *Totenkopf* Division.

Richter fought on the Russian Front and his division was involved in the Demjansk Pocket. Cut off by three Russian armies, the Germans managed to hold out and save themselves, though at great cost. Their actions in March 1942 tied down 18 divisions and six brigades that the Russians needed elsewhere. Richter commanded a strongpoint in a sector which had suffered particularly badly and fortified it against impending attack. Sixteen T-34s overran a part of the defences, but German anti-tank weapons destroyed six of the tanks before being eliminated. Grenadiers using teller mines dispatched a further five. Richter directed a barrage from the remaining artillery on the enemy held positions, which destroyed yet another tank. Husbanding all the available grenadiers, Richter stormed into the Soviet-held position. The enemy suffered heavy losses in the fierce hand-to-hand combat which ensued, and were forced to retreat. For his bravery and leadership, Richter was awarded the Knight's Cross of the Iron Cross.

Attached as an instructor to the SS-Junkerschule at Bad Tölz, he finally became deputy regimental commander in the 38th SS Panzergrenadier Division *Nibelungen*. It comprised the staff and cadets of various Junkershcule and was briefly deployed in Bavaria before surrendering to the American forces. Like most Waffen-SS divisions formed at the end of the war it was under-strength and poorly equipped, and suffered from shortages of fuel and ammunition. Richter died in Engehausen district, Falingbostel, in 1981 after a long illness.

ROESTEL, Franz
RANK: SS-Obersturmbannführer
BORN: 4 May 1902
DIED: 1974 (D)
PARTY NUMBER: 5468915
SS NUMBER: 457995
AWARDS: 1939 Iron Cross Second Class;
    1939 Iron Cross First Class; German
    Cross in Gold; Knight's Cross of the
    Iron Cross, 28 March 1945; 1939
    Wound Badge Silver Class.

An experienced officer of assault gun troops, Roestel was transferred to the Waffen-SS in order to teach his skills at the anti-tank gun school of the Waffen-SS. He later became the commanding officer of the 10th SS Anti-Tank Detachment, 10th SS Panzer Division *Frundsberg*. Here he was awarded the Knight's Cross of the Iron Cross which was personally presented to him by Field Marshal Ferdinand Schörner. In the last weeks of the war on the Eastern Front, he was the last commanding officer of the *Frundsberg* Division. He survived the war and died in Regensburg Danube in 1974.

ROSSNER, Erich
RANK: SS-Unterscharführer
BORN: 26 May 1913
DIED: 12 September 1941 (K.I.A.)
PARTY NUMBER: —
SS NUMBER: —
AWARDS: 1939 Iron Cross Second Class,
    25 July 1941; 1939 Iron Cross First
    Class, 3 August 1941; Knight's Cross
    of the Iron Cross, 25 August 1941.

In 1941 Rossner was attached to *Das Reich* Division, Army Group Centre on the Russian Front. In July he and his fellow gunners destroyed eight Soviet tanks in close combat near Jelnja. He displayed exceptional bravery and was awarded the Knight's Cross of the Iron Cross. A few weeks later he was again engaged in heavy fighting, but was fatally wounded.

ROTHARDT, Dr Bruno

RANK: SS-Brigadeführer
BORN: 21 August 1891—
PARTY NUMBER: 430880
SS NUMBER: 276754
AWARDS: 1914 Iron Cross Second Class;
1914 Iron Cross First Class; Cross of
Honour 1914-1918 Combatants; 1914
Wound Badge Black Class; 1939 Iron
Cross Second Class Bar; 1939 Iron
Cross First Class Bar; War Merit Cross
Second Class with Swords; SS Honour
Ring; SS Honour Sword.

One of the medical staff of the SS-Verfügungstruppe, Rothardt
was transferred in October 1939 to the *Totenkopf* Division, serving with Eicke (q.v.) as its physician until January 1941. From
then until November 1942, he worked in the Waffen-SS medical
service, and from the 20th of that month until 15 August 1943 was
assigned to the medical staff of the state security service. He
returned to the Waffen-SS in the autumn of 1943 for the remainder of the war, serving successively as physician to the 7th and 4th
Corps respectively.

RUCKDESCHEL, Ludwig

RANK: SS-Brigadeführer,
Gauleiter of Bayreuth
BORN: 15 March 1907—
PARTY NUMBER: 29308
SS NUMBER: 234190
AWARDS: Golden Party Badge; German
Cross in Gold; 1939 Iron Cross Second
Class; 1939 Iron Cross First Class; 1939
Wound Badge Black Class; SS Honour
Ring; SS Honour Sword.

Rucksdeschel commanded the SS unit that executed Fritz Wächtler
(q.v.), the Gauleiter of Bayreuth, on 19 April 1945 on charges of
defeatism. Ruckdeschel was Deputy Gauleiter and ran the district
during the period after Wächtler's death until the surrender.

RÜHLE VON LILIENSTERN, Hans-Joachim

RANK: SS-Hauptsturmführer der Reserve
BORN: 9 January 1915
DIED: 1983 (D)
PARTY NUMBER: 3287913
SS NUMBER: 151372
AWARDS: 1939 Iron Cross Second Class,
9 November 1940; 1939 Iron Cross First
Class, 22 January 1944; Knight's Cross of
the Iron Cross, 12 February 1944.

The son of a Hessian doctor Rühle served as a platoon comman-
der in the French campaign of 1940. Transferred to the Russian
Front as commander of I Battalion, SS-Freiwilligen Panzergrenadier
Regiment 48 *General Seyffardt*, he was part of the 23rd
Freiwilligen Panzergrenadier Division *Nederland*. The division

was composed of Dutch volunteers and in June 1944 had a strength of 6713 men. He was heavily involved in the actions on the Leningrad Front.

In February 1944 Rühle was rewarded with the Knight's Cross of the Iron Cross, but by June the division was in full retreat before the bludgeoning Red Army. In July it took part in the 'Battle of the European SS' at Narva, which lasted six months and held up the Red Army. In February 1945 they were evacuated by sea from Libau on the Baltic coast to Stetin. After only a brief respite they joined battle in Pomerania, moving south later to Fürstenwalde, where they surrendered. He died in Frankfurt in 1983.

RUMOHR, Jochim

RANK: SS-Oberführer
BORN: 6 August 1910
DIED: 13 February 1945 (S).
PARTY NUMBER: 216161
SS NUMBER: 7450
AWARDS: 1939 Iron Cross Second Class, 14 November 1939; 1939 Irson Cross First Class, 28 August 1940; German Cross in Gold, 23 February 1943; Knight's Cross of the Iron Cross, 16 January 1944; Oakleaves, 4 February 1945; SS Honour Ring; SS Honour Sword.

Rumohr was born in Hamburg and was the commanding officer of the SS-Artillery Regiment of the 8th SS Kavallerie Division *Florian Geyer,* Army Group South. While serving on the Russian Front he was awarded the Knight's Cross of the Iron Cross.

Rumohr took the command of the division in a temporary capacity on 1 April 1944, a position that was later confirmed and which he held until his suicide in 1945. In the autumn of 1944 the Rumanians defected from the Axis camp. This enabled the Soviet forces to increase pressure on the already weakened German line.

The army's 13th and 'Feldherrnhalle' armoured divisions were sent to Hungary to fight alongside the Waffen-SS. These troops, numbering some 50,000 men, became completely encir-

cled by New Year's Eve 1944 at Budapest. They were desperately fighting for their lives and for a time the garrison managed to hold the position. Hitler ordered the *Totenkopf* and *Wiking* divisions from the defence of Warsaw to the relief of Budapest, but after a fortnight of fighting it was called off. Rumohr's bravery and leadership won him the Oakleaves, the 721st recipient.

Only 800 defenders broke through the besiegers to reach the German lines

With the defenders exhausted, the defence area shrank by mid-January. The collapse came on 12 February 1945. Only 800 defenders broke through the besiegers to reach the German lines, among them 170 members of the 8th and 22nd Cavalry Divisions. Rumohr was wounded while attempting to escape from the city, and decided on suicide rather than fall into Russian hands.

SAUCKEL, Fritz

RANK: SS-Obergruppenführer,
Gauleiter of Thüringia 1927-45 and
Governor of Anhalt and Brunswick
BORN: 27 October 1894
DIED: 16 October 1946 (E.A.)
PARTY NUMBER: 1395
SS NUMBER: 254890
AWARDS: Golden Party Badge; Coburg
Badge, 14 October 1932; Gau
Thüringen Badge; SS Honour Ring;
SS Honour Sword.

Responsible for the Reich's labour procurement from 1942, Sauckel succeeded in deporting some five million people to Germany. Born in Lower Franconia, Sauckel became a seaman in 1910. His ship was captured in 1914 by the French and he was interned as a prisoner of war until 1919. On his return he joined the People's Defence Union and worked in a factory while attending engineering school. In 1921 he joined the NSDAP, and after holding a variety of posts he was appointed Gauleiter of Thüringia in 1927, a position he held until the war's end. He was made governor in 1933.

Sauckel was described by Göbbels as the 'dullest of the dull'

Sauckel was described by Göbbels as 'the dullest of the dull'. He was also perceived as quasi-literate, leading the life of an ordinary high-ranking Nazi political functionary until March 1942, when he was appointed Plenipotentiary General for Mobilisation to meet the labour demands of Speer's armament and munitions production programme. Speer found the flow of workers too slow and suggested that a tough Gauleiter be found to undertake the job. Sauckel was proposed. This prosaic little man, who in another time and place would have been a complete cipher, was entrusted with labour recruiting in the countries and territories overrun by Germany. He became the most notorious 'slave driver' in the history of man.

More than two million people came from the conquered East, about half of them women, but unlike those who came from the West, the *Ostarbeiter* (Eastern workers) were treated more as slaves than as fellow labourers in the German cause. Their presence was a constant anxiety to the German authorities, who felt that the aliens would have to be marked in some way, just as the Jews were, to ensure that they did not stray outside the strict prescribed confines of their life in the Reich. They were, for example, banned from all places of public entertainment, relaxation and refreshment. The first workers to be marked thus were the Poles. A second *Ostabzeichen* (Eastern Badge) was introduced in February 1942 which was to be worn by all other workers from the East.

The workers found wearing the patch deeply offensive, and Sauckel asked Himmler (q.v.) that the Ukranians, 80 per cent of whom were volunteers, be allowed to wear a Ukranian emblem instead. Himmler forcibly refused. Various German labour agencies, worried by the declining morale of these workers, contributed to pressure for an abolition of the detested badges, appreciating that low morale meant a decline in production. This morale decline, together with the Nazis' love of ritual, led in April 1943 to the granting of the medal of the Order of the German Eagle in Bronze without Swords to be awarded to outstanding foreign workers from countries without diplomatic representation in the Reich. The normal requirements for this dubious 'honour' was at least two years' good work connected with the German war effort, or a single act of merit.

Sauckel's teams went out on the streets all over Europe, even in Italy, to round up men and women, taking them from their homes, from shops and cinemas, by false arrest or by getting them drunk before signing them up. Sauckel recruited more than five million workers, thousands of whom died of malnutrition or disease in the labour camps and factories where they were subject to brutal treatment. Sauckel regarded himself as an agent supplying workers for factories. He was shocked when arrested in 1945 by the British, who put him on trial at Nuremberg. He claimed to have known nothing about the concentration camps and protested his innocence until the moment he was hanged in October 1946.

SCHÄFER, Max

RANK: SS-Standartenführer
BORN: 17 January 1907
DIED: 7 May 1987 (D)
PARTY NUMBER: 359242
SS NUMBER: 16362
AWARDS: 1939 Iron Cross Second Class, 3 June 1940; 1939 Iron Cross First Class 13 July 1941; Knight's Cross of the Iron Cross, 12 February 1943; Oakleaves, 24 January 1945; Honour Roll Clasp of the Army, 25 November 1944; SS Honour Ring; SS Honour Sword.

Schäfer was born in Karlsruhe, Baden, and saw service in the French campaign of 1940. He was transferred to the East with Operation 'Barbarossa'. In 1943 he was the commanding officer of the SS-Engineer Battalion, SS Division *Wiking*, LVII Panzer General Command, 4th Panzer Army, Army Group Don on the Russian Front, where he was awarded the Knight's Cross of the Iron

Cross. In January 1945, he commanded the Corps of Engineers of III (Germ.) SS Panzer Corps and was commander of a mixed battle group, again on the Eastern Front. Awarded the Oakleaves for his leadership, he became the 714th recipient. He survived the war and died in Steinbach, Baden, in 1987.

SCHALBURG, Count Christian Frederik von

RANK: SS-Obersturmbannführer
BORN: 1906
DIED: 2 June 1942 (K.I.A.)
PARTY NUMBER: —
SS NUMBER: —
AWARDS: 1939 Iron Cross Second Class; 1939 Iron Cross First Class; Demjansk Shield; Cross of the Danish Volunteer Battalion in Finland.

Born at Poltava in the Ukraine, the son of wealthy parents of Baltic German stock, Schalburg's family emigrated to Denmark after the Russian Revolution and he became a naturalised Dane. He served as a lieutenant in the Royal Danish Life Guards and was also National Youth Leader of Clausen's DNSAP. Schalburg served in the Danish battalion during the 'Winter War' in Finland and later he

was among the first to volunteer for the newly raised SS-Regiment *Nordland*. He went on to serve in the *Wiking* Division. In March 1942 he took command of the Freikorps *Danmark*, and by May it was ready for service. It went into battle as part of the *Totenkopf* Division in the Demjansk

Pocket, but von Schalburg was killed in the first action on 2 June 1942. The body of this very popular commander was brought back to Denmark and interred with full military honours. In April 1943 Martinsen (q.v.) set up what he called a 'Germanic' corps, which he renamed the *Schalburg* Corps in memory of the Freikorps' most popular commander. He also has the dubious honour of having a decoration created in his memory: the Cross of Merit of the Schalburg Corps.

SCHARFE, Paul

RANK: SS-Brigadeführer
PARTY NUMBER: 665697
SS NUMBER: 14220
AWARD: SS Honour Ring.

Scharfe was Chief of the SS Legal Services, being an SS judge and head of the SS court. He held the view that the SS man was not

subject to judgement by any court, either military or civil. This was born out of the assumption that the SS man naturally occupied a privileged place in society, primarily because it was his duty to protect the movement and its Führer, if necessary, at the sacrifice of his life. Nothing is known of his fate.

SCHAUB, Julius

RANK: SS-Obergruppenführer
BORN: 20 August 1898
DIED: 27 December 1967 (D)
PARTY NUMBER: 81
SS NUMBER: 7
AWARDS: Golden Party Badge; Coburg Badge 14 October 1932; Blood Order No 296; SS Honour Ring; SS Honour Sword.

Born in Munich, Schaub was one of the first members of the NSDAP. He became a member of the Stosstrupp which was formed under Julius Schreck (q.v.), took part in the 1923 Putsch and was imprisoned with Hitler, soon becoming a member of Hitler's inner circle. After their release, he became a member of the 1925-26 Schutzkommando which was the forerunner of the SS. Hitler made him number two adjutant and when Wilhelm Brückner was dismissed Schaub became Hitler's chief personal adjutant.

Schaub (left in picture) was influential because he controlled access to Hitler, who became increasingly isolated as the war progressed, and made him his confidante. He mentioned his secret dislike of Himmler, saying: 'I need such policemen, but I don't like them.' Schaub was sent to destroy Hitler's personal papers in Berchtesgaden and Munich just prior to the Führer's suicide in April 1945. At the end of the war he was caught in Bavaria. Subsequently he became a pharmacist and died in Munich.

SCHEEL, Dr Gustav-Adolf

RANK: SS-Obergruppenführer
Gauleiter of Salzburg 1941-45
BORN: 22 November 1907
DIED: 25 March 1979 (D)
PARTY NUMBER: 391271
SS NUMBER: 107189
AWARDS: Golden Party Badge; War Merit
Cross Second Class with Swords; War
Merit Cross First Class with Swords;
SS Honour Ring; SS Honour Sword.

Scheel became a member of the National Socialists' Student Bund
while he was a medical student. From 1930 he held various posts
in Nazi student groups and became Reich student leader in 1936.
He was in charge of both Nazi university students and the National
Student Bund. He was appointed Gauleiter of Salzburg in November
1941, retaining all his previous posts. In Hitler's will he was nominated to the position of Minister of Culture. After the war he was
sentenced to five years' imprisonment. After his release he went
into medical practice and died in Hamburg in 1979.

SCHELLENBERG, Walter

RANK: SS-Brigadeführer
BORN: 16 January 1910
DIED: 1952 (D)
PARTY NUMBER: 3504508
SS NUMBER: 124817
AWARDS: 1939 Iron Cross Second Class;
1939 Iron Cross First Class; War Merit
Cross Second Class with Swords; War
Merit Cross First Class with Swords;
SS Honour Ring; SS Honour Sword.

Schellenberg was a secret service agent who became Head of
Combined Secret Services in 1944. A law graduate of Bonn with
a strong interest and command of several languages, Schellenberg

---

Left: Soldiers of the Leibstandarte *Division fighting on
the outskirts of Kharkov in March 1943.*

joined the SS in 1934. His intelligence and culture won him
the patronage of the head of the
SD, Heydrich (q.v.).

Schellenberg was involved
in a number of plots, notably
investigating British intelligence
operations in 1939, when he
posed as a Resistance agent to
gain the confidence of two MI5
agents in Holland. This led to their kidnap by SS troops on neutral
territory. He is also believed to have been involved in the plot to
abduct the Duke of Windsor.

In 1938 he organised the notorious Einsatzgruppen (which by
March 1943 had murdered 633,000 Jews) under Heydrich's
orders. He was one of the first to enter both Austria and Poland
after their annexation, to carry out Himmler's (q.v.) secretive
objectives. In 1944, after the arrest of Canaris and the disman-
tling of the Abwehr, he became head of all the secret services.

In 1945 he assumed a leading role in Himmler's attempt to
arrange an armistice with the Western Allies. Schellenberg arranged
meetings in April 1945 between Count Bernadotte and Himmler,
and when the German surrender came he was in Denmark, still
apparently negotiating. He was released from prison in December
1950 and died two years later. Schellenburg's memoirs provide
a detailed account of life in the higher reaches of the Third Reich.

SCHMAUSER, Heinrich

RANK: SS-Obergruppenführer
BORN: 18 January 1890—
PARTY NUMBER: 215704
SS NUMBER: 3359
AWARDS: SS Honour Ring; SS Honour Sword.

During the Röhm Purge, Schmauser was the liaison officer between
the SS and the army. He accompanied Eicke (q.v.) and Lippert
(q.v.) to Stadelheim Prison and witnessed the proceedings between
Eicke and Röhm. He watched Röhm's execution by Eicke and
Lippert but took no active part himself. Several high-ranking SS
officers spent varying periods with Eicke in 1940-41 learning how

to command troops in the field; they later became very notorious for their activities as Higher SS and Police Leaders in the German-occupied East.

Schmauser joined Eicke's staff in March 1936 and spent one month training with the division. He became Higher SS and Police Leader for Upper Silesia, and in that capacity ruled as the supreme SS authority under Himmler (q.v.) Much of his time after 1942 was spent dealing with the logistical problems created by the immense mass killing operations which were taking place at Auschwitz and which came under his jurisdiction. His fate at the end of the war is unknown.

SCHMELZER, Heinrich

RANK: SS-Hauptsturmführer
BORN: 14 March 1914
DIED: 4 July 1985 (D)
PARTY NUMBER: —
SS NUMBER: —
AWARDS: 1939 Iron Cross Second Class, 1 July 1940; 1939 Iron Cross First Class, 27 July 1940; German Cross in Gold, 27 October 1942; Knight's Cross of the Iron Cross, 12 March 1944; Oakleaves, 28 February 1945; Close Combat Clasp Silver Class; General Assault Badge Silver Class.

Schmelzer was born in Nesselröden, Hesse. He joined the SS in 1935 and with the outbreak of war fought in Poland and France. He served in the Balkans before the start of Operation 'Barbarossa',

and then he went to fight on the Eastern Front.

In late December 1943, he was serving with SS-Pioniere Kompanie, Panzer Kampfgruppe *Das Reich*, when a Soviet offensive in the Zhitomir area forced back the opposing German forces, resulting in the capture of the only bridge over the River

Teteran. Panzer Kampfgruppe *Das Reich* was isolated on the wrong bank of the river with no means of escape. On 24 December 1944, despite heavy enemy fire, Schmelzer and his combat engineers set to work to construct a temporary bridge under cover of darkness. His endeavours saved the kampfgruppe from total annihilation, allowing a full panzer battalion, artillery and mortar battalions, an infantry regiment and all the support elements to cross the river. Schmelzer and his men defended the bridge and its perimeters until all had reached safety, earning him the Knight's Cross of the Iron Cross.

During the Ardennes Offensive in December 1944, Schmelzer's engineers and the Grenadier Regiment *Deutschland* were cut off near Magoure by an American tank advance. Schmelzer extricated the German troops and got them back to their own lines without major loss. He was rewarded with the Oakleaves, becoming the 756th recipient. He died in his home town in 1985.

SCHMIDT, Walter

RANK: SS-Obersturmbannführer
BORN: 28 January 1917
PARTY NUMBER: —
SS NUMBER: —
AWARDS: 1939 Iron Cross Second Class, 20 September 1939; 1939 Iron Cross First Class, 14 September 1941; German Cross in Gold, 9 April 1943; Knight's Cross of the Iron Cross, 4 August 1943; Oakleaves, 14 May 1944; Close Combat Clasp Silver Clasp.

Schmidt served in the Polish campaign in 1939 and was transferred to the Eastern Front with Operation 'Barbarossa'. In 1943 he was the commanding officer of the 2nd Battalion SS-Panzergrenadier Regiment *Westland*, *Wiking* Division, Army Group South on the Russian Front, where he was

awarded the Knight's Cross of the Iron Cross. In May 1944 he won the Oakleaves (the 479th recipient) while commanding the 2nd Battalion, 10th SS-Panzergrenadier Regiment *Westland* of the *Wiking* Division, again on the Russian Front. He survived the war and lives in his home town of Bremen.

SCHOLZ, Fritz Elder von Raranoze von

RANK: SS-Gruppenführer
und Generalleutnant der Waffen-SS
BORN: 9 December 1896
DIED: 28 July 1944 (K.I.A.)
PARTY NUMBER: —
SS NUMBER: —
AWARDS: 1914 Iron Cross Second Class; 1914 Iron Cross First Class; Cross of Honour 1914-1918 Combatants; 1939 Iron Cross Second Class Bar, 17 May 1940; 1939 Iron Cross First Class Bar, 29 May 1940; German Cross in Gold, 29 November 1941; Knight's Cross of the Iron Cross, 18 January 1942; Oakleaves, 12 March 1944; Oakleaves with Swords, 8 August 1944; SS Honour Ring; SS Honour Sword.

A scion of an Austrian noble family, von Scholz served as an artillery officer during World War I and afterwards in the Freikorps in Upper Silesia. In 1933, he went to Germany under political pressure for his beliefs. He joined the Austrian Legion and the SS-Verfügungstruppe in 1935. When war broke out he took over the SS-Volunteer Regiment *Nordland*. He died of his wounds on 28 July 1944 in a field hospital and was posthumously awarded the Swords, becoming the 85th recipient, and promoted to Generalleutnant der Waffen-SS.

SCHOLZ, Helmut

RANK: SS-Obersturmbannführer
BORN: 1 July 1920—
PARTY NUMBER: —
SS NUMBER: —
AWARDS: 1939 Iron Cross Second Class, 14 October 1941; 1939 Iron Cross First Class, 17 February 1943; Knight's Cross of the Iron Cross, 4 June 1944; Oakleaves, 21 September 1944; Close Combat Clasp Silver Class; Infantry Assault Badge.

A Silesian, Scholz was the commanding officer of the 7th Company, 49th SS-Volunteer Panzergrenadier Regiment *De Ruiter*, *Nederland* Division, III (Germanic) SS Panzer Corps, Army Group North, on the Northeastern Front in Russia in 1944. For his bravery and leadership he was awarded the Knight's Cross of the Iron Cross. Later in the year he gained command of the second battalion of *De Ruiter*, which was nearly destroyed at Narva, and became the 591st recipient of the Oakleaves.

SCHRECK, Julius

RANK: SS-Brigadeführer
BORN: 13 July 1898
DIED: 16 May 1936 (D)
PARTY NUMBER: 53
SS NUMBER: 5
AWARDS: Golden Party Badge; Blood Order No 349; Coburg Badge 14 October 1932.

Born in Munich, he was an early member of the party and one of the first members of the SA. He was well liked and apparently on very good terms with Hitler. A founder of the Stosstrupp, he participated in the 1923 Putsch and was incarcerated in Landsberg. In 1925, with the reformation of the party, he founded the Schutzkommando, which was charged with Hitler's safety and subsequently became the embryonic SS. From this time he was constantly at Hitler's side and succeeded Emil Maurice (q.v.) as his personal chauffeur. Hitler considered him to be the best driver imaginable. In 1936 he contracted meningitis and died. Hitler was deeply distressed and gave him the honour of a state funeral.

SCHREIBER, Gustav

RANK: SS-Hauptscharführer
BORN: 25 December 1916—
PARTY NUMBER: —
SS NUMBER: —
AWARDS: 1939 Iron Cross Second Class, 20 August 1940; 1939 Iron Cross First Class, 12 August 1941; German Cross in Gold, 14 January 1943; Knight's Cross of the Iron Cross, 2 December 1943; Infantry Assault Badge; Close Combat Clasp Gold Class, 7 December 1943.

Transferred to the Russian Front after serving in France in 1940, Schreiber continuously performed acts of personal bravery in numerous battles This was borne out by the award of the Close Combat Clasp in Gold, the highest infantry decoration short of the Knight's Cross of the Iron Cross bestowed personally by Hitler. By the end of the war only 403 had been presented.

Schreiber won both awards while he was company commander of the 10th Company, SS-Panzergrenadier Regiment *Germania*, 8th Army, Army Group South. Typical combat on the Eastern Front meant close-quarter fighting against Red Army tanks and hand-to-hand battles with Russian infantry, often with knives and entrenching tools. It was a particularly brutal type of warfare. Schreiber was taken prisoner by the Soviets in February 1944 and was repatriated to Germany in 1950.

SCHRYNEN, Remy

RANK: SS-Unterscharführer
BORN: 24 December 1921—
AWARDS: 1939 Iron Cross Second Class, 28 May 1944; 1939 Iron Cross First Class, 3 August 1944; Knight's Cross of the Iron Cross, 21 September 1944; Infantry Assault Badge Silver Class; 1939 Wound Badge Gold Class; Tollenaere Commemorative Badge; VNV Golden Party Badge Five Years' Service Bronze.

One of the most successful anti-tank gunners of the war, Schrynen was born in Kumtich, Flanders, and worked as a coal miner. He joined the VNV political party and volunteered for the Waffen-SS, joining the SS assault brigade *Langemarck*. He demonstrated his fortitude in many taxing situations: on 2 January 1944 he destroyed three Russian T-34 tanks; on 3 March he was wounded for the seventh time. On the fourth day of the Russian offensive his gun crew was neutralised, either killed or wounded, and the support grenadiers retreated. Schrynen, now alone, received orders to withdraw. He decided to stay at his post, loaded, aimed and fired at the advancing tanks. The Russian infantry attacked, as a dying naval radio operator directed artillery fire onto his own position. Behind the infantry came 30 tanks. In a dramatic firefight he destroyed three Stalins and four T-34s, putting others out of action, until a Stalin, at close range, blew up his gun, severely wounding him and catapulting him away. During a counterattack he was discovered surrounded by the shot-up Soviet tanks. He won his Knight's Cross for single-handedly knocking out seven tanks. After the war he was imprisoned from 1945-50. He was rearrested in 1953 and released in January 1955.

SCHUBACH, Joachim

RANK: SS-Obersturmbannführer
BORN: 17 September 1910
DIED: 8 November 1980 (D)
PARTY NUMBER: 555723
SS NUMBER: 17597
AWARDS: 1939 Iron Cross Second Class, 30 May 1940; 1939 Iron Cross First Class, 14 July 1941; German Cross in Gold, 26 September 1942; Knight's Cross of the Iron Cross, 3 April 1943; Infantry Assault Badge; 1939 Wound Badge Black Class; SS Honour Ring; SS Honour Sword.

Having served in the campaign in France in 1940, Schubach went to the Russian Front with the attack on the Soviet Union in 1941. In April 1943 he was the commanding officer of the 3rd Battalion, *Totenkopf* Division, Army Group South. He showed extreme bravery, while his battalion distinguished itself during the recapture of Kharkov, the Ukrainian capital, and he won the Knight's Cross. He continued to serve with his men despite the fact that he had been badly wounded. Still fighting in Russia near Kriwoj Rog, he was again wounded and lost his sight in both eyes. He survived the war and lived in Hanover, his birthplace, where he died in 1980.

SCHULDT, Heinrich

RANK: SS-Brigadeführer und Generalmajor der Waffen-SS
BORN: 14 June 1901
DIED: 15 March 1944 (K.I.A.)
PARTY NUMBER: 975664
SS NUMBER: 242677
AWARDS: 1939 Iron Cross Second Class; 1939 Iron Cross First Class 1941; German Cross in Gold, 21 April 1943; Knight's Cross of the Iron Cross, 5 April 1942.

Born in Blankensee near Hamburg, Schuldt was commissioned in the Reichsmarine in 1922, remaining until 1928 when he was discharged as a lieutenant. He served with several paramilitary training units until 1933, when he joined the elite *Leibstandarte*. He was given command of a company and was then promoted and joined the first battalion of the SS-Standarte *Germania*.

During the first winter of the Russian war a crisis developed for Army Group Centre. After returning from the siege of Leningrad, Schuldt and his regiment of about 2500 were transported by Junkers 52s to the middle of Army Group Centre's sector. They landed behind the frontline and immediately engaged a numerically superior force. The fighting was ferocious and the winter conditions extreme. In the spring the situation improved, but only 180 men out of a once proud regiment were still capable of fighting. Schuldt received the Knight's Cross of the Iron Cross for these actions.

The title *Langemarck* was conferred on the reformed 4th SS Totenkopf Infantry Regiment. Heinrich Schuldt continued to demonstrate his ability in the deployment of fast-moving units, for which he was honoured with the Oakleaves, becoming the 220th recipient.

In 1943 he took command of the Second Latvian Volunteer Brigade. Spurred by their inherent hatred of the Soviets, they became an elite unit under Schuldt's command. Schuldt was fatally wounded on 15 March 1944, and in recognition of his bravery and that of his men he was posthumously awarded the Swords, becoming the 56th recipient. He was also promoted to Generalmajor der Waffen-SS.

SCHULZE, Richard

RANK: SS-Obersturmbannführer
BORN: 2 October 1914—
PARTY NUMBER: —
SS NUMBER: 264059
AWARDS: German Cross in Gold; 1939 Iron Cross Second Class; 1939 Iron Cross First Class; 1939 Wound Badge Black Class; SS Honour Ring; SS Honour Sword.

Having begun his career as Ribbentrop's adjutant, a position he held from April 1939 until January 1941, Richard Schulze replaced his younger brother Hans-Georg as Hitler's SS ordnance officer on 3 October 1941. During this assignment he had short inter-

vals of combat duty. From October 1942 he was a personal adjutant to Hitler, who grew extremely fond of him and paid him great attention. Schulze was also made responsible for all SS men serving in the SS-Begleitskommando. He held this position with periods of combat duty and service at the SS training school, until he became the last commander of Bad Tölz in December 1944.

SEELA, Max

RANK: SS-Sturmbannführer
BORN: 15 July 1911—
PARTY NUMBER: 147126
SS NUMBER: 257323
AWARDS: 1939 Iron Cross Second Class, 31 May 1940; 1939 Iron Cross First Class, 22 June 1940; German Cross in Gold, 26 December 1941; Knight's Cross of the Iron Cross, 3 May 1942; General Assault Badge; Medal for the Winter Campaign in Russia 1941-1942; Infantry Assault Badge; SS Honour Ring; SS Honour Sword.

Seela was the company commander of the 3rd Company, SS-Engineer Battalion, *Totenkopf* Division, which was employed as a 'tank annihilation unit'. The division's anti-tank guns were ineffective against the new Russian T-34 tanks. In response Eicke (q.v.) created units consisting of two officers and 10 men, armed with bags of satchel charges, grenades, petrol bombs and mines, who had the extremely dangerous task of destroying tanks at very close quarters.

At Lushno on 26 September 1942, to demonstrate the proper finesse of tank destruction, Seela crawled up to one which had momentarily stopped. He placed a double satchel charge against the turret and detonated it with a grenade. He then led his men against a further six tanks, disabling or setting them on fire. When the Soviet crews abandoned their vehicles, Seela and troops shot them down. The Germans held Starey Russa mainly because of the stubbornness of the *Totenkopf* units deployed there, and Seela emerged as one of the heroes of the long siege. He led a combat group that fought for just over a month in the village of Dipovitzy. Here they endured air strikes and repeated Russian ground attacks without surrendering the village or the adjacent bridge over the Lovat river. Eicke recommended Seela for the award of the Knight's Cross of the Iron Cross.

SEYSS-INQUART, Dr Arthur

RANK: SS-Obergruppenführer
BORN: 22 July 1892
DIED: 16 October 1946 (E.A.)
PARTY NUMBER: 6270392
SS NUMBER: 292771
AWARDS: Golden Party Badge; Cross of Honour 1914-1918 Combatants; 1914 Wound Badge Black Class; War Merit Cross Second Class without Swords; War Merit Cross First Class without Swords; SS Honour Ring; SS Honour Sword.

Seyss-Inquart was an Austrian Nazi who prepared the way for the *Anschluss*. Born in Iglow, Moravia, he attended read law at Vienna University. During World War I he served in the Tyrol Kaiser Jägers with distinction. In 1921 he set up in practice and devoted himself, according to his own testimony, to working for the *Anschluss* through political means via the Austrian *Volksbund*.

As early as 1930 the SS Frauenfeld introduced black uniforms into Austria and recruited and equipped assault squads. Later, the SD infiltrated the Austrian police. SS officers entered Austria to conduct a campaign of intimidation, setting up an Austrian legion, controlled by them. In spite of the suppression of the SA and SS in Austria, and the closure of the Brown House, the Austrian Nazi organisation was never dismantled. Its spearhead was the SS Standarte 89, a clandestine unit meeting under the guise of an athletics association; 154 of its men took part in the attack on

Chancellor Dollfuss on 25 July 1934. His successor, Schuschnigg, concluded an agreement with Hitler which included secret clauses permitting the establishment of Nazi organisations in Austria.

Acting as secret representative for the Nazis while the party was still illegal, Seyss-Inquart finally came to power in 1938 when Hitler demanded, on threat of invasion, the legalisation of the Nazi Party and the appointment of Seyss-Inquart as Minister of the Interior, with control over the police. By February this was accomplished and he began taking his orders directly from Berlin, acting independently of the chancellor. On 11 March, with Hitler's troops at the border, he was appointed Chancellor. He forced a law through parliament making Austria a province of Greater Germany. He was subsequently appointed president, a title that eventually changed to governor.

In October 1939 he was made the Deputy Governor General, under Frankn, of the Polish General Government. In May 1940, he became Reich Commissioner of the Netherlands with complete control of the entire country's resources, which were directed exclusively to the demands of the German war machine. He ruled authoritatively, answering only to Hitler. He generally followed the 'carrot and stick' method of rule but did cooperate with Himmler in the deportation of 500 Jewish youths to Mauthausen

in February 1941. By March 1941 he had powers of summary justice in any case pertaining to dissension or suspected resistance. He forced five million Dutch to work for the Germans and deported 117,000 Jews. In early 1945, he did join with Speer in preventing the application of Hitler's scorched earth policy.

Canadian forces arrested him in May 1945 and he was sent for trial at Nuremberg, being indicted on four charges. As with regard to his defence, an interchange with American prosecutor Robert Dodd pretty well sums it up. Seyss-Inquart: "I have done many things in Holland that have been good". Dodd: "And you have done many things in Holland that have been bad". Seyss-Inquart: "Perhaps only harsh". Dodd: "It is easy to tell you are a lawyer". During the deliberations Seyss-Inquart's defence was brushed off with the comment that it is no defence that he was less oppressive than Himmler. He was convicted on three counts and there were no dissenting votes among the judges that he should receive the death penalty. This took place in the execution chamber of the Nuremberg Prison on 16 October 1946, when the first prisoner, von Ribbentrop, mounted the gallows at 11 minutes past 0100 hours. Seyss-Inquart followed as the 9th candidate.

SIEBKEN, Bernhard

RANK: SS-Obersturmbannführer
BORN: 5 April 1910
DIED: 20 January 1949 (E.A.)
PARTY NUMBER: 558752
SS NUMBER: 44894
AWARDS: 1939 Iron Cross Second Class; 1939 Iron Cross First Class; War Merit Cross Second Class without Swords; War Merit Cross First Class without Swords; Knight's Cross of the Iron Cross, 17 April 1945; Medal for the Winter Campaign in Russia 1941-1942; SS Honour Ring,; SS Honour Sword.

Siebken commanded the 2nd Battalion, 26th SS-Panzergrenadier Regiment, *Hitlerjugend* Division, during the Normandy invasion, when a British armoured assault group broke through and captured a German regiment's HQ on 8 June. The British used

several German officers as hostages in an attempt to regain their own lines. Colonel Luxemburger was fatally wounded after being tied to a British armoured vehicle, dying a few days later. British and Canadian troops were alleged to have killed and wounded German soldiers. The fighting was particularly brutal, and there were also numerous cases of British and Canadian prisoners being summarily executed. Two British prisoners were found shot in Siebken's battle area and he was placed on the British wanted list. Found in a POW camp after the war, he was tried before a military court for war crimes and hanged in the Hamlyn military penitentiary in 1949.

SIEGLING, Alfred

RANK: SS-Untersturmführer
BORN: 15 March 1918
DIED: 6 September 1984 (D)
PARTY NUMBER: —
SS NUMBER: —
AWARDS: 1939 Iron Cross Second Class, 1 August 1940; 1939 Iron Cross First Class, 1 April 1943; Knight's Cross of the Iron Cross, 2 December 1943; Bronze Tank Battle Badge.

Siegling joined the SS in 1938 and was attached to 16 Kompanie, SS-Standarte *Deutschland* in Ellwagen. He saw service in the Polish and French campaigns.

With Operation 'Barbarossa' he went east with 1 Kompanie, SS Panzer Aufklärungsabteilung 2, part of the *Das Reich* Division, and was involved in the fierce fighting in the Kharkov region. In late 1943 he was ordered to investigate Soviet movements in an area around a small village. Siegling's patrol, using Bussing-Nag eight-wheel armoured cars and travelling at high speed, reached the village where a number of Soviet armoured vehicles were concealed among the houses. He drove straight down its length. His patrol passed without incident. Siegling relayed the size and position of the column to HQ, ensuring that the Germans were now fully aware of the impending Soviet breakthrough. This reconnaissance mission earned him the Knight's Cross. He surrendered to the Americans in May 1945. He died in 1984 in Klingenberg.

SIMON, Max

RANK: SS-Gruppenführer
BORN: 6 January 1899
DIED: 1 February 1961 (D)
PARTY NUMBER: 1359576
SS NUMBER: 83086
AWARDS: 1914 Iron Cross Second Class; 1914 Iron Cross First Class; Cross of Honour 1914-1918 Combatants; 1939 Iron Cross Second Class Bar, 13 September 1939; 1939 Iron Cross First Class Bar, 2 October 1939; Knight's Cross of the Iron Cross, 20 October 1941; Oakleaves, 28 October 1944; German Cross in Gold, 9 October 1944; Wound Badge 1939 Black Class; Medal for the Winter Campaign in Russia 1941-1942; Demjansk Shield, 31 December 1943; Danzig Cross First Class, 24 October 1939; Italian Order of the Crown Officers Cross, 19 December 1941; SS Honour Ring; SS Honour Sword.

Born in Breslau, Silesia, Simon served in World War I and afterwards joined the Reichswehr. Simon was one of Eicke's (q.v.) most devoted protégés and having earned his complete confidence and trust, helped to form the SS-Totenkopf Standarte *Oberbayern*. This unit became a regiment of the newly formed *Totenkopf* Division.

Simon served in the Polish and French campaigns. Eicke chose him to command the first SS-TK Infantry Regiment in the Russian campaign and he performed with the measure of ruthlessness and bravery that Eicke expected, winning the Knight's Cross of the Iron Cross. His long association with Eicke and the SS-TK, coupled with his outstanding combat reports, prompted Himmler (q.v.) to give Simon command of the *Totenkopf* Division for a period.

On 16 October 1943 he was given command of the 16th SS Panzergrenadier Division *Reichsführer-SS*, a position he held until 24 October 1944; in recognition of his service, he was awarded the Oakleaves, becoming the 639th recipient. He then became commanding officer of XIII SS Army Corps, fighting on the Western and Southwestern Fronts in Germany.

After the war he was tried for war crimes, earning the special distinction of being condemned to death by both the Russians and the British. The unsubstantiated Russian charges stemmed from atrocities allegedly ordered during the German withdrawal from Kharkov (having said that, Simon is on record for urging his men to be ruthless, stating the Russians were 'bandits who must be slaughtered without pity').

The British sentenced him for the massacre of 2700 Italian civilians in reprisal for the activities of a partisan brigade in the Apennines. The sentence was commuted and he was freed in 1954. After his release he was tried twice by German courts for committing war crimes in Germany and was acquitted. He faced a third trial on the same charges, but before it began, he died, in 1961. Max Simon was lucky that he did not fall into Russian hands, for if he had have done his sentence would have been much harsher.

SIX, Prof Dr Franz

RANK: SS-Oberführer
BORN: 12 August 1909—
PARTY NUMBER: 245670
SS NUMBER: 107480
AWARDS: War Merit Cross Second Class
with Swords; War Merit Cross First
Class with Swords; SS Honour Ring;
SS Honour Sword.

Six joined the SD in the 1930s as a pupil of the economics expert, Professor Höhn. Himmler (q.v.) was acutely aware of the lack of competent professional men in the large bureaucracy. He constantly tried to recruit intellectuals, but in the main was unsuccessful with them, and both Höhn and Six tried to leave.

Six served in an Einsatzgruppe in Russia in 1941. Ribbentrop (q.v.) seconded him from the cultural activities section of RSHA to the cultural division of the Foreign Office as an expert on anti-Semitic matters. He was sentenced to life imprisonment after the war. This was commuted; he was released on 30 September 1952.

SKORZENY, Otto

RANK: SS-Sturmbannführer
BORN: 12 June 1908
DIED: 8 July 1975 (D)
PARTY NUMBER: 1083671
SS NUMBER: 295979
AWARDS: 1939 Iron Cross Second Class,
27 July 1941; 1939 Iron Cross First
Class; German Cross in Gold,
16 January 1945; Knight's Cross of
the Iron Cross, 13 September 1943;
Oakleaves, 8 March 1945; Combined
Pilot and Observer Badge in Gold with
Diamonds; SS Honour Ring.

Left: A Waffen-SS mortar team in action during the defence of the town of Narva in mid-July 1944. The weapon is an 80mm sGrW 34 model..

One of the Reich's most successful maverick soldiers, Skorzeny was born in Vienna. He joined the NSDAP in 1930 and was later accepted into the Waffen-SS and served with a field unit until he had a serious accident. After meeting him, Kaltenbrunner (q.v.) gave orders that he should form a special forces unit, as he was technically skilled and a linguist. He formed the commando unit *Oranienburg* in Amt II of the RuSHA in April 1943.

On Hitler's orders, Skorzeny rescued Mussolini from his Italian captors at the Gran Sasso Hotel in a daredevil paratroop raid on 12 September 1943. He helped stop a possible mutiny among the tank troops in Berlin after the 20 July Bomb Plot, and halted the indiscriminate execution of suspected conspirators. He kidnapped the son of the Hungarian premier, Admiral Horthy, thus forestalling Hungary's defection to the Allies. During the Battle of the Bulge, a brigade of English-speaking Germans led by Skorzeny masqueraded as American troops, causing havoc behind American lines. The Americans tried him for conducting illegal practices in the Ardennes Offensive, but acquitted him. He lived in Spain as a businessman and died in Madrid in 1975.

STADLER, Sylvester

RANK: SS-Brigadeführer
BORN: 30 December 1910—
DIED: 23 August 1995 (D)
SS NUMBER: 139495
AWARDS: 1939 Iron Cross Second Class,
    25 September 1939; Iron Cross First Class
    1939, 26 June 1940; Knight's Cross,
    6 April 1943; Oakleaves, 16 September
    1943; Oakleaves with Swords, 6 May
    1945; 1939 Wound Badge Black Class;
    Close Combat Clasp,12 December 1943.

Born in Fohnsdorf, Styria, Austria, he served bravely in the Polish and then the French campaigns, and was transferred to the Eastern Front. While serving as commander of the 2nd Battalion, 4th SS-Panzergrenadier Regiment *Der Führer*, he was awarded the Knight's Cross of the Iron Cross. Six months later he won the Oakleaves, becoming the 333rd recipient. He was transferred to the Western Front and saw action in the Ardennes Offensive. He was transferred to Hungary and fought a rearguard action to Vienna. As commander of the 9th SS Panzer Division *Hohenstaufen* and for actions he received the Swords two days before the surrender, becoming the 152nd recipient.

STAHLECKER, Franz-Walter

RANK: SS-Gruppenführer
BORN: 10 October 1900
DIED: March 1942 (K.I.A.)
PARTY NUMBER: 1069130
SS NUMBER: 73041

Stahlecker was an 'information officer' in the SD in 1938 and went on to become Head of Section VIa of the Reich Main Security Office. In early 1942 Heydrich (q.v.) sidelined Stahlecker by dubi-

ously promoting him to the command of an Einsatzgruppe in the Baltic states. Heydrich's reports claimed that Stahlecker's group liquidated 221,000 victims, although it is possible that such figures were reached carelessly and the same totals were added several times over. Heydrich stood to benefit from this misrepresentation, firstly by demonstrating his success in the 'final solution', and secondly to neutralise Nebe (q.v.), who is said to have opposed Heydrich's orders and to have disclosed them to the Oster Circle. Stahlecker was apparently killed by partisans in March 1942.

STANGL, Franz

RANK: Commandant of Treblinka
    Konzentrationslager
BORN: 26 March 1908
DIED: 28 June 1971 (D)

Stangl was commandant at Treblinka, an extermination camp located on the Bug River near Warsaw. He was extremely careful, however, to conceal his 'accomplishments' at the camp. This was a Herculean feat given that Treblinka is accredited with the extermination of nearly 700,000 people, second only to Auschwitz in numbers gassed. Himmler (q.v.) was aware Treblinka was operating very efficiently: during its operational life it contributed to the SS bank accounts $2,800,000, £400,000, 12,000,000 roubles, 145 kilograms of gold from rings and teeth, 4000 carats of diamonds, as well as hair and used clothing for SS factories. Himmler failed to bestow on Stangl the praise he deserved because of the latter's reluctance for publicity.

The Nazi authorities deemed it prudent to destroy the evidence that Treblinka would yield to the advancing Russians, by demolishing the camp and removing possible witnesses. They exterminated the inmates (only 40 people survived when the camp was demolished), and transferred the SS guards to fight the partisans in Yugoslavia, a virtual death sentence for them as well.

Stangl himself was among those who survived the war, however, and in 1945 returned to his wife and family in Austria. The destruction of the camp, coupled with his reluctance for publicity in part hid his identity, and he was arrested, not for his involvement, but on account of his SS rank. Consequently, those responsible for his arrest were in ignorance of his role in the Treblinka camp.

When his career was uncovered he was sent to Linz to await trial by the Austrian courts. At this stage the Allied control commission was still ignorant of his full involvement, and when he escaped from an outside working party, he was not considered important enough to pursue. He slipped away a few weeks later through Italy to Syria, where he was joined by his family, who had been assisted by Skorzeny (q.v.). Stangl reached Brazil and then worked in the Volkswagen factory in São Paulo.

Life was uneventful for 16 years, and then the Wiesenthal investigations caught up with him. In 1967 a disaffected cousin informed Wiesenthal of Stangl's whereabouts, and a former Gestapo man gave him the precise location. After much legal wrangling, he was returned to Germany for trial on 2 June 1969. He was tried three years later, where he stated: 'my conscience is clear. I was simply doing my duty.' Sentenced to life imprisonment, he died in 1971.

STEINER, Felix
RANK: SS Obergruppenführer und General der Waffen-SS
BORN: 23 May 1896
DIED: 12 May 1966 (D)
PARTY NUMBER: 4264295
SS NUMBER: 253351
AWARDS: 1914 Iron Cross Second Class; 1914 Iron Cross First Class; Cross of Honour 1914-1918 Combatants; 1914 Wound Badge Black; 1939 Iron Cross Second Class Bar, 17 September 1939; 1939 Iron Cross First Class Bar, 26 September 1939; German Cross in Gold, 22 April 1942; Knight's Cross, 15 August 1940; Oakleaves, 23 December 1942; Oakleaves with Swords, 10 August 1944; SS Honour Ring and Sword; Finnish Freedom Cross with Swords.

A career soldier from East Prussia who saw frontline service during World War I, Steiner joined the Freikorps and subsequently the Reichswehr. In 1933 he left the Reichswehr, enabling him to undertake special assignments with the Wehrmacht training department. In 1935 he joined the SS-Verfügungstruppe and helped to develop the 3rd Battalion of the SS-Standarte *Deutschland*, stationed in Munich and the SS training camp at Dachau. He applied his military training to the men, instituting training schedules in application of his motto 'sweat saves blood'.

While serving as commanding officer of the SS-Standarte *Deutschland*, attached to Army Group B on the Russian Front, he was awarded the Knight's Cross of the Iron Cross; as commanding general of the *Wiking* Division, he won the Oakleaves, becoming the 159th recipient. In 1943, using German and European volunteers including Latvians, he formed III (Germanic) SS Panzer Corps, which served on the Russian Front. He was awarded the Swords for his decisive leadership, becoming the 86th recipient.

As the war drew to a close, Hitler ordered his army group and the forces of General Wenck to break the encirclement of Berlin. Realising they had insufficient strength to accomplish the mission, Steiner directed his men to avoid Soviet capture. He was taken prisoner at Lüneburg on 3 May 1945. He died in Munich in 1966.

STRACHWITZ, Hyazinth Graf

RANK: SS-Standartenführer
BORN: 30 July 1893—
PARTY NUMBER: 1405562
SS NUMBER: 82857
AWARDS: 1914 Iron Cross Second Class;
1914 Iron Cross First Class; Cross of
Honour 1914-1918 Combatants; 1939
Iron Cross First Class, Bar; Knight's
Cross of the Iron Cross, 25 August
1941; Oakleaves, 13 November 1942;
Oakleaves with Swords 28 March 1943;
Oakleaves, Swords with Diamonds,
15 April 1944; Silesian Eagle First Class
with swords, (with the official recogni-
tion in 1933, the added devices were
discontinued); SS Honour Ring.

A skillful career soldier, Strachwitz became a cadet at Lichterfelde and was commis-sioned in the Garde du Corps Regiment as a leutnant in Potsdam. During World War I he saw service on the Western Front. After the war he was a member of the reserve and was promoted to oberleutnant.

Having joined the NSDAP and the SS, Strachwitz initially fought in Poland and France with the army. With Operation 'Barbarossa' he went to the East with the 16th Panzer Division, commanding the 1st Battalion, 2nd Panzer Regiment. German panzer divisions in 1941 usually comprised one panzer regiment of two battal-ions of around 60 tanks each. By 1944 this had risen to 90 tanks each. For bravery in the field near Werba he was awarded the Knight's Cross of the Iron Cross. He was further recognised with the Oakleaves for his bravery while commanding the same unit, becoming the 144th recipient. He was transferred to the Panzer Regiment *Grossdeutschland*, and the success of his tactics was borne out by the trail of burning Soviet tanks left by his men. Many engagements were undertaken at near point-blank range, and he

won the Swords, becoming the 27th recipient. A year later, he earned the ultimate accolade, the Diamonds, and was the eleventh person to win it. He assumed command of the 1st Panzer Division with a title broadened to Senior Panzer Leader in Army Group North. At the end of the war he was taken prisoner by the Americans and remained in captivity until 1946.

STRECKENBACH, Bruno

RANK: SS-Gruppenführer und
Generalleutnant der Polizei und
Waffen-SS
BORN: 7 February 1902
DIED: 28 October 1977 (D)
PARTY NUMBER: 489972
SS NUMBER: 14713
AWARDS: 1939 Iron Cross Second Class
(Polish Campaign); 1939 Iron Cross
First Class, 15 July 1943; German Cross
in Gold, 15 December 1943; Knight's
Cross of the Iron Cross, 27 August
1944; Oakleaves, 21 January 1945;
Close Combat Clasp Silver Class;
SS Honour Ring; SS Honour Sword.

A particularly brutal commander, Streckenbach was born in Hamburg, the son of a customs official. He joined the Hamburg police in 1933 and was appointed to lead it when the Gestapo absorbed it. He was an early member of the SS and commanded the first Stürm in Hamburg.

Streckenbach joined the RSHA and was Heydrich's (q.v.) deputy in Amt 1, the personnel office. He selected personnel for the various executive units of the security police and SD, as well as being responsible for their discipline. After the fall of Poland and the establishment of the General Government, he was appointed commander of its security police. He directed

the mass arrests of Polish intelligentsia, in Operation 'Action AB' in May 1940, and most of the Einsatzgruppen officers took their instructions from him. In May 1941, he held a course at the frontier police school at Pretzsch on the Elbe near Leipzig for over 100 candidates from the Gestapo or SD. Apart from lectures on the sub-human enemy, there were terrain exercises which one candidate described as games of hide-and-seek.

Streckenbach retained his position after Heydrich's death, but on 15 April 1944 he took over the command of the Latvian 19th Waffen-Grenadier Division der SS (Lettische Nr. 2). He was awarded the Knight's Cross of the Iron Cross and the Oakleaves, becoming the 701st recipient, for his leadership of the poorly equipped division during the heavy fighting in the Baltic area. He was taken prisoner by the Russians. He was not surrendered to the Nuremberg Tribunal to face the charges which were brought against Ohlendorf (q.v.) and his associates, nor was he hanged in Russia. He returned from the Soviet Union on 10 October 1955. He lived in Hamburg where he died in 1977.

STROOP, Jürgen

RANK: SS-Gruppenführer
BORN: 26 September 1895
DIED: 9 July 1952 (E.A.)
PARTY NUMBER: 1292297
SS NUMBER: 44611
AWARDS: 1914 Iron Cross Second Class; Cross of Honour 1914-1918 Combatants; 1914 Wound Badge Black Class; 1939 Iron Cross Second Class; 1939 Iron Cross First Class; 1939 Iron Cross Second Class Bar; War Merit Cross Second Class with Swords; Infantry Assault Badge, 21 January 1943; SS Honour Ring; SS Honour Sword.

Stroop was the SS and Police Chief of Warsaw in the spring of 1943 when Himmler (q.v.) decided to remove the remaining 56,000 Jews from the Warsaw Ghetto.

As an anti-partisan commander he was empowered to call on all troops in the Warsaw area, as well as the security police, and

his force included two training battalions, some Wehrmacht units and numbered 2096 men in total. The first Warsaw rebellion was treated as a military campaign. Himmler was at Zhitomir and did not personally visit Warsaw, but sent the police leaders Krüger (q.v.) and von Herff, to act as observers, and personally dispatched orders to Stroop.

Stroop sent daily situation reports to Himmler, dispassionate records of the numbers killed daily. They were bound as a sumptuous illustrated album entitled *There are no more Jews in Poland* for presentation to Himmler. Himmler reported on the action to Hitler at Rastenberg and tried, by means of photographs, to convince the high command that military emplacements had been built in the ghetto. Himmler was determined that this desperate resistance and the fag-end of the extermination of two million Polish Jews should figure as a genuine campaign and battle honour for the SS and police. Stroop personally supervised the deportation or summary execution of those Jews who surrendered, and blew up the venerated Tlomacki synagogue to celebrate the victory.

As a reward for his success, Himmler appointed him Higher Police Leader

As a reward for his Warsaw successes, Himmler appointed Stroop as the Higher Police Leader in Greece on 13 September 1943, a post then critically important in the wake of the surrender of Marshal Badoglio's Italian Government. Stroop established his headquarters in Athens, and for the next two months busied himself with directing the deportation of Jews from the Greek mainland to Auschwitz.

After the war Stroop was apprehended in the American zone and tried for war crimes by an American court at Dachau. The book he had submitted to Himmler convicted him, and he was condemned to death on 22 March 1947. He was then turned over to the Poles who tried him on 8 September 1951; he was publicly executed on 9 July 1952 on the site of the former ghetto.

STUCKART, Dr Wilhelm

RANK: SS-Obergruppenführer
BORN: 16 November 1902
DIED: December 1953 (D)
PARTY NUMBER: 378144
SS NUMBER: 280042
AWARDS: Golden Party Badge; War Merit
    Cross Second Class without Swords;
    War Merit Cross First Class without
    Swords; SS Honour Ring; SS Honour
    Sword.

Born in Wiesbaden, Stuckhart was a lawyer and a devoted supporter of Hitler. He drew up the Nuremberg laws, which were made public at the 1935 Nuremberg Rally and enforced from September of that year.

The first Reich law of citizenship recognised two degrees of humanity: the *Reichsbürger*, described as the citizens of pure German blood, and *Staatsangehörige* for all other categories of person who were the subjects of the state. The law for protection of German blood and honour forbade intermarriage between the two groups.

Stuckart replaced Hans Pfundtner as Chief State Secretary in Frick's Ministry of the Interior, and Himmler controlled it through him from 1935. After the death of the Minister of Justice, Gürtner, on 22 January 1941, Himmler wanted the administration of civil law to be handled by the Ministry of the Interior, which he also would control through Stuckart.

Stuckart was appalled by the 'final solution' and he tried to persuade Eichmann (q.v.) to spare the fringe categories of Jews, half-castes and those born of mixed marriages. Eichmann remained adamant. Stuckart appealed directly to Himmler, suggesting sterilisation, although having secretly ascertained from Dr Conti (q.v.) that this was impractical. Himmler was convinced by his appeal and issued an edict to spare the lives of Jews born of mixed marriages, saving 28,000 people. After the 20 July Bomb Plot, Stuckart interrogated one of the leading conspirators, Paul

Kanstein, and released him. Kaltenbrunner (q.v.), convinced of his guilt, was furious with Stuckart and never forgave him for his meddling and leniency.

After the war Stuckart was tried in the Wilhelmstrasse Case in 1949. The humane acts he carried out during the war at considerable personal risk brought a sentence of three years and 10 months' imprisonment. He was released the day after his sentence. He was killed near Hanover in a car accident in December 1953.

SUHR, Friedrich

RANK: SS Obersturmbannführer
BORN: 6 May 1907
DIED: 1946 (D)
PARTY NUMBER: 2623241
SS NUMBER: 65824
AWARDS: 1939 Iron Cross Second Class,
    20 May 1943; 1939 Iron Cross First
    Class, 16 December 1943; Knight's
    Cross of the Iron Cross, 11 December
    1944; War Merit Cross Second Class
    with Swords; Commemorative Medal of
    13 March 1938; Commemorative Medal
    of 1 October 1938; Prague Castle Bar;
    Close Combat Clasp Bronze Class; Anti-
    Partisan War Badge Silver Class; 1939
    Wound Badge Black Class.

A member of RSHA, Suhr was part of Amt IV B/4 working for Eichmann (q.v.) on the transportation of Jews from France.

In December 1944 he commanded a combined battle group under the high command of the German security forces in France and under the direct control of the Higher SS and Police Leader attached to the military governor. Suhr was awarded the Knight's Cross and survived the war, only to die in mysterious circumstances in Wuppertal-Elberfeld in 1946.

THALER, Johann

RANK: SS-Oberscharführer
BORN: 6 February 1920
DIED: 7 April 1945 (K.I.A.)
PARTY NUMBER: —
SS NUMBER: —
AWARDS: 1939 Iron Cross Second Class, 7 April 1943; 1939 Iron Cross First Class, 7 April 1943; Knight's Cross of the Iron Cross, 14 August 1943; Medal for the Winter Campaign in Russia 1941-1942; Silver Tank Battle Badge; 1939 Wound Badge Silver Class.

Thaler was a tank driver with the 6th SS-Panzer Regiment, 2nd SS Panzer Division *Das Reich*, on the Russian Front, driving a Panzerkampfwagen Mk IV with two others when they came face to face with several Soviet tanks. Despite first entering service in 1938, the Panzer IV continued to fight with German units until the end of the war. Various versions were produced, the most potent being the Ausf H and Ausf J. Their long-barrelled 75mm guns were adequate against most opposition, and they were far more reliable than the Panthers. Indeed, by 1943 panzer regiments in the German Army were supposed to have one battalion equipped with Mk IVs and the other equipped with Panthers, but because of the problems with the Panthers many regiments had nothing but Mk IVs.

Thaler's detachment immediately destroyed three of the enemy tanks, but Thaler's took a direct hit that immobilised it. He not only repaired the damage despite being subjected to heavy enemy fire, but went on to destroy several more Soviet tanks. He was awarded the Knight's Cross of the Iron Cross for his bravery and is only one of two tank crew members within the Waffen-SS to be so honoured. He was killed in action against the Russians near Vienna on 7 April 1945.

THOMAS, Dr Max

RANK: SS-Gruppenführer
BORN: 4 August 1891
DIED: 1944 (K.I.A.)
PARTY NUMBER: 1848453
SS NUMBER: 141341
AWARDS: 1914 Iron Cross Second Class; 1914 Iron Cross First Class; Cross of Honour 1914-1918 Combatants; 1939 Iron Cross First Class Bar; War Merit Cross Second Class with Swords; War Merit Cross First Class with Swords; 1939 Wound Badge Black Class; SS Honour Ring; SS Honour Sword.

Thomas was the SS Police Chief in France from 1940 until 1942, when one of Heydrich's (q.v.) plots to bomb two of Paris's synagogues went farcically wrong. Stülpnagel, the military governor of France, discovered accidentally the involvement of Knochen (q.v) and the implied involvement of Thomas.

Highly incensed, Stülpnagel complained to Keitel, commander of the High Command of the Armed Forces, that the Gestapo was intensifying his difficulties with the French. In response, Keitel politely wrote to Heydrich on 22 October requesting the recall of Thomas and Knochen from France. Heydrich answered Keitel from Prague with a letter to Quartermaster-General Wagner, which

Thomas was transferred to Russia to take over an Einsatzgruppe

he worded in the most insulting terms: 'My director of services in Paris did not think it necessary to tell Stülpnagel because our experience gave little hope of his comprehension. I was well aware of the political consequences of these measures, the more so since I have been entrusted for years with the final solution of the Jewish problem.' However, Thomas was transferred to Russia, where Heydrich saddled him with an Einsatzgruppe. He went on to become the SS Police Chief for the Ukraine, and it is thought he was killed in action sometime in 1944, though his ultimate fate is unknown.

TRABANDT, August-Wilhelm

RANK: SS-Brigadeführer
     und Generalmajor der Waffen-SS
BORN: 21 July 1891
DIED: 19 May 1968 (D)
PARTY NUMBER: —
SS NUMBER: 218852
AWARDS: 1914 Iron Cross Second Class;
     1914 Iron Cross First Class; Cross
     of Honour 1914-1918 Combatants;
     1939 Iron Cross Second Class Bar,
     18 September 1939; 1939 Iron Cross
     First Class Bar, 25 September 1939;
     German Cross in Gold, 22 October
     1943; Knight's Cross of the Iron Cross,
     6 January 1944; SS Honour Ring;
     SS Honour Sword.

Trabandt served as an infantry-man during World War I and joined the *Leibstandarte* in May 1936. He demonstrated his leadership qualities in the Polish campaign commanding the 3rd battalion LSSAH.

After leading the battalion through the severe winter fighting near Weliki-Luki in 1941-42, he went on to take command of the 1st SS-Infantry Brigade on 18 October 1943. This served as the 'fire brigade' for Army Group Centre, being deployed wherever it was deemed appropriate. For his leadership of the unit he was awarded the Knight's Cross of the Iron Cross. On 25 January 1944 he became the commanding officer of the *Horst Wessel* Division, a position he held until 3 January 1945. In the autumn of 1944 he fought with his command in Slovakia. Trabandt handed his command over to SS-Oberführer Georg Bochmann (q.v.) on 3 January 1945 and went on to command SS-Panzergrenadier-Schule Kienschlag from 17 February until April 1945, and SS Kampfgruppe *Trabandt*. Captured by the Soviets, he did not return to Germany until 1954. He died in Ahrenburg near Hamburg in 1968.

TYCHSEN, Christian

RANK: SS-Obersturmbannführer
BORN: 3 December 1910
DIED: 28 July 1944 (K.I.A.)
PARTY NUMBER: —
SS NUMBER: —
AWARDS: 1939 Iron Cross Second Class,
     30 May 1940; 1939 Iron Cross First
     Class, 18 July 1940; German Cross in
     Gold, 13 May 1942; Knight's Cross of the
     Iron Cross, 31 March 1943; Oakleaves,
     10 December 1943; Close Combat Clasp
     Silver Class; Infantry Assault Badge; 1939
     Wound Badge Gold Class.

Tychsen was born in Flensburg, Schleswig-Holstein. On 1 October 1934, he joined the SS-Verfügungstruppe and four years later served with the SS-Reconnaissance detachment. When Tychsen's division entered the Soviet Union he commanded a motorcycle company, operating as the advance guard for SS Division *Das Reich*. Tychsen was a tough and heroic leader, and it was during the fighting around Kharkov in 1943, after taking command of a panzer unit, that he was awarded the Knight's Cross.

As commander of the 2nd Battalion, *Das Reich*, he became the 253rd recipient of the Oakleaves for his actions against the Soviets when they attempted to establish bridgeheads across the Dnieper river, near Chodoroff.

After being wounded nine times, his luck ran out during the fighting in Normandy. Tychsen, accompanied by an NCO and a driver, was in a Kübelwagen when they were intercepted by an American tank. The driver was killed and the NCO was severely wounded and managed to escape, but Tychsen was critically wounded. He died while receiving medical treatment. He was buried in an unmarked grave, after souvenir hunters had removed his tunic, decorations and identification. It took many years of verification to identify his remains.

ULLRICH, Karl

RANK: SS-Oberführer
BORN: 1 December 1910—
PARTY NUMBER: 715727
SS NUMBER: 31438
AWARDS: 1939 Iron Cross Second Class,
18 May 1940;1939 Iron Cross First Class,
1 July 1940; Knight's Cross of the Iron
Cross, 19 February 1942; Oakleaves,
14 May 1944; Commemorative Medal of
13 March 1938; Commemorative Medal
of 1 October 1938; Prague Castle Bar;
Medal for the Winter Campaign in
Russia 1941-1942; Demjansk Shield,
General Assault Badge; SS Honour Ring;
SS Honour Sword.

Ullrich saw service in the French campaign of 1940 as the commanding officer of the 3rd Company, SS-Engineer Battalion of the SS-Verfügungs-division. During the heavy winter fighting of 1941-42 in Russia he commanded a small battle group and was awarded the Knight's Cross of the Iron Cross. His achievements were further rewarded with the bestowal of the Oakleaves, which he received personally from Hitler at his 'Wolf's Lair' headquarters. He was the last commander of the 5th SS Panzer Division *Wiking*, a position he held from 9 October 1944 until 5 May 1945. In the final months of the war, *Wiking* fought a stiff defensive action from Stuhlweissenburg, west of Budapest, back into Czechoslovakia, just south of Fürstenfeld. before capitulating on 8 May 1945.

VAHL, Herbert-Ernst

RANK: SS-Brigadeführer
    und Generalmajor der Waffen-SS
BORN: 9 October 1896
DIED: 22 July 1944 (A)
PARTY NUMBER: —
SS NUMBER: 430348
AWARDS: 1914 Iron Cross Second Class;
1914 Iron Cross First Class; Cross
of Honour 1914-1918 Combatants;
1939 Iron Cross Second Class Bar,
2 October 1939; 1939 Iron Cross First
Class Bar, 13 July 1941; German Cross
in Gold, 18 September 1941; Knight's
Cross of the Iron Cross, 31 March 1943.

A Prussian, Vahl joined the Reichswehr after serving in World War I. He became a lieutenant in the First (Prussian) Motorised Detachment on 1 April 1925, with promotion to captain in 1931 and to commanding officer of a motorised company in 1935. Vahl commanded an armoured unit in the army during the Polish campaign, and later with the rank of lieutenant-colonel, an army tank unit in 1941.

On 13 July 1944 he was given command of the SS-Polzei *Division*

On 1 August 1942 he transferred to the Waffen-SS and took over command of the panzer regiment of the *Das Reich* Division on the Russian Front, winning the Knight's Cross of the Iron Cross. Vahl was in temporary command until he was relieved by Walter Krüger (q.v.) when Georg Keppler (q.v.) left the division. Vahl was appointed as inspector general of all SS panzer units. On 13 July 1944, he was given the command of the 4th SS

Panzergrenadier Division *SS-Polizei*, which had been reformed, and then underwent training before being sent to the mountainous area of northern Greece. There, the division engaged in comparatively quiet anti-guerrilla warfare, apart from savage reprisals which followed the ambushing of a German convoy near Klissura. Vahl's command lasted only nine days as he was killed in a car accident on the way to his command in Greece on the July 1944. He is buried at Dionyssos-Rependoza.

VANDIEKEN, Anton

RANK: SS-Sturmbannführer der Reserve
BORN: 4 July 1909—
PARTY NUMBER: —
SS NUMBER: —
AWARDS: 1939 Iron Cross Second Class, 1 December 1941; 1939 Iron Cross First Class, 24 February 1942; German Cross in Gold, 22 December 1943; Knight's Cross of the Iron Cross, 26 December 1944; Close Combat Clasp Silver Class.

Vandieken joined the Waffen-SS as a reservist on 15 January 1940. He became the commanding officer of the 6th Company SS-Cavalry Regiment 1, *Florian Geyer* Division, LVII Panzer Corps, Army Group South. He was on the southeastern front in the autumn of 1944 and fighting in Hungary when units of the allied Hungarian forces defected to the Soviets. Cut off for a short time from the German lines, his unit managed to stop the advancing Soviet forces. For his bravery and leadership he was awarded the Knight's Cross of the Iron Cross.

VEESENMAYER, Dr Edmund

RANK: SS-Brigadeführer
BORN: 12 November 1904—
PARTY NUMBER: 873780
SS NUMBER: 202122
AWARDS: War Merit Cross Second Class with Swords; War Merit Cross First Class with Swords; Knight's Cross of the War Merit Cross with Swords, 29 October 1944; SS Honour Ring; SS Honour Sword.

Rabidly anti-Semitic, Veesenmayer joined the Allgemeine-SS and became a protégé of Wilhelm Keppler (q.v.).

Keppler's failure to become minister of economic affairs channelled his ambitions towards diplomacy. During the plotting which preceded the Austrian *Anschluss*, Himmler (q.v.) secured his appointment as Secretary of the Vienna Embassy. Keppler fulfilled similar missions in Slovakia and Danzig on the eve of their digestion, and Veesenmayer accompanied him.

Veesenmayer became a recognised member of the Foreign Office at the beginning of the war, with the post of Plenipotentiary for Ireland, and with Admiral Canaris, he concocted schemes for using Irish nationalist terrorists against England in early 1940.

Veesenmayer's professional home was not the Foreign Office, but the SS, and he had to serve two masters: his immediate chief, von Ribbentrop, and Kaltenbrunner (q.v.) at the Reich's main security office. His position was often tricky, because Kaltenbrunner, having swallowed Canaris's Abwehr, was trying to absorb the Foreign Office too. However, there could never be any quarrel between Kaltenbrunner and Ribbentrop over the extermination of European Jewry. For this purpose Veesenmayer was not ill-chosen. He composed long reports to Ribbentrop on Hungary's failure to deport Jews in May 1943 and on Slovakia's failure to renew the deportations in December.

On the strength of these cold, inhumane and ill-informed documents (which Veesenmayer insisted later were amended by Ribbentrop before he signed them), this insignificant person became Plenipotentiary to Hungary, a position he held from March to October 1944 due to Hewel's forcing Admiral Horthy, Hungary's Regent, with the threat of kidnapping, to accept a German occupational force. He was really appointed for little other purpose than to provide Eichmann (q.v.) with diplomatic cover to continue deporting Jews from Hungary.

After the war Veesenmayer was tried for war crimes and sentenced to 25 years' imprisonment. This sentence was commuted to 10 years; he was released from Landsberg in December 1951, having played a part in the murder of at least 300,000 persons.

VEISS, Woldemars

RANK: Waffen-Standartenführer der SS
BORN: 7 November 1899
DIED: 16 April 1944 (K.I.A.)
PARTY NUMBER: —
SS NUMBER: —
AWARDS: 1939 Iron Cross Second Class; 1939 Iron Cross First Class; Knight's Cross of the Iron Cross, 9 February 1944.

Born in Riga, Latvia, Veiss joined the Latvian anti-Soviet forces under Colonel Kalpak when he was a student in 1918, and was quickly made an officer. He went on to join the Latvian regular army, holding many commands and serving as military attaché in Finland and Estonia in 1939. The three independent Baltic states were occupied in June 1940 by the Soviets as a result of the Russo-German Pact of 1939, when Stalin announced their 'voluntary incorporation' into the Union of Soviet Socialist Republics. There followed a year of terror and repression when Veiss had no alternative than to go underground until the German invasion of June 1941. To the Baltic people, everyone who took up arms against the Stalinist regime had to be regarded as a protester, if not as a friend.

Veiss assisted in the formation of security forces which attempted to rid the country of Soviet soldiers and communist partisans who had banded together. Hitler and the SS main office in 1943 ordered the expansion of the Latvian forces, and Veiss was instrumental in forming the new unit. He became the commanding officer of the new 40th Volunteer Brigade of the SS, and fought for several months against advancing Soviet forces in the Wolchov area. Veiss and his men displayed considerable heroism in both offensive and defensive actions, and for this he was awarded the Knight's Cross of the Iron Cross. Later, he was seriously wounded and died of his wounds in a military hospital in Riga. He was given a formal funeral which was attended by several high-ranking German officers, including the army commanding general, Georg Lindemann.

VOGT, Fritz

RANK: SS-Sturmbannführer
BORN: 17 March 1913
DIED: 3 April 1945 (K.I.A.)
PARTY NUMBER: 3302347
SS NUMBER: 97799
AWARDS: 1939 Iron Cross Second Class, 23 September 1939;1939 Iron Cross First Class, 27 May 1940; Knight's Cross of the Iron Cross, 4 September 1940; Oakleaves, 30 March 1945

Vogt was born in Munich, Bavaria, and joined the SS-Verfügungstruppe in 1935. During the invasion of the Low Countries and France in 1940, he served with the 2nd Company, SS-Reconnaissance Detachment of the SS-Verfügungsdivision. In the surrounding area of the Meuse-Waal Canal near Heerbosch

WÄCHTLER, Fritz

RANK: SS-Obergruppenführer,
Gauleiter of Bayreuth 1935-45
BORN: 7 January 1891
DIED: 19 April 1945 (E.R.)
PARTY NUMBER: 35313
SS NUMBER: 209058
AWARDS: Golden Party Badge; 1914 Iron
Cross Second Class; Cross of Honour
1914-1918 Combatants; 1914 Wound
Badge Black Class; SS Honour Ring;
SS Honour Sword.

were a line of fortified Dutch bunkers which he successfully attacked and destroyed, thus enabling the advancing German troops to pass without hesitation. A few days later near Lys, he captured an entire French battalion, an action which earned him the Knight's Cross of the Iron Cross.

In Operation 'Barbarossa', he distinguished himself commanding the SS-Volunteer Battalion *Norge* of the *Wiking* Division. In late December 1944, *Wiking* and *Totenkopf* were removed from the defence of Warsaw and rushed to Hungary in an attempt to rescue the besieged city of Budapest and its garrison. On New Year's Day 1945, the armoured attack opened and continued for nearly two weeks, but the SS divisions could not break into the city. *Wiking* was again repulsed by formidable Soviet defences in late January, and in February the battered division was on the defence against the pressure of increased Soviet attacks. Vogt was commanding officer of the 1st Battalion of the 23rd SS-Volunteer Panzergrenadier Battalion, and his leadership during the battles made him the 685th recipient of the Oakleaves. In the final months of the war Wiking fought a defensive action west of Budapest, back into Czechoslovakia, where Vogt was killed on 3 April 1945.

Born in Triebes in Thüringia, Wächtler was a leutnant in a machine-gun company during World War I, and after the war returned to his profession as a teacher. In 1926 he founded the local NSDAP group in Triebes and was appointed Deputy Gauleiter in 1929. In 1933 he was made Minister for National Education and Minister of the Interior for Thüringia. After the death of Hans Schemm in an air crash on 5 March 1935, he was sent to the Bavarian Ostmark as Gauleiter of Bayreuth; he was appointed on 5 December 1935, and held the position until his execution. Schemm had founded and led the Nazi teachers' league and this post also fell to Wächtler. Nazi education placed the emphasis on physical training and biology. In the latter natural selection theories became a dominant teaching strand. At the same time, religious instruction was greatly reduced (Hitler was not only fanatically anti-church, he also believed that Nationalism Socialism itself would supplant Christianity as a religious faith). The House of Education was at Bayreuth and in contemporary writings was described as a memorial to Schemm.

Wächtler was a heavy drinker and in the last days of the war fell foul of Bormann (q.v.). He was charged with defeatism and was executed by an SS unit commanded by Deputy Gauleiter Ludwig Ruckdeschel (q.v.) on 19 April 1945.

WÄCHTER, Dr Otto

RANK: SS-Gruppenführer
BORN: 8 July 1901—
PARTY NUMBER: 301093
SS NUMBER: 235368
AWARDS: Commemorative Medal of
   13 March 1938; Commemorative Medal
   of 1 October 1938; Prague Castle Bar;
   SS Honour Ring; SS Honour Sword.

Dr Otto Wächter was a key figure in the formation of the Ukrainian SS divisions after the invasion of Russia.

The Stalin-Hitler 'Pact of Friendship' in August 1939 put Galicia in the Russian sphere of influence. With Poland's partition in September, Galicia was among the territories ceded to the USSR and for the next 21 months was subject to Stalinist rule. It was therefore with something akin to relief that the Galicians welcomed the arrival, in June 1941, of Hitler's armies. In August 1941 Galicia was made a fourth district of the General Government. Dr Otto Wächter, who was attached to the staff of the SS-Oberabschnitt Ost,

had been promoted to the purely SS rank of SS-Brigadeführer on 9 November 1939, and was made Governor of Galicia in 1941, a position he held until 1944. Under his governorship it enjoyed a fair degree of autonomy.

Wächter (left in picture) was one of the more enlightened German administrators of the eastern territories, seeking to win the local population's cooperation rather than bludgeoning them into submission. As a result, Galicia was one of the most peaceful regions of the occupied Ostgebiete. Wächter had been in Lvov since 1941 and knew and understood the people; he was anxious to obtain from his fellow countrymen a better understanding of the Ukrainians and a closer collaboration between the Ukraine and Germany. He believed that raising a Ukrainian division to fight Bolshevism alongside the Germans was a step in the right direction. He suggested the idea to Himmler (q.v.), and in March 1943 obtained approval for the raising of a 'police regiment Galicia'. Disaster at Stalingrad in January 1943 made Himmler more receptive to the idea of recruiting slaves for the Waffen-SS, and he proposed that the police regiment be transferred into a combat division. Wächter's ultimate fate is unknown.

WAGNER, Jürgen
RANK: SS-Gruppenführer
  und Generalleutnant der Waffen-SS
BORN: 9 September 1901
DIED: August 1947 (E.A.)
PARTY NUMBER: 707279
SS NUMBER: 23692
AWARDS: 1939 Iron Cross Second Class,
  16 May 1940; Iron Cross First Class,
  7 July 1940; German Cross in Gold,
  14 December 1942; Knight's Cross,
  24 July 1943; Oakleaves, 29 December
  1944; 1939 Wound Badge Black Class;
  SS Honour Ring; SS Honour Sword.

Born in Strassburg-Neudorf, Alsace, Wagner joined the *Leibstandarte* in July 1933, and was transferred to the SS-Standarte *Deutschland* in 1939. He became regimental commander of Panzergrenadier Regiment *Germania*, 5th SS Panzer Division *Wiking*, on the Russian Front, where he was awarded the Knight's Cross of the Iron Cross.

Wagner assumed command of the 23rd Freiwilligen Panzergrenadier Division *Nederland* when Himmler (q.v.) wanted to pool all 'Nordic' volunteers into a single division. Mussert, the Dutch Nazi leader, was outraged by this suggestion and complained that since the Dutch outnumbered all the rest, they were entitled to an ethnic unit of their own. Hitler supported this and ordered Himmler to withdraw the Dutch complement from the projected *Nordland* Division. Eventually sufficient numbers – some 5500 men – were obtained, to advance the unit as a battalion.

It was raised in Croatia in 1943, where it first saw action against Tito's partisans. Wagner was awarded the Oakleaves, becoming the 580th recipient. The unit acquired an excellent combat reputation and Wagner went on to lead his unit with considerable success against the advancing Russian forces. He surrendered the remnants of his unit to the American forces at Tangermünde on the River Elbe on 1 May 1945. He was handed over to the British military authorities, who then sent him on to Belgrade after a request from the Yugoslav Government to have him extradited as a war criminal. He was tried by a military tribunal for war crimes, found guilty and sentenced to death. He was executed in 1947.

WAHL, Karl
RANK: SS-Obergruppenführer,
  Gauleiter of Schwabia 1928-45
BORN: 24 September 1892
DIED: 18 February 1981 (D)
PARTY NUMBER: 9803
SS NUMBER: 228017
AWARDS: Golden Party Badge; 1914 Iron
  Cross Second Class; 1914 Iron Cross
  First Class; Cross of Honour 1914-18
  Combatants; 1914 Wound Badge Black
  Class; SS Honour Ring; SS Honour
  Sword.

Wahl volunteered for military service in the army when he was 18, and served with distinction in World War I, leaving the ranks in 1921. He joined the NSDAP, becoming one of the first SA men in Schwabia. He was present at the 1923 Putsch and was instrumental in the conversion of the Bavarian People's Party to the Nazi cause. In 1928 he was appointed Gauleiter of Schwabia, a post he held until 1945 (*gau* was an old Frankish word for a political division within a state; in 1942 there were 40 Nazi Party districts in Greater Germany).

Wahl was continually at variance with Bormann (q.v.), who made strenuous attempts to have him removed from office, which he successfully resisted. After the war he was tried by a de-Nazification court and received a short sentence. He went into the textile industry and died in Augsburg.

WAHL, Kurt

RANK: SS-Sturmbannführer
BORN: 20 August 1914
DIED: 23 December 1988 (D)
PARTY NUMBER: —
SS NUMBER: —
AWARDS: 1939 Iron Cross Second Class,
    1 September 1941; 1939 Iron Cross
    First Class, 1 April 1942; Knight's Cross
    of the Iron Cross, 23 August 1944;
    Oakleaves, 1 February 1945; Tank Battle
    Badge 25; Close Combat Clasp Silver
    Class.

Kurt Wahl was born in Meinigen Thüringen and saw service on the Russian Front with the commencement of Operation 'Barbarossa' in June 1941. In August 1944 he was the regimental adjutant of the 38th SS-Panzergrenadier Regiment, 17th SS Panzergrenadier Division *Götz von Berlichingen*, Army Group B on the Western Front, where he was awarded the Knight's Cross of the Iron Cross. He became the 720th recipient of the Oakleaves during the bitter fighting in the Ardennes in the winter of 1944-45. He survived the war and died in Germany at the end of 1988.

WEBER, Christian

RANK: SS-Brigadeführer
BORN: 25 August 1883
DIED: April 1945 (K.I.A).
PARTY NUMBER: 15
SS NUMBER: 265902
AWARDS: Stosstrupp Cuff Band; Blood
    Order No 84; Coburg Badge,
    14 October 1932; SS Honour Ring;
    SS Honour Sword.

Born in Polsingen, Weber was a lifelong horse fancier, becoming a bookmaker and publican. He was one of the first members of Hitler's Stosstrup, whose headquarters were established in the Torbräu public house. The formation was commanded by Berchtold and Schreck (q.v.), accompanied by Ulrich Graf (q.v.), Emil Maurice (q.v.), 'Sepp' Dietrich (q.v.) and Weber himself. All were linked by a strong sense of camaraderie and by an absolute commitment to protect Hitler, even at the risk of losing their own lives. In this privileged position Weber became part of Hitler's inner circle and was involved in the Röhm Purge of 1934.

The sanctity of the Blood Order, its award and the social benefits conferred upon its holders was carefully scrutinised by the office of '9 November'. It also looked after the participants of the 1923 Putsch. Although he faded from prominence, Hitler entrusted him with his safety during the 'old guard's' annual gathering on 8 November in Munich. Had the police or SS been responsible for security on these occasions, the bomb that exploded on 8 November 1939, nearly killing Hitler, would probably have been detected. In the event, Weber was compromised. He was killed in April 1945 during the Bavarian separatist uprising.

WEGENER, Paul

RANK: SS-Obergruppenführer,
　Gauleiter of Weser-Ems 1942-45
BORN: 1 October 1908—
PARTY NUMBER: 286225
SS NUMBER: 353161
AWARDS: Golden Party Badge; 1939 Iron
　Cross Second Class; War Merit Cross
　Second Class with Swords; War Merit
　Cross First Class with Swords;
　SS Honour Ring; SS Honour Sword.

Wegener was a businessman who held a number of positions in
the NSDAP. In 1936 he was appointed Deputy Gauleiter of Mark-
Brandenburg. He saw service as a Luftwaffe war correspondent
in 1940. After the Gauleiter of Weser-Ems, Karl Röver, died on
15 May 1942, he was appointed to the post which he held till the
end of the war. He was tried by a de-Nazification court, found
guilty and sentenced to six years' imprisonment.

WEIDINGER, Otto

RANK: SS-Obersturmbannführer
BORN: 27 May 1914
DIED: 10 January 1990 (D)
AWARDS: 1939 Iron Cross Second Class,
　15 July 1939; 1939 Iron Cross First
　Class, 25 July 1940; German Cross in
　Gold, 26 November 1943; Knight's
　Cross of the Iron Cross, 21 April 1944;
　Oakleaves, 26 December 1944; Swords,
　6 May 1945; War Merit Cross Second
　Class with Swords; Commemorative
　Medal of 13 March 1938;
　Commemorative Medal of 1 October
　1938; Close Combat Clasp Bronze
　Class; 1939 Wound Badge Black Class;
　SS Honour Ring; SS Honour Sword.

Weidinger was born in Würzburg on the Main river and volunteered
for the SS-Verfügungstruppe in 1934. He attended the SS officers'

school in Brünswick, graduating in 1935. He was the adjutant
of a reconnaissance unit that was the eyes and ears of the
Standarte *Deutschland* in the campaigns in Poland and
France. Having served in Yugoslavia and then on the
Russian Front, he returned to the SS officers' school at
Brünswick in October 1943, this time as an instructor in tactics.
Later that year he was transferred to the *Das Reich* Division in
Russia. There he was awarded the Knight's Cross of the Iron Cross
for actions on the Russian Front.

In 1944 he took command of the Battle Group *Das Reich*. His
unit was transferred to France, where he commanded the 4th SS-
Panzergrenadier Regiment *Der Führer*. With the American advance
into northern France, thousands of German troops were threatened with encirclement but Weidinger's leadership enabled the
German forces to escape north. In recognition of his leadership
and bravery he was awarded the Oakleaves, becoming the 688th
recipient. His unit was transferred to Hungary where it fought a
rearguard action and Weidinger was awarded the Swords, becoming the 150th recipient. He surrendered his unit on 9 May 1945.

Weidinger and some of his men were tried by the French for
war crimes, but were acquitted. He died in Aalen.

WEISE, Erich

RANK: SS-Obersturmbannführer
BORN: 12 August 1911—
PARTY NUMBER: —
SS NUMBER: —
AWARDS: 1939 Iron Cross Second Class,
　10 August 1942; War Merit Cross
　Second Class with Swords, 15 August
　1941; War Merit Cross First Class with
　Swords, 20 April 1942; German Cross
　in Silver, March 1945; Knight's Cross
　of the War Merit Cross with Swords,
　16 November 1945.

From Blankenburg, Thüringen, in the Harz Mountains, Weise was an SS-Untersturmführer and technical repair officer with the 5th SS-Panzer Regiment, 5th SS Panzer Division *Wiking*, on the Eastern Front in November 1943. For his technical service to the division he was awarded the Knight's Cross of the War Merit Cross with Swords on 16 November 1943. His fate is unknown, but it is not unlikely that he was killed in the Cherkassy Pocket at the end of 1943 and beginning of 1944, when the Russians trapped over 75,000 German troops.

WERNER, Heinz
RANK: SS-Sturmbannführer
BORN: 2 December 1917
DIED: 9 August 1978 (D)
PARTY NUMBER: —
SS NUMBER: —
AWARDS: 1939 Iron Cross Second Class, 28 May 1940; 1939 Iron Cross First Class, 26 October 1941; German Cross in Gold, 29 May 1943; Knight's Cross of the Iron Cross, 23 August 1944; Oakleaves, 6 May 1945.

Werner saw service in the invasion of France and the Low Countries in 1940, and was transferred to the Russian Front in 1941. In August 1944 he was the commanding officer of the 3rd (Armoured) Battalion, 4th SS-Panzergrenadier Regiment *Der Führer*, 2nd SS Panzer Division *Das Reich*, Army Group B on the Western Front, where he was awarded the Knight's Cross of the Iron Cross. He was further recognised for his leadership by the bestowal of the Oakleaves, becoming the 864th recipient, as the Waffen-SS fought desperately to stem the massive Allied tide that was storming east towards the Reich. He survived the war and died in Essen in 1978.

WINKELMANN, Otto
RANK: SS-Obergruppenführer und General der Polizei
BORN: 4 September 1894
DIED: 24 September 1977 (D)
PARTY NUMBER: 1373131
SS NUMBER: 308238
AWARDS: War Merit Cross with Swords Second Class, 20 April 1941; War Merit Cross with Swords First Class, 30 January 1942; German Cross in Silver, 5 November 1943; Knight's Cross of the War Merit Cross with Swords, 21 December 1944; Silesian Eagle First Class; Wound Badge; SS Honour Ring; SS Honour Sword.

Born in Otterndorf near Bordesholm Hrlothew, Winkelmann joined the army as a cadet in 1912, was commissioned as a lieutenant in 1913 and fought through World War I. In 1919, he joined the Prussian Schutzpolizei, and from 1933 to 1937 he was the State Police Director in Göritz. In November 1937, he was transferred to the headquarters of the Ordnungspolizei, and in March 1944 he was appointed Higher SS and Police Leader in Hungary by Hitler himself.

Winkelmann was a colourless individual who had been Daluege's (q.v.) successor as the head of the German regular police. He was not a violently indoctrinated SS man; he was good-natured and lazy, and left his nasty responsibilities in the hands of Edmund Veesenmayer (q.v.) and the two Hungarian special commissioners, Endre and Baky. An Einsatzgruppe of the security police had been assembled in Mauthausen concentration camp for use in the Hungarian region. The real purpose of it was to remove all Jews from Hungary when the country became a combat area. Hitler's brief to Winkelmann was 'to perform tasks of the SS and police concerning Hungary and

especially duties in connection with the Jewish problem'. By December 1944 Winkelmann had become combat commander of Budapest, and he was awarded the Knight's Cross of the War Merit Cross for his services. Himmler (q.v.) proposed treating Budapest like Warsaw, smashing all resistance and making the defence of the city against the Russians a purely German matter. Finally he declared it an area of partisan warfare and sent in von dem Bach-Zelewski (q.v.). The position in Budapest and with Horthy became very fraught and Bach-Zelewski was recalled by Himmler for more important tasks. Winkelmann was again in control. He survived the war and died in Kiel in 1977.

WIRTH, Christian
RANK: SS-Oberführer
DIED: 1945 (K.I.A.)
PARTY NUMBER: —
SS NUMBER: —

A former Stuttgart police officer, Wirth was recommended to Himmler's (q.v.) euthanasia programme by Nebe (q.v). He was an expert in all three phases of the programme: incurables, direct extermination by special treatment, and experiments in mass sterilisation. When Himmler complained that a better method had to be found to liquidate Polish Jews, Grawitz (q.v.) suggested Wirth for the task. Wirth was immediately assigned to Poland to work under Odilo Globocnik (q.v.), with the brief to find a method of dispatching one million Polish Jews more efficiently than the gas vans and firing squads. He selected an area along the Lublin-Lwow railway for his first experimental camp and went on to head an organisation of four extermination camps.

Wirth decided he wanted nothing to do with gas vans or mobile death units, using instead a stationary unit with three 'shower rooms', constructed at the centre of the camp. He camouflaged them by planting geraniums and trimming the surrounding grass. The victims were pacified by the thought of a shower, but inside were killed by exhaust gas from diesel engines. Wirth fitted wide doors on both front and back walls to make the removal of gassed victims easier. He was so pleased with the killing centre that he added three more to allow the camp to deal with 1500 Jews daily. In a particularly sick touch, he hung a sign over the gate that

read, 'Entrance to the Jewish State'. Above the entrance to the gas chamber was a banner made from a synagogue curtain which stated in Hebrew, 'This is the gate of the Lord into which the righteous shall enter'.

Wirth was an egotist without conscience. An eyewitness remembers him striking a woman across the face with five lashes of a whip to encourage her into the chamber. Worse, the engines failed to work and the victims were crammed in for two hours and 49 minutes before they started. A further 35 minutes passed before all were dead. Then, the workers prised open the victims' mouths with iron bars, searching for gold teeth, and checked their private parts for hidden valuables.

Wirth was dubbed, 'the death camp king' but this title aroused the jealousy of others determined to topple him, in particular Höss (q.v.), who eventually succeeded him. Wirth accompanied Globocnik to Trieste in September 1943 and it is said that he was ultimately killed by Tito's partisans.

WISCH, Theodor
RANK: SS-Brigadeführer
und Generalmajor der Waffen-SS
BORN: 13 December 1907
DIED: 11 January 1995 (D)
PARTY NUMBER: 369050
SS NUMBER: 4759
AWARDS: 1939 Iron Cross Second Class, 24 September 1939; Iron Cross First Class, 28 November 1939; German Cross in Gold, 25 February 1943; Knight's Cross of the Iron Cross, 15 September 1941; Oakleaves, 12 February 1944; Oakleaves with Swords, 28 August 1944; Black Wound Badge; SS Honour Ring, SS Honour Sword.

Early in spring 1933 Wisch was one of the first volunteers to join the *Leibstandarte*. He served as a company commander during the Polish campaign and a battalion commander in the campaign in France. During the bitter battles in Russia he served as a battalion and regimental commander. As commanding officer of the 2nd Battalion, *Leibstandarte* Division, he was awarded the Knight's Cross of the Iron Cross for actions on the Russian Front while attached to Army Group South, and while commanding the 1st SS Panzer Division LSSAH he was awarded the Oakleaves, becoming the 393rd recipient. He succeeded 'Sepp' Dietrich (q.v.) to command the *Leibstandarte*. He had achieved the leadership of the Waffen-SS's most prestigious and battle-hardened unit at the tender age of 36. It was no mean feat to fill Dietrich's shoes, and certainly Wisch did not have the charisma possessed by his predecessor. However, he was a very able commander, and held the affection and confidence of his men. This was all the more remarkable in the last year of the war when the Reich was falling apart and its armies collapsing.

On 6 June 1944, when the Allies invaded Normandy, the LSSAH Division was there to mount an aggressive defence. For this he was awarded the Swords, becoming the 94th recipient. He had to relinquish command of the LSSAH in the autumn of 1944 after he was severely wounded, and spent the rest of the war on attachment to the SS-Fürhungshauptamt.

WISLICENY, Dieter
RANK: Sturmbannführer
BORN: 1899
DIED: July 1948 (E.A.)
PARTY NUMBER: —
SS NUMBER: —

Born in East Prussia, Wisliceny joined the SS and became an official in Eichmann's (q.v.) Jewish resettlement office, part of the Gestapo Büro IV A,4b. He became a key figure in devising schemes and making collective bargains for Jewish lives in Slovakia, Hungary and Greece. In 1942, Himmler (q.v.) received a proposal through him, from the Bratislava Zionist Relief Committee, that two million Dollars' worth of foreign currency would be available for Jewish lives. Ultimately this money did not materialise, but the offer was a bridge not only to immense international funds which might be extracted from world Jewry, but also towards peace discussions with the West.

Wisliceny was transferred to Budapest and his first proposals to the head of the Hungarian Jewish community were modest, but on 5 May 1944 a staggering offer was made by Eichmann to Joel Brand of the Budapest Joint Distribution Committee. The author of this plan is unclear: Becher (q.v.), Schellenberg (q.v.) or Himmler (q.v.) himself. Brand was to go to Istanbul and offer the lives of 700,000 Jews of Greater Hungary in exchange for 10,000 lorries from the Allies which would be delivered to the port of Salonika. Eichmann promised that the Jews, who had already been deported to Germany, would be kept alive for a fortnight, but if he heard nothing, he would 'let the Auschwitz mills grind'. On 14 June Eichmann made the Budapest Jews a new proposal – 20 million Swiss Francs would save the lives of 30,000 Jews who were to be deported from old Hungarian communities west of the River Theisses. Meanwhile, Jewish international charity found the 20 million Francs and 1684 Jews were taken from Belsen and released in Switzerland in two trains on 21 August and 6 December 1944. However, only five million Swiss Francs were transferred to Himmler, and this only after a further 1100 Jews were released in Switzerland in February 1945.

After the war, Wisliceny was arrested and became a prosecution witness at Nuremberg. He was returned to Czechoslovakia where he was tried, and hanged at Bratislava in July 1948.

WISLICENY, Günther-Eberhard

RANK: SS-Obersturmbannführer
BORN: 5 September 1912
DIED: 25 August 1985 (D)
PARTY NUMBER: 1187703
SS NUMBER: 41043
AWARDS: 1939 Iron Cross Second Class,
27 July 1941; 1939 Iron Cross First
Class, 1 November 1941; German Cross
in Gold, 25 April 1943; Knight's Cross
of the Iron Cross, 30 July 1943;
Oakleaves, 27 December 1944; Swords,
6 May 1945; Close Combat Clasp Gold
Class, 31 March 1945; 1939 Wound
Badge Gold Class.

From a wealthy East Prussian family, Wisliceny joined the Allgemeine-SS in Berlin-Lichterfelde on 18 March 1933. He was assigned to the LSSAH and rose steadily through the ranks to a combat command. He was severely wounded in action for the second time near Moscow in December 1941; he eventually received the Gold Wound Badge. While serving as commanding officer of the 3rd Battalion, SS-Panzergrenadier Regiment 3 *Deutschland*, he was awarded the Knight's Cross of the Iron Cross for his actions at the Battle of Kursk (the battle had been a nightmare for the Waffen-SS; total German losses amounted to 100,000 men, with the Wehrmacht losing over 300 tanks on one day of fighting alone, and Hitler had failed to win back the initiative on the Eastern Front). His unit was transferred to France and participated in the breakout from the Falaise Gap in 1944. He fought in the German counteroffensive in the Ardennes at the end of 1944 and beginning of 1945 and won the Swords, becoming the 151st recipient. Two days later he marched at the head of his men into American captivity and was then handed to the French, who held him until 1951. Released from captivity, he died in Hanover in 1985.

WITT, Fritz

RANK: SS-Brigadeführer
und Generalmajor der Waffen-SS
BORN: 27 May 1908
DIED: 16 June 1944 (K.I.A.)
PARTY NUMBER: —
SS-NUMBER: —
AWARDS: 1939 Iron Cross Second Class,
19 September 1939; 1939 Iron Cross
First Class, 25 September 1939;
Knight's Cross, 4 September 1940;
German Cross in Gold, 8 February
1942; Oakleaves, 1 March 1943.

Born in Westphalia, Witt was one of the 120 men who made up the original *Leibstandarte*. In 1935, he joined the SS-Standarte *Deutschland*, and was a company commander in the Polish campaign. His skills as a leader were clear early in the war. On 10 May 1940, he led his command against heavily fortified Dutch positions, and in the French campaign he was engaged in the fighting around the La-Bassée Canal and subsequently the battle for the Plateau of Langres. In recognition of these actions he was awarded the Knight's Cross of the Iron Cross.

In October 1940, he was transferred to the *Leibstandarte* and fought in the Balkans and in Russia. He saw continuous service on the Russian Front and was awarded the Oakleaves for his leadership and bravery, becoming the 200th recipient. When the *Hitlerjugend* was raised, he was given command of the unit which later bore the brunt of the fighting in Normandy. He was killed by Allied naval gunfire 16 June 1944. Witt must surely be considered as one of the great panzer commanders of not only the Waffen-SS but the German Army as a whole.

Right: A young soldier of the Hitlerjugend *Division receives medical attention during the fierce fighting in Normandy in June 1944.*

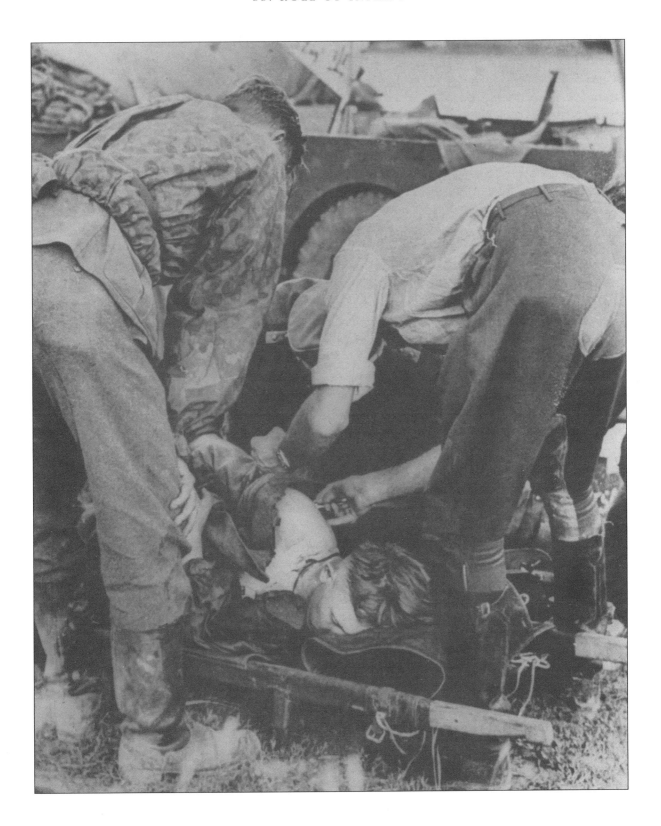

WITTMANN, Michael

RANK: SS-Hauptsturmführer
BORN: 22 April 1914
DIED: 8 August 1944 (K.I.A.)
PARTY NUMBER: —
SS NUMBER: —
AWARDS: 1939 Iron Cross Second Class, 12 July 1941; 1939 Iron Cross First Class, 8 September 1941; Knight's Cross of the Iron Cross, 14 January 1944; Oakleaves, 30 January 1944; Swords, 22 June 1944.

Wittmann was one of the most successful tank killers in World War II. He was born in Vogenthal, Upper Palatinate, and joined the *Leibstandarte*, remaining with this unit until his death. He saw action in the Polish campaign followed by Holland, France, Greece, Russia and then returning to France.

In early 1943, Wittmann received his first Tiger tank on the Eastern Front. The secret of his success was patience and steady nerves – he often waited for his victim to come within close range. By the end of the Kursk Offensive, Wittmann had destroyed some 38 enemy tanks and 45 artillery pieces. He was awarded the Knight's Cross of the Iron Cross as a platoon leader on the Russian Front, where he achieved the majority of his kills. Two weeks later he won the Oakleaves, becoming the 380th recipient.

When the D-Day invasion came, I SS Panzer Corps, to which the LSSAH was attached, quickly engaged the invading force. During the fierce counterattacks against the Allies in the area of Caen and Villers-Bocage, Wittmann and his crew performed almost superhuman feats. When total chaos reigned among the British, Wittmann suddenly appeared in the middle of a column of tanks and motorised units, wreaking havoc. He was awarded the Swords for his actions, being the 71st recipient. At this time he was accredited with 138 tanks and 132 vehicles destroyed. Wittmann was killed with his crew on 8 August 1944 by either a bomb or tank shell, near Gaumesnil just south of Caen.

WOLFF, Karl

RANK: SS-Obergruppenführer
BORN: 13 May 1900
DIED: July 1984 (D)
PARTY NUMBER: 695131
SS NUMBER: 14235
AWARDS: 1914 Iron Cross Second Class; 1914 Iron Cross First Class; Cross of Honour 1914-1918 Combatants; 1914 Wound Badge Black Class; German Olympic Games Decoration First Class, 29 October 1936; 1939 Iron Cross Second Class Bar; 1939 Iron Cross First Class Bar; NSDAP Long Service Medal 10 Years, 30 January 1941; Commemorative Medal of 13 March 1938; Commemorative Medal of 1 October 1938; Prague Castle Bar, 19 December 1939; Commemorative Medal for the return of the Memel Region, 19 December 1939; SS Honour Ring; SS Honour Sword; Italy: Grand Cross of the Order of the Crown.

Having served in World War I, Wolff subsequently joined the Hessian Freikorps. He joined both the NSDAP and SS in 1931 and served briefly as Ritter von Epp's personal adjutant in 1933. Himmler (q.v.) noticed him and in 1935 appointed him as his own adjutant. Wolff headed Himmler's personal staff and was liaison officer for the Reichsführer with Hitler from 1939 until 1943, when Himmler dismissed him because of his insistence on divorcing his wife, against Himmler's wishes. Throughout this period, he was a close confidant of Himmler's and shared in the development of the SS and its Teutonic mystique.

Wolff was transferred to Italy as military governor of northern Italy and Plenipotentiary General of the Wehrmacht in 1943, helping Mussolini to re-establish a Fascist regime under German domination. By February 1945 he was convinced that the war was lost, but real power in the region lay with Kesselring, commander of the German armed forces. Wolff attempted to make peace with the Allies in Italy, making contact with Allen Dulles, the American head of the capital's OSS (Office of Strategic Services). Although forbidden by Hitler to negotiate peace in Italy, he went ahead and a surrender was signed on the day of Hitler's suicide.

After the war Wolff was sentenced by a de-Nazification court to four years, but only served one week of his sentence before being released. He was living quietly as a successful public relations man when, during the Eichmann trial (q.v.), he wrote an article on Himmler. He was then tried in July 1964 and eventually charged with organising additional rolling stock to transport Jews to extermination camps. This rather flimsy charge resulted in a 10-year prison sentence.

WOLL, Balthasar
RANK: SS-Oberscharführer
BORN: 1 September 1922—
PARTY NUMBER: —
SS NUMBER: —
AWARDS: 1939 Iron Cross Second Class, 23 July 1942; 1939 Iron Cross First Class, 14 October 1943; Knight's Cross of the Iron Cross, 16 January 1944.

Woll was an SS-Rottenführer and gunner for Michael Wittmann (q.v.) with the 13th (Heavy) Company, 1st SS-Panzer Regiment, 1st SS Panzer Division LSSAH, on the Russian Front. For his skill, he was awarded the Knight's Cross of the Iron Cross. In the great panzer battle at Kursk, Wittmann and his crew claimed eight enemy tanks and seven artillery pieces on the first day alone. By the end of this offensive Wittmann had added a further 30 tanks and 38 guns to the tally.

Wounded in an Allied bombing raid and confined to hospital, Woll was not killed with the rest of Wittmann's tank crew in August 1944. He returned to active service in March 1945, and fought the US armoured forces advancing on Bielefeld. He survived the war and became an electrician.

WOYRSCH, Udo von
RANK: SS-Obergruppenführer
BORN: 24 July 1895—
PARTY NUMBER: 162349
SS NUMBER: 3689
AWARDS: Golden Party Badge; 1914 Iron Cross Second Class; 1914 Iron Cross First Class; Cross of Honour 1914-1918 Combatants; War Merit Cross Second Class with Swords; War Merit Cross First Class with Swords; SS Honour Ring; SS Honour Sword.

Von Woyrsch served as a first lieutenant during World War I and joined the frontier protection service afterwards. He organised the SS in Silesia on Himmler's (q.v.) direction. During the Röhm Putsch of 30 June 1934 he took command in Silesia, and on the orders of Göring arrested a number of SA leaders, disarmed all SA headquarters' guards and occupied the Breslau police headquarters. Von Woyrsch's men murdered some of the SA officers as a result of an on-going private feud.

A particularly barbaric man, Woyrsch headed an Einsatzgruppe in September 1939 that was to operate in the Katowice area to liquidate the Jews and Poles. The plan was to transport 50,000 Jews from West Prussia and Danzig into Poland's interior. However, German officers in the area strongly objected, so brutal were his troops and so frequent were the mass murders. These officers also called for Woyrsch's men to be transferred to the front and face real fighting rather than rounding up and murdering defenceless civilians. On their insistence, particularly that of General

German officers in the area strongly objected to the mass murders

Gerd von Rundstedt, Commander-in-Chief East, Himmler withdrew Woyrsch's special task force and called a halt to the massacres, albeit very grudgingly. From 20 April 1940, he was Higher SS and Police Leader in military IV and district leader in Dresden until February 1944. Like many others, Von Woyrsch's ultimate fate is unknown.

WÜNNENBERG, Alfred

RANK: SS-Obergruppenführer
und General der Waffen-SS und Polizei
BORN: 20 July 1891
DIED: 30 December 1963 (D)
PARTY NUMBER: 2221600
SS NUMBER: 405898
AWARDS: 1914 Iron Cross Second Class;
1914 Iron Cross First Class; Cross of
Honour 1914-1918 Combatants; 1939
Iron Cross Second Class Bar, 18 June
1940; 1939 Iron Cross First Class Bar,
21 August 1941; Knight's Cross of the
Iron Cross, 15 November 1941;
Oakleaves, 23 April 1942; SS Honour
Ring; SS Honour Sword.

Born in Saarburg, Lorraine, Wünnenberg fought in World War I as an infantry officer and later as a pilot. After the war, he served with the Freikorps in the Baltic area and then joined the police.

In World War II, he was posted to Russia and was commanding officer of the 3rd Police Infantry Regiment. His regiment fought bravely at Leningrad, and in recognition of this he was awarded the Knight's Cross of the Iron Cross. He became the commanding officer of the 4th SS Panzergrenadier Division *SS-Polizei* on 15 December 1941. The division was generally poorly armed and equipped – the army believed that policemen were not proper soldiers and therefore deserved second-rate hardware. It generally suffered on the Leningrad Front, though improved later with combat experience. Wünnenberg defeated the Second Soviet Assault Army commanded by General Vlassov near Wolchov. He was awarded the Oakleaves for his bravery and leadership, becoming the 93rd recipient. His last command, towards the end of the war, was as commanding general and head of the Ordnungspolizei. He survived the war and died at Krefeld in 1963.

WÜNSCHE, Max

RANK: SS-Obersturmbannführer
BORN: 20 April 1914—
PARTY NUMBER: —
SS NUMBER: 491403
AWARDS: 1939 Iron Cross Second Class;
1939 Iron Cross First Class, 31 May
1940; Medal for the Winter Campaign
in Russia 1941-1942; Silver Infantry
Assault Badge; 1939 Wound Badge
Silver Class; German Cross in Gold,
25 February 1943; Knight's Cross,
28 February 1943; Oakleaves,
11 August 1944.

Max Wünsche joined the SS in 1934. He served in France and then in the Greek and Yugoslav campaigns. During Operation 'Barbarossa' he fought in the *Leibstandarte*'s panzer regiment. He was involved in the battle for Kharkov, and his bravery and masterful leadership during the intense fighting won him the Knight's Cross of the Iron Cross. He was transferred to command the newly raised Panzer Regiment 12 in the *Hitlerjugend*. He trained the new recruits, aided by experienced personnel from his old unit and in conjunction with some experts from army panzer units.

When the Allies landed in Normandy, Wünsche's regiment had only Panther and Mark IV tanks. He successfully defended Hill 112 near Caen, and *Hitlerjugend* was responsible for the destruction of over 250 Allied tanks. During the fighting in the Falaise Pocket with the remnants of army units, his unit held open a gap,

enabling part of the German 7th Army to escape. These actions surely averted a 'Stalingrad' in Normandy, and Wünsche justly deserved the Oakleaves, of which he was the 548th recipient. He was wounded again just prior to his capture on 14 August 1944. He was held prisoner by the British until 1948, when he was released.

ZEHENDER, August

RANK: SS-Brigadeführer
und Generalmajor der Waffen-SS
BORN: 28 April 1903
DIED: 11 February 1945 (K.I.A.)
PARTY NUMBER: 4263133
SS NUMBER: 224219
AWARDS: 1939 Iron Cross Second Class,
14 September 1939; 1939 Iron Cross
First Class, 18 June 1940; German Cross
in Gold, 16 October 1942; Knight's
Cross of the Iron Cross, 10 March
1943; Oakleaves, 4 February 1945;
Infantry Assault Badge; Close Combat
Clasp Silver Class.

Zehender first saw service in the Polish campaign in September 1939 and then fought in the invasion of the Low Countries and France in the spring of 1940. At the beginning of 1943, he was the commanding officer of 2nd SS-Cavalry Regiment, *Florian Geyer* Division, 2nd Panzer Army, Army Group Centre. Placed under the Second Armoured Army's XXXXVII Armoured Corps, which was also known as Corps *Lemelsen* after its commander, he fought south of Orel in February 1943 when the Wehrmacht was attempting to stem the Russian tide. The division was refitted northwest of Bobruyal in April and May while in reserve for the Second Armoured Army, and then waged guerrilla warfare under the SS and police leader for partisan warfare in June and August. In March 1943, Zehender was awarded

the Knight's Cross of the Iron Cross. He went on to become the commanding officer of the 22nd Freiwilligen-Kavallerie Division der SS *Maria Theresia* and was further honoured with bestowal of the Oakleaves, becoming the 722nd recipient. He was killed in action seven days later in Budapest. The *Maria Theresia* Division was made up of Hungarian recruits. It was destroyed in the fighting in and around Budapest in early 1945, when only 790 men of the 70,000 who had left the city reached German lines.

ZIEREIS, Franz

RANK: SS-Standartenführer
BORN: 13 August 1905
DIED: May 1945 (K.I.A.)
PARTY NUMBER: 5716146
SS NUMBER: 276998
AWARDS: War Merit Cross Second Class
with Swords; War Merit Cross First
Class with Swords; German Horseman's
Badge Bronze; SS Honour Ring;
SS Honour Sword.

Ziereis was commandant of Mauthausen concentration camp. In the closing days of the war Hitler ordered Pister (q.v.), who was in command of the camps in the south, that Dachau, Mauthausen and Theresienstadt were to be blown up, with their inmates if they could not be evacuated before the arrival of the Allies. It would have fallen to Kaltenbrunner (q.v.) to implement Hitler's murderous order, but he had no motive for doing so. An affidavit from an assistant to the Gauleiter of Munich reported that he was going to bomb Dachau from the air, while a Swiss Red Cross observer, who was allowed into Mauthausen, learned that Ziereis planned to blow up all the inmates in a subterranean aircraft construction hangar at Gusen. However, he never attempted to put the plan into action, preferring to disguise himself and hide in the camp. After the liberation he was shot by an American Army patrol while resisting capture. In a dying testimony taken down by a camp inmate in the presence of the American officers who spoke no German, Ziereis denounced Kaltenbrunner as the author of the Gusen plan, whereas Kaltenbrunner had in fact signed an order that the camp should be handed over to Patten's troops intact.

ZIEGLER, Joachim

RANK: SS-Brigadeführer
    und Generalmajor der Waffen-SS
BORN: 18 October 1904
DIED: 1 May 1945 (K.I.A.)
PARTY NUMBER: —
SS NUMBER: 491403
AWARDS: Iron Cross Second Class,
    23 September 1939; Iron Cross First
    Class, 28 June 1940; German Cross in
    Gold, 15 March 1943; Knight's Cross
    of the Iron Cross, 5 September 1944;
    Oakleaves, 28 April 1945.

Ziegler was born in Hanau, Main. He saw service in Poland and then in the Low Countries and France in 1940.

On 28 July 1944, he became the commanding officer of the 11th SS Freiwilligen-Panzer-grenadier Division *Nordland*, III (Germ.) SS Panzer Corps, Army Group North, and was awarded the Knight's Cross of the Iron Cross two months later. *Nordland* joined a variety of elements under Army Group *Steiner* in a desperate offensive in Pomerania on 16 February 1945. The aim was to thrust to the northwest against the northern flank of Marshal Zhukov's First Russian Front. In two days the offensive ground to a halt. Fighting followed around Storgard, but *Nordland* was forced to leave on 3 March. Defensive battles followed around the Altdamm Bridgehead until the division was withdrawn on 20 March and sent to the Schwedt-Angermünde area, some 44 miles (70km) northwest of Berlin. Ziegler established his staff quarters at Angermünde. It was here that a number of Britons were added to the division's ranks: members of the British Freikorps. The *Nordland* Division was now desperately trying to hold the Russian drive to Berlin.

The final Soviet offensive against the city opened on 16 April, and two days later the division was ordered into the city. In the face of vastly superior numbers it fell back towards the govern-

ment quarter. Plans had been made for *Nordland* to escort Hitler in a desperate breakout through Grunewald, but even Hitler realised that this was impossible. An enraged Führer relieved Ziegler of his command on 26 April and placed him under arrest in the bunker, although strangely he bestowed the Oakleaves on him two days later, making him the 848th recipient. After Hitler's suicide Ziegler was freed, and while he was trying to negotiate a truce was killed near the Friedrichstrasse railway station in Berlin on 1 May 1945.

ZINGEL, August

RANK: SS-Untersturmführer
BORN: 20 January 1922—
PARTY NUMBER: —
SS NUMBER: —
AWARDS: 1939 Iron Cross Second Class,
    10 October 1941; 1939 Iron Cross First
    Class, 27 February 1942; Knight's Cross
    of the Iron Cross, 5 September 1942;
    Medal for the Winter Campaign in
    Russia 1941-1942; Army Long Service
    Medal Four Years; Infantry Assault
    Badge, Commemorative Medal of
    13 March 1938; Commemorative Medal
    of 1 October 1938; Prague Castle Bar;
    1939 Wound Badge Black Class.

In 1942 Zingel was NCO commanding an assault troop of the *Totenkopf* Division in Russia. His unit, Battle Group *Krauth*, was pitched against a Soviet defensive line consisting of several machine-gun bunkers. This experienced NCO successfully broke through and opened a gap for his unit. On another occasion he was wounded in a similar assault and was hospitalised. He was awarded the Knight's Cross for his bravery, and was presented with the award while in hospital.

Table of SS Ranks and their US and British equivalents

SS	BRITISH ARMY	US ARMY
Reichsführer-SS	Field Marshall	General of the Army
SS-Oberstgruppenführer	General	General
SS-Obergruppenführer	Lieutenant-General	Lieutenant-General
SS-Gruppenführer	Major-General	Major-General
SS-Brigadeführer	Brigadier	Brigadier-General
SS-Oberführer	(not applicable)	Senior Colonel
SS-Standartenführer	Colonel	Colonel
SS-Obersturmbannführer	Lieutenant-Colonel	Lieutenant-Colonel
SS-Sturmbannführer	Major	Major
SS-Hauptsturmführer	Captain	Captain
SS-Obersturmführer	Lieutenant	1st Lieutenant
SS-Untersturmführer	2nd Lieutenant	2nd Lieutenant
SS-Sturmscharführer	Regimental Sergeant-Major	Sergeant-Major
SS-Hauptscharführer	Sergeant-Major	Master-Sergeant
SS-Oberscharführer	(not applicable)	Technical Sergeant
SS-Scharführer	Staff Sergeant	Staff Sergeant
SS-Unterscharführer	Sergeant	Sergeant
SS-Rottenführer	Corporal	Corporal
SS-Sturmann	Lance-Corporal	Corporal
SS-Oberschütze	(not applicable)	Private 1st Class
SS-Schütze	Private	Private

Appendix

Main German Concentration Camps and their Staff

AUSCHWITZ (established 1940)

1,500,000 million deaths

Built in May 1940. In June 1941, under Himmler's orders, it was greatly extended. Gas chambers disguised as 'Bathhouses' were added and *Leichenkeller* (corpse cellars) were built to house the dead before they were burned. A factory area which developed as part of the Auschwitz-Birkenau complex housed I. G. Farben and Krupp's, who worked their slave labourers to death.

Aumeir: SS-Hauptsturmführer, Deputy Commander

Baur, Richard: SS-Hauptsturmführer

Bodmann, von: SS-Obersturmbannführer

Boger: SS-Oberscharführer

Burgen: SS-Sturmbannführer

Caesar, Joachim Dr: SS-Standartenführer

Drechsler: SS-Untersturmführer

Grabner, Max: SS-Untersturmführer

Grese, Irma: SS-Kriegshelferinnen

Hartenstein, Fritz: SS-Sturmbannführer

Hasselbroek, Johannes: SS-Sturmbannführer

Höss Rudolf: SS-Obersturmbannführer Camp Commandant

Kirschner: SS-Oberscharführer

Kremer, Johann Paul Dr: SS camp doctor

Lachman: SS-Oberscharführer

Langermann, Armand: SS-Hauptsturmführer

Mandl: SS-Kriegshelferinnen, Senior Wardress

Mengele, Josef Dr: SS-Hauptsturmführer

Muhsfeldt, Erich: SS-Hauptsturmführer

Mummenthey, Karl: SS Sturmbannführer

Rödl: SS-Obersturmbannführer, Camp Commander

Schneider, Thilo: SS-Sturmbannführer

Schoppe: SS-Unterscharführer

Schwarz: SS-Hauptsturmführer

Sell: SS-Untersturmführer

Stibitz: SS-Unterscharführer

Stocker, Emil: SS-Hauptsturmführer

Uhlenbrock, Kurt Dr: SS-Hauptsturmführer

Voznitza: SS-Untersturmführer

Wirths, Edward Dr: SS-Sturmbannführer, Garrison MO

Ziemesen: SS-Hauptsturmführer

BELZEC (established 1942)

600,000 deaths

It opened in March 1942 and for nine months was the main extermination camp. Jews were taken from the villages of eastern Galicia and Rumania, Czechoslovakia and Germany. It had six gas chambers allowing the SS to murder 15,000 Jews a day.

BERGEN-BELSEN (established 1943)

50,000 deaths (disease and starvation)

A labour camp in northwest Germany. Intended for political prisoners and considered a 'soft' camp. It was intended for 10,000 prisoners but 70,000 arrived from other camps in the East. The murderous neglect by the commander, Kramer, lead to the discovery of 30,000 living prisoners, many on the point of death, and the bodies of over 30,000 lying in heaps or in uncovered pits on the day of liberation.

Ehlert, Herta: SS-Kriegshelferinnen

Grese, Irma: SS-Kriegshelferinnen

Hössler, Franz: SS-Obersturmführer

Kramer, Josef: SS-Hauptsturmführer Camp Commandant

Lotte, Ilse: SS-Kriegshelferinnen

BIRKENAU (established 1941)

A hastily constructed extermination camp for Russian officers which began operations in 1941. It was part of Auschwitz and had a railway siding disguised as a normal railway station.

Hartjenstein, Friedrich: SS-Sturmbannführer, Camp Commandant

BUCHENWALD (established 1933)

In 1945 there were 47,500 prisoners in the camp.

Barnewald, Otto: SS-Sturmbannführer, Leiter der Lagerverw

Florstedt: SS-Sturmbannführer, 1 Lagerführer

Foerschner, Otto: SS-Sturmbannführer

Hoven, Dr: SS-Hauptsturmführer, Garrison MO

Koch, Ilse: SS-Kriegshelferinnen

Koch, Karl: SS-Standartenführer, Camp Commander

Krone, Heinrich: SS-Hauptsturmführer

Pister, Hermann: SS-Standartenführer, Camp Commander

Plaza: SS-Obersturmbannführer

Schober: SS-Hauptsturmführer, 2 Lagerführer

Voss, Franz E.: SS-Obergruppenführer, Camp Commander

Weisenboln: SS-Hauptsturmführer, 1 Lagerführer

CHELMO (established 1941)
The first extermination camp

DACHAU (etsablished March 1933)
Under the administration of Eicke, Dachau became a model camp. The slogan over the gate read: *arbeit macht frei*. At the end of World War II it was used to house the 'prominents', prisoners Himmler hoped to bargain with at the war's end.

Brachtel, Dr: SS-Hauptsturmführer, doctor at the camp

Breuer, Prof: psychiatrist

Eichele, Hans: SS-Obersturmbannführer

Fronapfer: SS-Oberscharführer, 2 Rapportführer

Grünewald, Adam: SS-Sturmbannführer, Deputy Camp Commander

Hofmann: SS-Untersturmführer, 1 Lagerführer

Jarolim: SS-Untersturmführer, 2 Lagerführer

Klaitenhof: SS-Hauptsturmführer

Loritz, Hans: SS-Oberführer, Camp Commander.

May: SS-Oberscharführer

Niedermayer: SS-Oberscharführer, Cell Leader

Pfeifer: SS-Oberscharführer

Piorkowski: SS-Sturmbannführer, Camp Commander

Preiss: SS-Oberscharführer, Cell Leader

Rascher, Sigmund: SS-Untersturmführer

Redwitz: SS-Hauptsturmführer

Reinecke, Otto: SS-Untersturmführer

Remetz: SS-Oberscharführer, Cell Leader

Remmele: SS-Hauptscharführer, 1 Rapportführer

Schlemmer: SS-Oberscharführer, Cell Leader

Stumpf: SS-Untersturmführer, Politische Abteilung

Tiedchen: Gestapo Kommissar

Wagner: SS-Hauptscharführer, laundry

Weiss, Martin: SS-Obersturmbannführer

Wolter, Dr: SS-Hauptsturmführer, Senior Camp MO

Zeiss: SS-Hauptscharführer, Cell Leader (Brothers)

Zeiss: SS-Hauptscharführer, Cell Leader (Brothers)

Zilie: SS-Hauptsturmführer, Lagerführer

ESTERWEGEN (established March 1933)
The earliest major camp, converted to a special punishment camp. First run by the Ministry of Justice.

FLOSSENBÜRG (established 1939)
Many Gestapo prisoners were taken here as the war ended and executed. Canaris, Oster and Bonhöffer were executed here.

Fassbender, Willy: SS-Untersturmführer

Fritzsch: SS-Hauptsturmführer, Deputy Camp Commander

Koegel, Max: SS-Obersturmbannführer, Camp Commander

Koermann: SS-Untersturmführer

Künstler, Karl: SS-Obersturmbannführer, Camp Commander

Schnabel, Alfred Dr: SS-Sturmbannführer, garrison MO

Zill, Egon: SS-Sturmbannführer, Camp Commander

GRINI (established May-June 1941)
Former Norwegian women's prison. Inmates from Äneby Hakadal were transferred here. In December 1943 there were about 2000 inmates, of which 100 were women. Some 700 were deported to Germany in late 1943, but the number was kept up to 2000 in throughout 1944.

Blatner: SS-Oberscharführer

Deutzer: Lagerkommandant

Heilemann: SS-Scharführer

Jenzer: SS-Untersturmführer

Jønichen: SS-Obersturmbannführer, Gestapo (permanently stationed)

Koch, Karl: SS-Standartenführer (see Buchenwald)

Kuntz: SS-Untersturmführer

Kuntze: SS-Untersturmführer

Kuntze: SS-Scharführer

Lenzer: SS-Untersturmführer

Lüdtke: SS-Scharführer

Nemitz: SS-Oberscharführer

Niebel: SS-Untersturmführer, connected with Work's Directorate

Nunz: SS-Oberscharführer

Reich: SS-Obersturmbannführer, Gestapo (permanently stationed)

Reinhardt: SS-Sturmbannführer, Gestapo

Schwartz: SS-Untersturmführer

Schwarz: SS-Oberscharführer

Seidel: SS-Untersturmführer

Stange: SS-Untersturmführer

Stange: SS-Hauptscharführer

Warnecke: SS-Hauptscharführer

Zeidler: SS-Hauptsturmführer, Gestapo (permanently stationed)

GROSSROSEN (established 1938)

Erzberger: SS-Obersturmbannführer, Lagerführer

Eschner, Helmuth: SS-Unterscharführer, 1 Rapportführer

Gray: SS-Hauptsturmführer, Camp Commander

Hasselbroek, Johannes: SS-Sturmbannführer, Camp Commander

Henneberg: SS-Obersturmbannführer, Verwaltungsführer

Lindstedt: SS-Oberscharführer, SS Clothing Store

Marienfeld: SS-Unterscharführer, Prisoners' Kitchen

Ottohall: SS-Unterscharführer, SS Handicrafts

Remmeling: SS-Rottenführer, Blockführer

Roedel: SS-Hauptsturmführer, Camp Commander

Schramm: SS-Rottenführer, Blockführer

Schrammel, Erich: SS-Rottenführer, 2 Rapportführer

Schwarze: SS-Unterscharführer, Arbeitsführer

Stoerzinger: SS-Obersturmbannführer, 1 Company

Thumann: SS-Untersturmführer, Lagerführer

Witte: SS-Rottenführer, Blockführer

LUBLIN-MAJDANEK (established 1942)

200,000 deaths. In the autumn of 1942 the camp was installed with gas chambers.

Fasstedt: SS-Hauptsturmführer

Florstedt: SS-Hauptsturmführer

Fuss: SS-Hauptsturmführer

Trommer, Richard: SS-Obersturmbannführer

MAUTHAUSEN (established 1938)

Over 40,000 deaths

Located near Linz in Austria, it was not designated as an extermi-

nation camp. Dutch, Italian and Hungarian Jews were sent there.

Kitt, Bruno: SS-Untersturmführer

Krebsbach, Eduard Dr: SS-Sturmbannführer, garrison MO

Quirsfeld, Eberhard: SS-Sturmbannführer

Sand: SS-Obersturmbannführer, Chief Administration Officer

Vetter, Helmuth Dr: he ran medical trials for Bayer

Ziereis, Franz: SS-Obersturmbannführer, Camp Commander

NATZWEILER (established 1941)

Eisele D.: SS-Obersturmbannführer, MO

Fasching-Baur: SS-Obersturmbannführer

Hacker: SS-Oberscharführer, 1 Kasernenführer

Hartjenstein, Friedrich: SS-Sturmbannführer, Camp Commandant

Hinkelmann: SS-Obersturmbannführer, 2 Lagerführer

Kaseberg: in charge of Strafkamando punitive detail (a prisoner)

Kramer, Josef: SS-Hauptsturmführer, 1 Lagerführer (then Belsen)

Rödl: SS-Obersturmbannführer, Camp Commander

Rohrschach: Lagerältester (a prisoner)

Schlachter: SS-Obersturmbannführer

Strasser: SS-Oberscharführer in charge of the motor pool

Witzig: SS-Scharführer in charge of the quarry

Zill, Egon: SS-Sturmbannführer (then Flossenbürg)

NEUENGAMME (established 1940)

Kitt, Bruno: SS:Untersturmführer

Wirth, Christian: SS-Oberführer

Wirths, Eduard Dr: SS-Sturmbannführer

ORANIENBURG (established 1933)

This became a satellite for Sachsenhausen.

RAVENSBRÜCK (established 1938)

92,700 deaths

For women prisoners. Included industries such as a clothing factory and remodelling furs. Many totally useless medical experiments were undertaken on the female inmates, most ending in a painful death for the victim. Originally built to accommodate 6000 prisoners, by 1944 the number in the camp had doubled. Ann Frank and her mother died here.

Oberhauser, Herta Dr: admitted administering lethal injections to Polish women who had suffered experimentation

SACHSENHAUSEN (established 1933)

Over 100,000 deaths in this camp and its satellites. Used as the Gestapo interrogation centre in 1936.

Baranowski, Hermann: SS-Oberführer, Camp Commander

Bogdala: SS-Oberscharführer

Böhm, Wilhelm: foreman of crematorium and burial squad

Braun: SS-Schütze

Brum: SS-Untersturmführer, Leader of the Administrative Company

Bugdalle: SS-Schütze

Büttner: SS-Obersturmbannführer

Campe: SS-Untersturmführer

Cornelli: SS-Obersturmführer

Eicke, Theodor: SS-Obergruppenführer, Camp Commander

Eisfeld: SS-Brigadeführer, Camp Commander

Fickert: SS-Oberscharführer

Forster: SS-Hauptsturmführer

Gensior: SS-Untersturmführer, Bauleiterführer

Grim: SS-Obersturmbannführer, Adjutant

Grünewald Adam: SS-Sturmbannführer, Lagerführer

Heidrich: SS-Hauptsturmführer, Deputy Camp Commander

Hoffmann, R: SS-Schütze

Hohmann: SS-Hauptscharführer, Blockführer

Kaindle, Anton: SS-Standartenführer, Camp Commandant

Kilinger: SS-Hauptsturmführer

Klinger: SS-Hauptsturmführer

Kampe: SS-Schütze

Knittel: SS-Schütze

Kolb: SS-Hauptsturmführer, Camp Commander

Krämer: SS-Scharführer, Blockführer

Laver: SS-Sturmbannführer

Lehmann: SS-Unterscharführer

Lorenz: SS-Oberführer, Camp Commander

Meyer: SS-Schütze, Blockführer

Nowacki: SS-Oberscharführer

Radicke: SS-Oberscharführer

Saathoff: SS-Schütze, Blockführer

Schitli: Rapportführer, later Blockführer

Schröter: SS-Unterscharführer, Blockführer

Schubert: SS-Oberscharführer

Seifert: SS-Oberscharführer, Blockführer

Sommer: SS-Schütze

Sorge: SS-Oberscharführer, known as Eiserner Gustav Iron Gustave

Sorger: SS-Untersturmführer, Bauleiter

Suren: SS-Hauptsturmführer, Grünewald's predecessor as Lagerführer

Todden, von: Gestapo

Volk: Gestapo Chief

Weymann Hans: SS-Hauptsturmführer

SOBIBOR (established 1942)

250,000 deaths

It opened in April 1942 near the frontier of the Ukraine Reich Commissariat. Prisoners at Sobibor rebelled on 14 October 1943, and of the 300 who escaped 100 were caught and killed. Wirth calculated that it allowed the SS to murder 20,000 Jews a day.

STUTTHOF (established 1940)

Hoppe, Paul Werner: SS-Sturmbannführer

THERESIENSTADT: (established 1939)

Special ghetto for Jews, later converted to extermination camp.

TREBLINKA (established 1942)

700,000 deaths

The camp began operations in July 1942. The 700-1000 Jews who worked for the SS decided in August 1943 to rebel. Kerosene was used to spray buildings instead of disinfectant by a group of prisoners. They then set fire to the buildings and snatched the guards' weapons (15 guards were killed in total). Of the 350-400 prisoners who escaped during the uprising, which destroyed most of the camp, about 150-200 avoided immediate capture. However, only about 70 survived the war. The remainder were caught and killed. No SS man from Treblinka was executed as they were all tried by the Germans, who abolished the death penalty after the war.

Kurt, Franz: Deputy Commander

Lambert, Hermann: helped construct the gas chambers.

Marchenko, Ivan: 'Ivan the Terrible'

Matthes, Arthur: Chief officer of camp No 2 and the gas chambers.

Munzberger, Gustav: assistant to Matthes

Nikolai, Shulayev: worked in operating the gas chambers.

Stangl, Franz: SS-Hauptsturmführer, Camp Commandant

Suchome, Franz: collected and processed gold from Jewish victims

Glossary

Abwehr: German military intelligence organisation.

Amtsgruppe: a branch of the Hauptamt.

Anschluss: the movement in Germany and Austria for the union of the two in a Greater Germany. Strongly supported by Nazi parties in Germany and Austria, the *Anschluss* took place in March 1938.

Beer Hall Putsch: abortive Nazi coup in November 1923 in which Hitler attempted to take over Bavaria.

Berghof: Hitler's mountain retreat in the Bavarian Alps.

Blood Order: *Blutorden*, the prestigious Nazi decoration, awarded to those who took part in the 1923 Munich Beer Hall Putsch.

Brown House: the headquarters of the Munich Nazi Party.

Condor Legion: name of the military force Hitler sent to aid the Nationalists in the Spanish Civil War.

Demjansk Shield: medal given to those who fought in the Demjansk Pocket, northern Russia, in early and mid-1942.

Einsatzgruppen: SS Special Action Groups responsible for the extermination of Jews and communists in Eastern Europe.

Frontbann: paramilitary organisation raised by Ernst Röhm after the Munich Putsch, when the SA and NSDAP were banned.

Gau: the main territorial division of the Nazi Party.

Gauleiter: highest-ranking party official in a Gau.

Gestapo: Geheimes STAatsPOlizei, the Third Reich's secret police.

Hauptamt SS: the Central Office of the SS.

Iron Cross: originally a Prussian award for valour. It had three grades: Second and First Class and the Grand Cross.

Kampfgruppe: battle group.

Kapp Putsch: attempted right-wing coup in Germany in January 1920. Supported by the Freikorps, it was defeated by a general strike throughout Germany and armed left-wing workers.

Knight's Cross: higher Iron Cross award for valour. Knight's Crosses went upwards in degrees: Oakleaves, Oakleaves with Swords, and Diamonds.

Kripo: Kriminalpolizei, the Criminal Police headed by Nebe.

LSSAH: *Liebstandarte SS Adolf Hitler.* Originally Hitler's bodyguard, it later became the *Leibstandarte* Division.

NSDAP: *Nationalsozialistische Deutsche Arbeiterpartei* (National Socialist German Workers' Party).

Reichsleiter: the highest-ranking Nazi Party official.

Reichstag: home of the German parliament in Berlin until it was burnt down in February 1933.

Reichswehr: the 100,000-strong army of the Weimar Republic.

RFSS: Reichsführer-SS Heinrich Himmler.

Ritterkreux: Knight's Cross.

Röhm, Ernst: leader of the SA who was murdered on Hitler's orders during the 'Night of the Long Knives' in June 1934, Röhm advocated a continuing revolution in Germany after the Nazi rise to power in 1933, which Hitler perceived as a threat to himself.

RSHA: Reichssicherheitshauptamt, the Reich Central Security Department. Created in 1939, it combined the Security Police (Gestapo and Kripo) and the SS Security Service (SD).

RuSHA: Rasse-und Siedlungshauptamt, the SS Race and Resettlement Department, responsible for SS racial purity and SS colonisation in the conquered Eastern territories.

SA: Sturmabteilung. The Brownshirts, unemployed ex-soldiers, who were first recruited to protect Nazi speakers at meetings.

Sipo: Sicherheitspolizei, the Security Police under Heydrich consisting of the Gestapo and Kripo.

SD: Sicherheitsdienst, the Nazi Party's intelligence and security organisation. Created by Himmler, it was headed by Heydrich.

Sonderkommando: special SS detachment for police and political tasks in occupied areas.

SS Honour Ring: silver death's head signet ring, a personal reward for service from Himmler himself.

SS Honour Sword: finely crafted sword which was presented to SS personnel by Himmler for services rendered.

SS-Verfügungstruppe: military formations of the SS, renamed Waffen-SS in early 1940.

Standarte: SS unit equivalent to a regiment.

Stosstrupp Adolf Hitler: Shock Troop Adolf Hitler, an early bodyguard unit formed to protect the life of Hitler in 1922-23.

Totenkopfverbände: death's heads units. The concentration camp guard units which were the nucleus of the *Totenkopf* Division.

'Werewolves': underground army raised in Germany in 1945 to wage guerrilla warfare against the invading Allies.